St Andrews
The Evolution of the Old Course

The Impact on Golf of
Time, Tradition & Technology

Scott Macpherson
Foreword by Peter Thomson

Hazard Press
publishers

Published by Hazard Press Limited
PO Box 2151, Christchurch, New Zealand
Email: info@hazard.co.nz
www.hazardpress.com

ISBN 978-1-877393-22-3

Front cover photo: S. Macpherson
Title page & half-title page photos: S. Macpherson
Book design & page layout by Quentin Wilson
Printed in India through Kalamazoo

This page: The Road Hole (17th) green.
Iain Lowe

CONTENTS

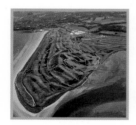

FOREWORD

by Peter Thomson
Five Times Open Champion – 1954, '55, '56, '58, '65.

The Old Course on the St Andrews links is the rock on which the game of golf anchors itself. It was not the first piece of ground over which the game of golf was played. But it was the place where the game as we know it now evolved and refined itself. In the beginning, three or four hundred years ago, it was a wild place on which to hit a small ball across country and it did not enjoy a sunny, warm climate, except for the high summer months of the year. Yet the game of golf not only survived, it flourished. Today, this place is called 'the Home of Golf', although truthfully, golf has no 'home'. It is worldwide. But St Andrews is the true base of the Royal and Ancient Golf Club (of St Andrews) in whose hands the game is entrusted by all the world of play outside the United States. This book tells the story of how this came about. The R&A made the Old Course what it is, and in its turn, the course made the R&A. Had the Club not nurtured and enhanced its dignity, the custody of golf would probably have drifted somewhere else.

Scott Macpherson, the author, researcher and compiler of this work, is a New Zealander by birth, but perhaps it was a deep tribal instinct that lured him from half the world away to the Highlands of his forbears and steep himself in the lore and fable of the game he learnt as a child. He has given us a chronological view of how the Old Course emerged out of the strip of territory that started at the town steps and took in a crooked path along the coastal route until it ran out of land at the estuary of the Eden River. The golfers then reversed their progress and returned from whence they came, ending their game at the town limit.

As history tells us, originally there were 22 'stages' along the golfing journey there and back, but in the mid-nineteenth century the golfers of the Club decided that some of the stages were too short, and that there was merit in joining a few together and settling for 18 holes as adequate. This as it turned out was the first of many momentous decisions that were made in the refining of the game. Eighteen holes consequently became universally accepted as the standard number of holes to comprise a full course.

Above: Peter Thomson retains the Claret Jug after defending his Open Championship title at St Andrews in 1955.
Cowie Collection, St Andrews University Library

The Old Course at St Andrews is the model and prototype for courses everywhere. All courses are, to varying degrees, copies of the Old. Not only have they accepted and followed the number of holes set, but also courses everywhere have sand bunkers in emulation of the links features, and a fair ratio of 'fair ground' to 'rough' areas to complete what has come to be accepted as a full-featured playing arena. The lakes and swamps of Florida courses, for example, are imitations of the Swilcan Burn, albeit by a considerable distortion of dimension. Yet the innumerable illogicalities of the St Andrews course have largely been ignored in other places. Who indeed would tolerate a golf hole with a green sliced in half like the Road Hole, or put up with a hole without a visible fairway like the 7th?

These things no doubt troubled the minds of the early Greens Committees, and their judgment to leave the course as nature had left it was no doubt cursed by many who suffered the punishment of insufficient shots. Even so, the appointment of 'Old Tom' Morris as the Keeper of the Greens charged with widening the course to make more space for the increasing number of golfers, was a momentous step.

We can only surmise that the ordering of this exercise was a bold assertion that more fairway and less hazard would make the game of golf a more enjoyable experience. Certainly it made a huge difference. More freedom to divert from the rigid 'straight and narrow' must have brought joy to many hearts!

As a result of this work the Old Course took up approximately 92 acres, which is its scope today. More than 80 per cent of its territory now is given to clean-cut 'fairground', and the broken sward (112 bunkers) adds up to just one acre in total catchment area – always surprising when one hears of its fearsome reputation.

But such decisions have proved their weight. The course of today is not entirely virginal territory. The hand of man has added and subtracted from the original landform at just about every juncture. And nature itself is a dynamic force that has its own way of changing things. What we have in the Old Course is an environmental partnership that arranged a playing arena and gave the game of golf a suitable shape, contour and dimension. Yet the major issue, as this book tells us, was the battle that the 'keepers' of the course fought to match these dimensions with the ever-developing technology of the balls and clubs that threatened to render the course irrelevant.

At various times the governing body set specifications for the ball that were intended to control its performance. A weight limit of 1.62 ounces was set and a minimum size of 1.62 inches was added to attempt to limit the balls' flying performance. Later still, in more modern times, a speed restriction was imposed. This particular imposition was thought to be the ultimate 'stopper' to the ball's seemingly increasing length of flight. Alas, what was overlooked was its aerodynamics. Balls have been carrying greater distances than ever, so that this battle still goes on today.

No one anywhere in the world has been foolish enough to try to copy the Old Course. It wouldn't work. On another piece of ground in a different climate, it might look ridiculous. It is just as well. The Old Course is unique, as this story tells us, and long may it be so.

When two stranger golfers meet on some neutral ground, one of the first questions that will pass from one to the other will most certainly be, "Have you been to St. Andrews?" – and should the answer be in the negative, the questioner will immediately deem himself justified in assuming a tone of patronage which the other will feel he has no right to resent.
– H.G. Hutchinson, *The Badminton Library: Golf*, 1890

INTRODUCTION

'Far and Sure.' A common golfing motto.

Early changes to the Old Course were always somewhat serendipitous. Golf was an adventure then. If the length of a hole varied by 20, 30, or 60 yards from one day to the next it was inconsequential to golfers playing a match. In fact, the length of holes and the course were never recorded in the earliest days, and it was only towards the end of the nineteenth century with the growing popularity of stroke play that the length of the championship course at St Andrews was measured accurately at all.

While history records the Old Course was at one time 22 holes, the modern configuration is 18 – a configuration developed when the first two and last two holes were eliminated. No plan of the 22-hole layout is known to exist and because of that, and the fact that 18 holes has become the 'standard' course, this study begins with the first known plan of the Old Course, which was produced in 1821.

In that era, the feathery ball was used. The invention of the gutta percha ball in 1848 brought the first big wave of changes to the Old Course, and perhaps more significantly,

it established the process by which golf would forever evolve. The relationship between new inventions and their subsequent adoption by golfers triggered physical changes to the golf course. Changes to the physical features of a course were, and generally remain, a response to new technology.

Improving skill levels and supportive rules have contributed to the impact new technology has had on golf and the Old Course. The Haskell ball, surlyn, steel shafts and graphite have all subsequently contributed to the pace of the evolution. Given these developments and other challenges, it is of great credit to the Old Course that it has exhibited such extraordinary adaptability to survive as a viable and legitimate test of championship golf through the centuries. As Alister MacKenzie wrote in 1933 in his book *Spirit of St Andrews*,

In discussing the question of finality it is well to enquire if there are any really first class courses in existence which have been unaltered for a considerable number of years and still remain not only a good test of golf

Opposite page: The Principal's Nose. See extended caption on page 78.
Iain Lowe

but a source of pleasure to all classes of players; to see if there is any golf course which not even the rubber cored ball has spoilt; and if so to find the cause of its abiding popularity.

The only one I know is the Old Course at St Andrews, Scotland. It was the most popular course in the world in the days of the feather ball, the guttie and the Haskell, and today Bobby Jones considers that not only is it the best course in the world, but he says he gets more joy in playing it than a hundred other courses. Today, with the exception of the lengthening of some of the tees, St Andrews remains substantially the same as it was seventy years ago.

There have been some significant physical changes to the Old Course, not least of which was the construction of the new first green in 1870. Since then the width of the course has expanded, two holes cut on each green and many bunkers added, and for that matter, some removed. Most recently a series of new tees outside the recognised boundaries of the course have also been constructed. Other changes have been more naturally induced, such as the coastal erosion, and continual weathering of the dunes. Due to time and treatment, the grasses of the course have also developed into a mosaic of varying turf grass species. Throughout these changes, while now less daunting, the Old Course has not only remained an exacting and complete test of golf, but its

popularity has also multiplied with around 43,000 rounds now being played annually.

This research looks to provide a greater understanding of the physical changes to the Old Course, particularly since the Open Championship was first played on it in 1873. Viewing changes in correlation with the advancements in equipment and the rules provides a new look at the evolution of the Old Course and raises many questions, such as: How did it evolve? What balance between the hand of man and serendipity was responsible for the making of the physical features on the Old Course? Is Par still a valid method of course standardisation? Has there been a time, taking into consideration course set-up, scoring and equipment, when the Old Course was the best test of golf? What is the future for this celebrated links?

The Old Course has been of greatest interest to golfers and golf course architects for many, many years. The best have played it, studied it, marvelled at it, borrowed from it, been perplexed by it, and some have even disputed the quality of its unique features – though usually for only a short period of time. Understanding the virtues of this slowly evolving, living, growing masterpiece often only comes with time, even for the most fervent admirers. Because of this, and perhaps in spite of it, the Old Course justifiably remains a focal point of the design industry and golf world. I hope this study is enjoyed by those whose spirit is lifted by golf, St Andrews, or the Old Course.

*'I loved the greens, but learnt
the most in the bunkers.'
– Anon.*

CHAPTER ONE

PILMOUR LINKS
Setting the course boundaries

What lends golf the variety which is its chief fascination is that the game is played, not upon lawns,
but over long reaches of broken country, the surface of which is diversified by sand-hills,
patches of "whins" or gorse, rushes, stone walls, coarse grass, cart-ruts, and other
obstacles, upon which has been bestowed the generic name of 'hazards'.
— W.E. Norris, 1892

Golf historians claim golf has been played on the Links in St Andrews for up to six centuries, and in the reduced 18-hole format since 1764. But it was not until 1821 that the first map was produced entitled the 'Plan of Pilmour Links belonging to James Cheape of Strathtyrum'. This plan defined on paper the boundaries of the course and quantified the length and width of the holes.

Prior to this time, the course route was not marked by anything more than the edge of the whins (gorse). So, together with the survey, Mr Cheape had a set of stones commissioned that would act on the ground as property boundary markers. These were called 'march stones' and clearly defined the location of the links for all parties.

With this act, James Cheape, Laird of Strathtyrum, who was a local landowner and keen golfer, had saved the links from a war which had started twenty years earlier when 'temporary impecuniosity' or bankruptcy, had forced the St Andrews Town Council to sell off some sections of the Links. The war was between local golfers and merchants who

had bought sections and turned them into rabbit farms. By repurchasing the land in 1821, Mr Cheape ended the fierce hostilities. The march stones were as much little monuments to his victory as boundary markers. When Mr Cheape had the stones set in 1821, the width of the corridor that the 1st hole or 'Bridge Hole' played down was measured as being 72 yards (it is now 129 yards). Prior to this delineation, however, the future of this area – bordered to the north by the beach and to the south by private property ownership – was endangered, and only protected from gross encroachment by fiercely devout golfers. According to old minutes of the Royal and Ancient Golf Club in May and July 1820,

…an extraordinary meeting was convened, to take into consideration the action of the Magistrates and Town Council of St Andrews who, having 'feued', or let, to several individuals, portions of the course between the first and second holes, had thereby illegally encroached upon the links, to the detriment of golfers… Having

Opposite page: This aerial view was taken during the 2000 Open Championship. The grandstands, tented village, car parking and courses can be clearly seen along with the West Sands, Eden Estuary and the ancient Town of St Andrews.
Ian Joy Photography

14

Far right & right (detail):
Mr William Chalmer of
Perth, Scotland surveyed
this more detailed plan
in 1836. Though
difficult to imagine
nowadays, the sand from
the west sands would
often blow up as far as
the R&A Clubhouse.
Rough unshaven
hillocks covered what are
now the 1st and 18th
fairways, and the 18th
green. The road across
the Links, now known
as Granny Clark's Wynd,
is simply a series of cart
ruts. Half way to the
Swilcan Burn is a large
bunker known as
Halket's*. The Swilcan
Burn is a natural sandy-
edged water hazard.

*Halket's Bunker was
filled in sometime
between the making of
this plan in 1836 and
1842, about when Mr
Balfour's recollections
*Nine holes of St.
Andrews* was written.

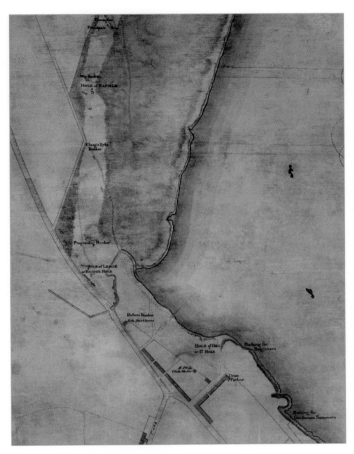

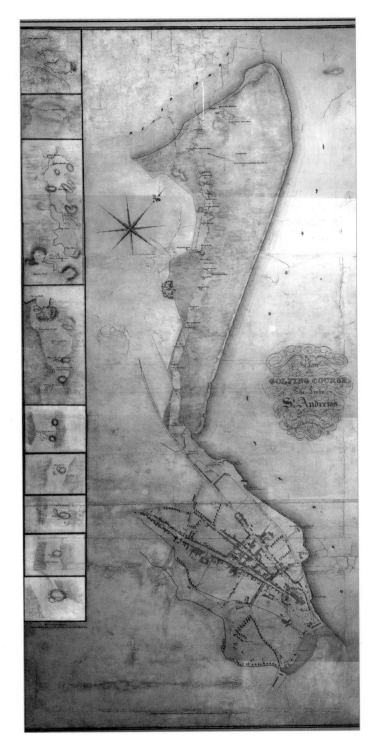

*the most earnest desire to see the matter amicably settled,
and having inspected the ground in question, the club
committee caused a line to be staked off as the southern
boundary of that part of the course.*
(*Everard,* Golf Illustrated, *Nov, 1900*)

A large committee was also nominated 'to take care that a
road of ten feet is preserved from the south-west corner of
Mr. Richard's park, to the first hole.' However, records show
that Magistrates persisted in their encroachments and not
only 'ploughed up and cropped' the land in question, but
'erected several houses' on it as well.

No record has been found of what happened in this debate
between 1820 and 1850, but the second survey of the course
was made in 1836. By then the course was nine holes out and

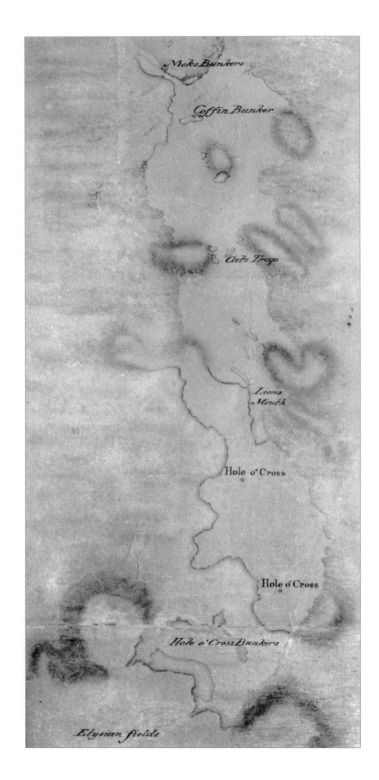

Nicks Bunkers

Coffin Bunker

Cat's Trap

Lions Mouth

Hole o' Cross

Hole o' Cross

Hole o' Cross Bunkers

Elysian fields

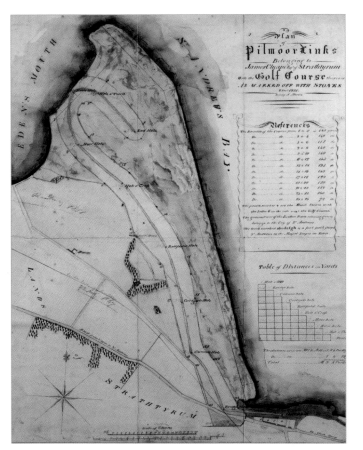

Plan of Pilmoor Links

Left: Surveyed by A. Martin on 8 December 1821, this plan shows the area of the Links purchased from the Town Council of St Andrews by James Cheape. Boundary stones distinguish the Old Course from the remainder of the Links.
Plan Courtesy of National Archives of Scotland.

Far left: Old Daw Anderson is credited for creating the first 'double green' as late as 1832 by cutting a second hole on the fifth green (Hole o'Cross), but references also credit Allan Robertson as a likely co-conspirator. This plan shows the first physical evidence of that change. Here the two holes, both named Hole o'Cross, are separated by a distance of approximately 60 yards.
Plan courtesy of Royal and Ancient Golf Club

nine holes back with double holes that had been introduced by 1832. There were no tee boxes in that period and the rules simply stated that the ball be teed upon a mound of sand which was within two club-lengths of the last hole played. It was not until 1875 that separate teeing grounds were introduced.

In March 1853 the strained relationship between the Royal and Ancient Golf Club and the municipal authorities arose again. According to the minutes,

> *The meeting having taken into consideration that in the year 1820 an agreement was entered into between the City of St Andrews and this Society, whereby in consideration of the club abandoning their opposition to the Town Council fencing part of the links eastward from the Swilcan Burn for building purposes, the Town*

Small plan featuring Halket's Bunker from 1855. Also note the lifeboat house and the track to the beach that is later to be straightened to become Granny Clark's Wynd.

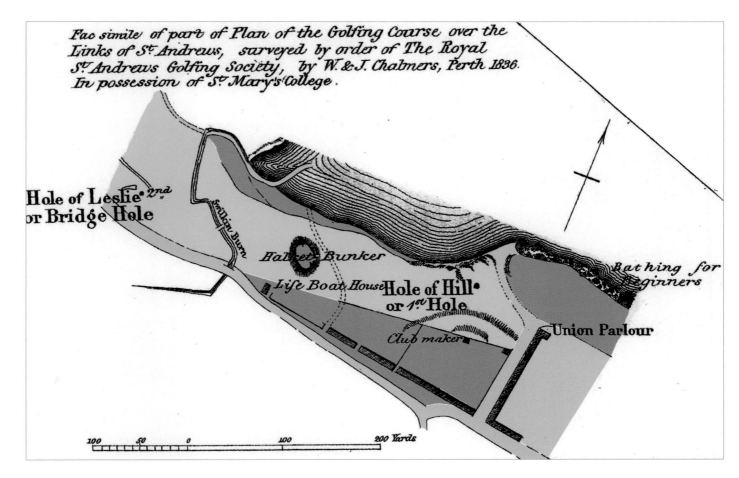

Fac simile of part of Plan of the Golfing Course over the Links of S.t Andrews, surveyed by order of The Royal S.t Andrews Golfing Society, by W. & J. Chalmers, Perth 1836. In possession of S.t Mary's College.

Hole of Leslie. 2nd or Bridge Hole

Swilcan Burn

Halket Bunker

Life Boat House **Hole of Hill.** or 1st Hole

Club maker

Union Parlour

Bathing for Beginners

100   50   0   100   200 *Yards*

Council by Minute of 13th October, 1810 inter alia, became bound to give the club a piece of ground east of the first hole for the site of a new Golf house…

This defined the eastern boundary in front of the present Royal and Ancient Clubhouse.

Regarding the boundary resolution and process of negotiations, prominent author, golfer and R&A member H.S.C. Everard researching the matter in 1900 concluded,

On the whole then, it seems that the committees in 1820 acted with judgement, and arranged what must be regarded as a satisfactory compromise. The whole episode seems to have been not without some beneficial effect upon the Municipal authorities, for, four years later, in 1824, on the encroachment question again cropping up, the attitude assumed by them, so far as being high handed or masterful, is eminently the reverse. A site was required for a Life Boat House; and a piece of ground just east of the Swilcan Burn, adjoining what was then the turnpike road (now the road to the old Station) was selected.

Care was taken that the building would 'not interfere with or encroach upon the golfing course' and it did not.

After the Life Boat House was built,

…the magistrates proposed to close a road through the

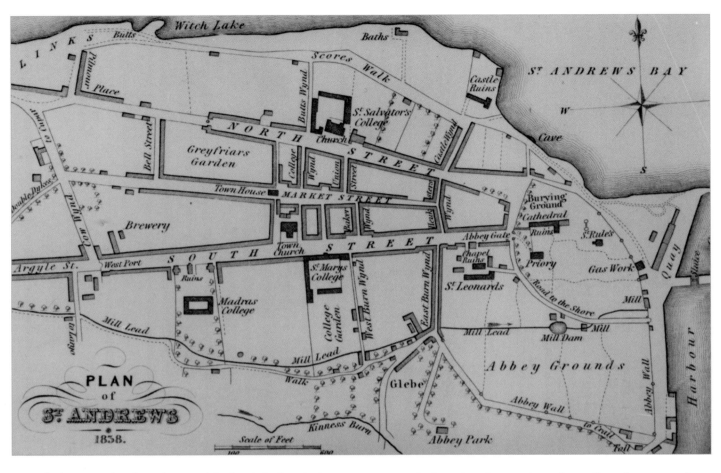

Map of St Andrews
from 1838 showing
where the Links are in
relation to the town.

*links, immediately to the east of the first hole, by which
means a considerable portion of ground would be
gained for Golf; this was agreed to…*

During this negotiation, in October 1845, the Royal and
Ancient Golf Club was increasingly alert to any encroachment on the links. The next challenge would soon come, but
this time by rail. In 1847 visitors destined for St Andrews
could only get as far as Leuchars by train. They had to travel
the remaining four miles by horse-drawn coach. But this
situation was about to change. An extension to the track was
planned. A report in 1901 read:

…a survey had been made with a view to the construction

*of a branch railway to St Andrews, from the station of
the Edinburgh and Northern Company's line at Guard
Bridge; and it was apprehended that the golfing course
would be interfered with. The proposed plan would
have had the effect of separating the putting green at
the burn hole* [the current 17th green] *from the
remainder of the course. A committee appointed to
safeguard the interests of the Club, remonstrated with
the Company, who, in consequence, agreed to modify
their scheme, and construct their line further to the
south, so as to avoid the links altogether…*

It took five years before the track to the Links station was

Right: On Martin's 1821 plan, the following reference is made: 'The points marked + are the march stones with the letter G on the side next to the golf course. They defined the outside limits of the course.' Nowadays, however, due to the expanding width of the course, some march stones sit in the middle of fairways. For example, here on the 5th hole. Reports state that this march stone was originally set in the whins but since the 1870s has been visible to golfers.
Iain Lowe

Far right: This march stone is located between the 10th green and the 11th tee. On this stone the G is still clearly legible.
S. Macpherson

completed, but when the route of the line was finalised and opened, in 1852 this set the western boundary of the 16th and 17th holes. The station was located where the Old Course Hotel now sits.

The famous Links Road war, which had begun around 1820, reached its climax in 1880. This was an important issue because it would ultimately define the boundary along the southern perimeter of the 18th hole. What occurred was a long running debate caused by the sale of land between Pilmour Links and the Old Course for the purpose of housing. Many people believed the land had been '…in 1799, specially reserved by the Town Council for the inhabitants of the city of St Andrews for the purpose of playing golf.' But many houses were built on these plots, often right up to the limits and facing the links. So the course itself became the boundary to these houses, instead of the road provided in the titles, meaning access was only possible via the Old Course. The report in the *St. Andrews Citizen* in May 1879 continued,

> *…since 1870 a strip of ground at the back of these houses has been used by carts and carriages, and the defenders have been accustomed to use this strip of ground as an access for vehicles to their houses…This has seriously interfered with the servitude and privilege of playing golf enjoyed by the citizens from time*

immemorial. The ground in question, which is close to one or more of the golf holes, has ceased to be covered with grass, and is ploughed up with cart ruts, in consequence of the use to which it is now put.

To resolve the contention, residents of the new houses had petitioned the town council in 1874 to build a road twenty-one feet wide, from Golf Place to Granny Clark's Wynd, at their own expense. The proposal included a chain and post fence between the road and the Links, but the town council could not decide. After a long, and in hindsight, reasonably humorous battle, the road was built though the cost had become extortionate, to such point that the curb and channel planned could not be afforded.

The fence alongside the 18th fairway was an ongoing issue.

A fence had been erected at some point to protect the putting green at the last hole on its south side. However in 1877 it was accidentally destroyed. To repair this fence should have been an easy task but it was not until 1880 that the matter was resolved.

'It was stated that the Town Council, at their last meeting, had empowered the Links Road Committee of the Council to erect a fence of posts and chains on the south side of the links, at the first hole from Golf Place to Swilcan Burn... It was also stated that the cost of the post and chains would be about £38.' The final fence was erected in 1914, and three months later it was painted white, and it is still there today.

In 1894 the town purchased the Links which had previously been owned by the Laird of Strathtyrum, Mr Cheape. Negotiations had begun in 1890 with the valuation of £5000 finally being agreed. However, the proprietor of the Strathtyrum Estate had reserved certain rights, including digging in the shell pits, laying drains and stipulating that he and all his family and guests resident at Strathtyrum should have the right to play on any new course that might be made. In terms of the golf, it was recently estimated that should the Cheape family exercise their rights, it could amount to

7000 rounds per year. While this was discomforting to the townsfolk, it was more unsettling to the Links Trust, who began to imagine the family calling up for a tee time during the Open Championship week – possibly leading to scenes reminiscent of the second Open held at St Andrews where Championship contenders and weekend golfers shared the Links. It was this image that motivated the authorities to visit the Cheape family prior to the Open Championships and request that they kindly not exercise their rights during the Open Championship week. To settle the situation long-term, in 1992 the Links Trust began negotiations with Mrs Gladys Cheape. An agreement was reached, and for £245,000 payable at a rate of £35,000 per year until 1998, the Cheapes relinquished their rights.

By the 1880s more track was laid and a new station opened in the town, relegating the Links station to a freight depot. After the bridge spanning the Firth of Forth opened in 1890, St Andrews became an easily accessible destination, especially from Edinburgh. This resulted in a tourist boom as golfers and holiday-makers descended on the town. The town's popularity only started to wane, when by WWII travel by automobile overtook train travel. The service to St Andrews ceased in 1969. Today only the original stationmaster's home remains but is now the popular 'Jigger Inn'.

Left: Used by visitors, joggers and golfers going to practice, a pathway now takes the place of the old railway line. The 16th hole still plays around the old railway line and the fence remains out of bounds – and a fearsome hazard when the wind blows left to right (east to west)!
Iain Lowe

Right: Taken in the late 1840s, this coloured photo is believed to be the first taken of the links at St Andrews. Here the Swilcan Burn Bridge can be seen, but also note the location of the Home Hole green – it is noticeably short of its current position.
Courtesy of David Joy

The design and development of the 'New Course' by Tom Morris in 1895 fairly much set the eastern boundary and northern corner of the Old Course. The Old Course would not have much room to move – not that there was any desire for it to do so.

The northern boundary of the first hole took somewhat longer to establish. It had previously been defined only by the bay – often referred to on maps as St Andrews Bay. But in 1908 the road across the course known as 'Granny Clark's Wynd' had become dangerous to cross, and those attempting to do so often faced a barrage of strong language from golfers whose game was temporarily hindered. So with the double

objective of averting the danger of people being struck by golf balls and stopping the unnecessary ruffling of golfers' feathers, the town councillors considered constructing a wide road with a footpath from the Royal and Ancient Club to the bridge over the burn at the ladies' putting course. This road inadvertently became the new boundary.

In 1910 a new question of local importance came to the fore. Mr Cheape suggested that the field bordering the Long Hole-In (the 14th) should be made out-of-bounds, as should the field beyond the railway going to the Corner of the Dyke (the 16th). It had been a burning question between two parties within the Royal and Ancient Club for some time,

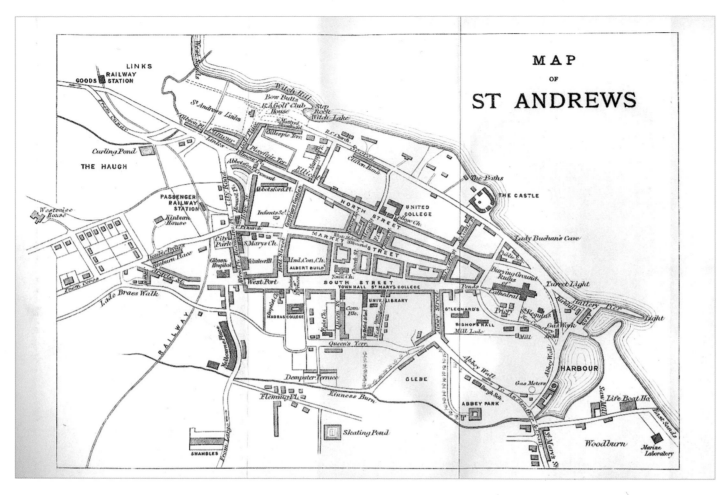

Left: 1897 map of St Andrews. Note the road down the right side of the 1st hole.
From: Hay Flemming's *Guide to St Andrews*

but it was brought to a head by negotiations between the town council of St Andrews and Mr Cheape relating to the proposed Eden Course. A delay in the decision was upheld because a considerable group of members also felt that the railway should be included in the out-of-bounds rule.

Previously, the only area ruled out-of-bounds was the Stationmaster's garden and the other ground at the goods station, which is enclosed by a wall, the Corner of the Dyke and the 17th. If this new ruling was to be introduced, it would affect the drive from four tees, namely the 14th, 16th, 17th and 18th. It would also include the now non-existent 'Children's putting green' that was beyond the road and over

the wall at the 17th green. The announcement was well received even though many golfers remembered Vardon, the current popular Open Champion, had hit his second shot on the 18th hole on to the roof of one of the houses, and been able to play to the green!

At the spring meeting in 1911 the decision reached by the St. Andrews Links Green Committee the previous year was passed and came into force on 17 July. The area west of the Elysian Fields, the railway and the Clifton Bank School Park at the 16th became out-of-bounds. To cement this, the town council took steps to rebuild the dilapidated boundary wall along the 14th hole and the neighbouring parks.

Above: Granny Clark's Wynd is barely visible as it skirts across the 1st fairway but the popular pedestrian path, leading to the new ladies putting course and the Jubilee courses, now forms one boundary of the course.
S. Macpherson

The final boundary of the Old Course to be set was that abutting the Eden Course. This was completed in 1913 when Harry Colt had laid out his course. From then the 12th, 13th and 14th holes on the Old Course were surrounded, and the current boundaries set.

In 1914, few would have expected any more alterations to these boundaries. However, in very recent years, changes have occurred. What is somewhat ironic about these latest events is that at a time when the course has been increasing in length, the acreage of the course has been decreasing!

Not for the first time, the north-western edge of the Links bore the brunt of the damage. One of the first reported times was in the 1940s and 'coast protection works' had been undertaken in 1948/49 and in 1955/56. But in 1957 the banks were still eroding and experiments planting sea lyme grass and sloping the overhanging banks were conducted. More recently, twenty feet of the coastline that bordered the New and Old and Jubilee courses eroded between late 1998 and 2000 from constant winds and rain. If the erosion continues at that rate, and if left unchecked, the Old Course

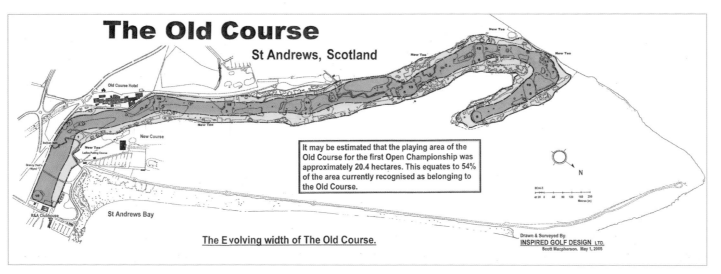

The Old Course

St Andrews, Scotland

Old Course Hotel

New Course

Ladies Putting Course

Greency Club's

R&A Clubhouse

St Andrews Bay

New Tee

It may be estimated that the playing area of the Old Course for the first Open Championship was approximately 20.4 hectares. This equates to 54% of the area currently recognised as belonging to the Old Course.

N

SCALE

The Evolving width of The Old Course.

Drawn & Surveyed By:
INSPIRED GOLF DESIGN LTD.
Scott Macpherson, May 1, 2005

Left: It is well known that the width of the Old Course, and the total playing area of the course, have drastically changed over the last two hundred years. The gradual widening of the course in the early years has been followed by a slow drift outwards of the tees, and this has resulted in a playing area almost double what it was in 1821.

could lose key tees and the 'High Hole' green over the next 100 years.

After the first loss, the Links Trust recognised the seriousness of the threat and responded with pace and decisiveness. To minimise and stop the erosion the Links Trust spent almost £100,000 on a steep-faced rock-filled wire gabion. Unfortunately, while the wall has worked, another storm and high tide cut into the banks just south of the new gabion and created further havoc.

Swift decisions were again made to shore up the shoreline. However, in late 1999 the town council denied approval for a second gabion. Because part of the coastline of the Eden estuary was deemed a Site of Special Scientific Interest (SSSI) the council desired greater consultation. It was a fraught time for the Links Trust and the green keepers, as the 12th tee on the Old Course and the 8th fairway of the Jubilee were in danger of being washed into the Eden estuary just as the coastal path had done previously. Finally, after an independent study was completed that sought involvement from groups as wide ranging as Scottish Natural Heritage and the Ministry of Defence, approval was granted in August of 2000.

Work began hastily, but this time the shoreline support planned was designed differently to that installed further

south. The large gabions would be built on an angle so the erosive force of the tidal estuary would be calmed. Equally, it was thought such a design would prevent the problem being moved to another stretch of the coastline – a hope shared by the MOD, based at Leuchars across the estuary. The second component of the new design was a large backfill. Approximately 12,000 cubic metres of sand was poured behind the 100m-long gabions to bridge the gap between the unstable dune shoreline and the new wire and stone wall. It is estimated this work cost £200,000.

For now, this final and most vulnerable boundary of the Old Course is set, almost literally, in stone. Within these boundaries however, the course has constantly evolved. Aside

Below left & below: Two different types of sea gabions now help to control erosion behind 11th tee and 12th green.
Iain Lowe

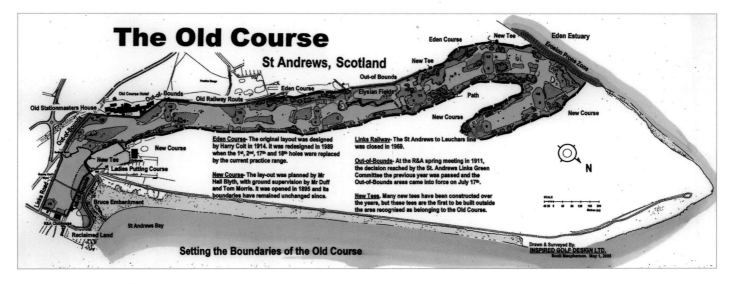

Right: Map of the Old Course showing various boundaries described in this chapter. For example, the out-of-bounds wall, erosion zone, railway line, neighbouring courses and the Ladies Putting Course.
S. Macpherson

from natural processes such as erosion, changes in technology, foot traffic, rules and improved scoring have all inspired physical changes to the course. Long gone is the rough, untamed, rabbit-infested sandy wasteland. The links is now one of the world's foremost championship venues, and is widely recognised as the Home of Golf.

THE LADIES PUTTING COURSE, OR 'THE HIMALAYAS'.

Women are known to have participated in golf from the early eighteenth century – particularly at Musselburgh. Their acceptance on the Old Course, however, was not always unanimous. There were raids on the links by women, and they had a good many allies. To avert any clash, Mr D.L. Burn in 1867 gallantly suggested that some quieter corner

Right: The Ladies Putting Course in 1920. Perhaps the biggest change to this most enjoyable putting course since this photo was taken has been the addition of the tarmac path (see opposite page).

of the Links might be found on which short holes could be made, 'where ladies could play short golf without being made the cynosure of too curious and inquisitive spectators'. The piece of ground selected was between the Swilcan Burn and the Flagstaff. A short course was laid out, and Mr Burn was nominated by Miss Boothby – the sister of Col. R.T. Boothby – as the secretary of the new Club. The Club was limited to one hundred ladies and fifty gentlemen associate members.

Originally the course was laid out as a miniature links rather than as a putting green. Hazards, both whins and bunkers, few of which were inconsequential, sharpened the challenge. However the ball finding a resting place in a deep rabbit hole, or on the fisherman's path that crossed the course could also spoil a good score. This path was pitted with deep ruts, many of which would render a ball unplayable, and heavy sand had to be carried on the holes nearest the sea. Those captured in these large traps usually had to take a drop under the penalty of one stroke, as playing out with only a putter was most impractical.

As described, 'the existence of the rule prohibiting the use of any club except a wooden putter', has led to the present alteration of the links. The course has been made suitable for a putter and all obstacles have been cleared away. Bunkers have been filled in and rough areas turfed. The course is shorter than it once was. Holes once varied from 25 to 75 yards, but now with the Links Clubhouse occupying a corner of the original course, present holes rarely exceed 40 yards. Holes continue to be moved around every week, however, and rarely are they considered easy. Holes are often cut into hollows and upon humps, with one or two holes also crossing the macadamised pathway.

Permission to erect the clubhouse was granted in 1898 by the council. It replaced a tent that members tried to shelter in previously – often without success.

Nowadays the course is enjoyed by members, but also by the annual summer throng of boys, girls, women and men. Open between April and October, the green fee of £1 offers little deterrent as eager golfers line up to tackle the perilous putting course. Long may this continue.

Above: This is the view from atop the new clubhouse. On the putting green townsfolk and visitors alike enjoy the challenge offered by these compelling undulations.
Iain Lowe

CHAPTER TWO

THE GUTTA PERCHA BALL – 1848–1902
and the first responses

*Let us but ask ourselves why golf originated on links land and immediately it becomes clear.
Here was terrain to be battled with – terrain which called forth skill, adroitness, finesse, power,
daring and other fine qualities possessed by the athlete and the sportsman. Here were the great dunes
to be carried, problems to be met and solved, masterly strokes to be made, dangers to be faced, Scylla here
and Charybdis there, a path strewn with pitfalls on this side, a route secure but long on the other.
These were the attractions which first drew men to the links and which have held them there ever since.*
– Robert Hunter, 1926

Physical changes to the Old Course can be directly linked to changes in the rules of golf, the sport's increasing popularity, and advancements in the game's equipment. The first of the major changes to the ball came with the invention of the gutta percha ball or 'gutty' around 1850.

Prior to this period, the feathery was the ball of the day. Old Tom Morris, one of the greatest authorities on the subject was asked about the construction of the feathery and wrote: 'The balls were stuffed with ordinary cocks' and hens' feathers, and their covering was made of bull's hide, and neither the feather nor the leather were boiled.' Relatively speaking, they were not great balls. Indeed, they were time-consuming to make and expensive to buy.

It was a Divinity student at St Andrews University by the name of Rob Paterson who supposedly invented the first ball made of gutta percha – a rubber-like substance obtained chiefly from the latex of thirty varieties of trees growing along the Malaysian peninsula, notably the giant *Dichopsis* gutta, after a revelation in 1845. Too poor to buy the featheries, he

fashioned his solid golf balls from gutta percha shavings he had first received as packing material in a gift box, and then worn on the sole of his shoes!

Paterson's brother made the first substantial batch of balls in 1846, all painted white and branded with 'Paterson's Composite-Patented'. They proved popular with some, but Allan Robertson, who first saw one in 1848, considered them a threat to his feathery business and deliberately moved against them. However, his assistant, Tom Morris, who had been banned by Robertson from using gutties or even playing in a group that was using them, became so excited with the new ball that he left the employment of Robertson and in 1851 moved to Prestwick and opened his own shop. The new ball quickly ousted the old feathery.

The gutta percha ball or 'gutta' was improved around 1850 by the introduction of special additives to the gum. These later balls were known as gutties. The material for these balls was collected by felling the trees, cutting the bark, and gathering the emergent juice. Impurities were removed by

A replica feathery ball.
S. Macpherson

Opposite page: A summer's evening – the Swilcan Burn bridge in calmer times.
S. Macpherson

Far right: Elevated view of 1st/18th fairway showing Granny Clark's Wynd.
S. Macpherson

Below: By 1855 Clark's Wynd (now known as Granny Clark's Wynd) was formalised. It took a more direct north route across the links, as opposed to the north-westerly curve indicated in Martin's 1821 survey. Perhaps more importantly it shows a 'Medal Hole' being located less than 20 yards west of the bottom of the steps leading up to the R&A clubhouse; approximately where it is located today, but eleven years before Morris is recorded as building his green there in 1866!

heating the gum, before it was cooled and moulded for use. In the 1880s and 1890s there were dozens of different makes of gutty, both British and American. C.B. MacDonald, who did much to popularise golf in America, said in *Scotland's Gift – Golf* (1928) that he had a list of 166 makes.

Robertson finally accepted the new infidel ball when he realised he was fighting the tide and that he could make and paint as many gutties in an hour as he could make featheries in one day!

The next few years saw some changes that would impact on St Andrews and the Old Course. Firstly, in 1852 the St Andrews branch railway line opened, and secondly, two years later, the Royal and Ancient Club began to build their clubhouse.

Mr D. Salmond described the Old Course in 1855 in his book *Reminiscences of Arbroath and St Andrews*. He wrote,

> *The links at St Andrews were then much rougher than I have found them on subsequent visits. There was but one course and the same nine holes served for the outward as for the inward play. Each hole was marked*

> *by a small iron pin with a bit of red flag attached. The greens were in the "rough", and the bunkers were in their natural state. If a player went off the narrow course of good ground he was at once landed in a very rough country, and the course at the ninth hole was all heathery and difficult across its whole breadth. It seems to me that many of the bunkers have been filled up since the days of which I write... Not so much is the driving nowadays easier on St Andrews links as is the putting on the bowling-green-like putting-greens which are so much affected now... I think that putting then was a much more "scientific" as well as more difficult thing than it is now.*

An anonymous writer, published around the turn of the twentieth century, described his memories of how the Old Course played in the 1850s:

> *The golf course was then very narrow, no wider, if as wide, sometimes than a good broad street. Occasionally a bunker stretched right across the course. It was risky to attempt to drive over it by one shot, so that the first shot had to be played short of the bunker, and the*

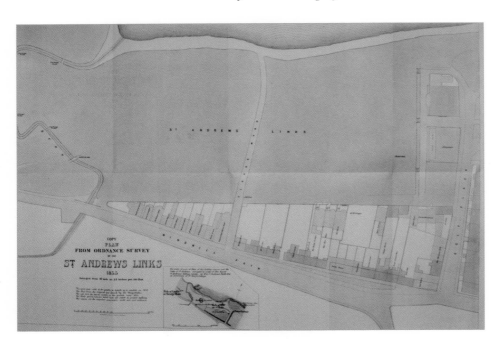

player was lucky if he carried it with his second. This narrow course was bordered by whins, and if the ball was not driven straight, it landed in a whin bush. Then followed a tussle for possession of the ball between the whin and the heavy iron, not always to the glory of the iron. The ground also was not carefully kept. In some places it was coarse, rough and reedy, and one was not always sure of getting a good lying ball. Now all that is changed under the skilful management and loving attention given to the Links for many years past by old Tom Morris. The whins have disappeared, the course has been widened, so that if one is afraid to face the bunkers he can go around their corners. The risks and penalties which long ago attended the playing of a weak or faulty game are very considerably reduced. Perhaps the most critical place in those old times going out, was when, driving off from the 4th hole, one had to cross the bunker called Hell to get into the Elysian Fields. It was not always easy to escape this awful pit and get into the better country.

W.T. Linskell wrote an article for *Chamber's Journal* called 'St Andrews Links in the Days of Young Tom Morris.'

Describing the changes to the Old Course between the 1860s and 1906 he wrote:

As I have stated before, the Links were formerly very narrow. Between the Royal and Ancient Golf Club and the burn at the first hole, many acres of land have been reclaimed from the German Ocean. Where I can remember the seashore once existed there are now excellent lies for the players' balls. There are, I believe, three sea-walls buried under the golf-green…

As the bunkers were honeycombed with rabbit-holes, and all the grassy hollows were overgrown with long, rank, benty grass or rushes, an iron niblick became a necessity to dislodge the ball. Now one can easily use a play-club in these well-mown hollows. While all the eighteen holes are considerably changed, I can notice the greatest difference at the long holes, out and in— the Heathery Hole and the High Hole. Formerly, at the long hole going out, one was obliged to cross the Hell Bunker, a fearful place, and approach the hole from what are still known as the Elysian Fields. The present valley course (new course) on the north side of the Links was at that time all rough ground, whins, and benty grass. I remember one of the old school golfers— I think it was the late Mr Whyte-Melville— remarking to me that the above-mentioned valley was getting gradually quite easy and playable, and that it ought to be ploughed up thoroughly to keep the players on the old line. At the Heathery Hole, just over "Walkinshaw's grave", there is a large bunker filled up, and new bunkers have to take the place of the former dense thickets of whins or gorse. At one time the tee-shot to this hole had to be kept far away to the left, or the consequence was a fearful lie or a lost ball. The same may be said of the drive off the tee to the High or Eden Hole; to the right all was coarse grass and whins, long since vanished.

Far left: Car, mowers, golfers and pedestrians all crossing or using Granny Clark's Wynd. Note that the road is 'in play' and golfers must hit their ball off the tarmac if they are unfortunate enough to finish on it – as Bobby Jones did during his victory in 1927 (refer page 72).
S. Macpherson

With the railway and clubhouse in place, Sir Hugh Lyon Playfair was appointed Captain of the R&A in 1856 and it was under his watch that many of the described changes evolved. Though it had already been trialed, a recording in an R&A minute on 2 May 1856 read:

> It was agreed that henceforth there shall always be two holes on the green at the High Hole, and THAT on Medal days as well as at other times.

In December 1856 the programme was expanded. A report in a local newspaper read:

> In consequence of the golfing course being much out of order by the greatly increased number of golfers... the

Above: High on the outside wall of the R&A clubhouse, facing the first tee, there is a plaque of Old Tom. It was put there after his death to commemorate the huge contribution he made to the Links. From there he now forever overlooks the Old Course.
S. Macpherson

Right: Old Tom Morris standing outside the Royal and Ancient Golf Club.

> Royal and Ancient deemed it necessary to vote a sum of £25 to have turf and bunkers repaired. Although just about half the sum is yet laid out the course wears a better look... Along with this is another improvement, viz., the two holes in each putting green, with the exception of the first and end hole, white flags going out and red ones coming in. The bent and whins have been cleared to widen the course when necessary.

The investment proved worthwhile, as results were impressive. A report on 7 May 1857 recorded:

> St Andrews Links were never in better condition for golfing purposes than now. Since the meeting in October, the Club has spent some twenty pounds in repair of the course in strengthening the walls of most of the bunkers, which had become much breached by frequent visitations, and filling up other little holes and corners. The putting greens have had a thorough overhaul, re-turfed, and otherwise improved. On each green, with the exception of the first and return, two holes have been placed; the one is played to by parties going outwards, the other in the in-coming. To prevent mistakes, the outgoing hole is supplied with a white flag, and its neighbour sports a red one, that being the colour for all the return.

Morris had moved back to St Andrews in 1864, and in 1865 was appointed Custodian of the Links by the R&A. Changes had occurred to the course in his absence, perhaps most notably that most greens now had two holes cut in them! With golf's popularity growing – largely due the inexpensive new gutty ball – Morris intended to continue the modifications. He embarked on widening the greens to give incoming and outgoing players greater safety. To meet the same ends, new tees were constructed. These new tees, however, had benefits beyond providing greater safety: they

extended the length of holes, and helped protect the surface of the putting areas from ill-directed blows with a driving club.

Ultimately Morris was to have several great and lasting influences at St Andrews. Around 1866 Morris moved the 18th green back from Granny Clark's Wynd possibly 50 or 60 yards to its current location. Until that point, the green had been on broken ground in a hollow with the ground sloping down on both sides. The ground where the green sits today was a hollow in front of Morris's shop. To make the green, Morris filled the hollow up with a variety of materials including refuse from the town, for the 'formation of an artificial table land'. Perhaps only the base of the hollow known as the 'Valley of Sin' is representative of the original ground level.

Interestingly, there is also a reference to the new 18th green by the famous American golf architect A.W. Tillinghast, who was a friend and student of Old Tom Morris. He stated that Morris told him that the Home Green 'had been built over the bones of dead men', indicating that perhaps the site had at one point been an informal cemetery! This may be

confirmed by a reference in *My Fifty years of Golf* by Andrew Kirkaldy who wrote, 'What is now the eighteenth green on the Old Course was built up from a rubbish heap that had also served at some time as a burial ground'. Either way, prior to 1860 the green had been very different, and indeed earlier in the century, it had had the sea and sand dunes coming up alongside it almost to where the steps of the R&A Clubhouse are today.

Published at the end of March 1866:

Great improvements and preparations are going on for the ensuing golfing season… The road across the Links leading to the West Sands is to be substantially formed so soon as the weather will permit.

A few weeks later another report stated:

The recent showers had made the green to be in excellent condition for this year's May meeting of the Royal and Ancient Club. The recently formed road across the Links is no longer the mess it was, and it will soon be a great boon to every one who visits the locality. The starting hole was placed farther west, nearer to the road than ever we saw it, and was as good as a stroke less than on former years. It was

Far left: From ground level, this green gives no indication it may have a dark history. What hides in the valley of sin, no one can be absolutely sure. But from this angle the front of the green looks pregnant with secrets…
Iain Lowe

Left: Perched on the edge of the Swilcan Burn the 1st green, built by Tom Morris, provides the opening test for all golfers. This photo was taken during the 2005 Open Championship.
Iain Lowe

Right & far right: A close-up of the scorecard and a section of the Hodge plan (c. 1875). Note that the 'scorecard' averages the length of the two dashed lines on each hole. That is, the 5th and 14th holes are given an average length of 470 yards.

Right: The Thomas Hodge plan. This plan features prominently in Robert Clark's book, generally recognised as a masterpiece of golf literature, *Golf: A Royal and Ancient Game*. Published in 1875, Thomas Hodge's plan must slightly precede Clark's compilation, but it is thought by not very much. Regardless, the plan is of greater accuracy than those before it and provides a further window into how the Old Course played in the 1870s.
Courtesy of The Trustees of the National Library of Scotland

The size of the hole was not mentioned until the code of 1893 when, for the first time, it was recorded that its diameter should be 4¼ inches and its depth not less than 4 inches.

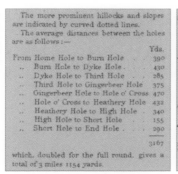

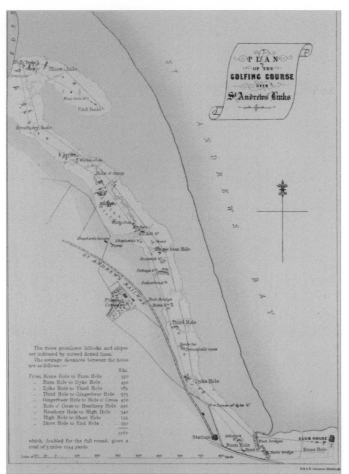

certainly a well-chosen starting point.... Tom Morris has entered upon his new premises, and his hands were busy at the club...

The second of Morris's great alterations was the construction of a new first green just west of the Swilcan Burn in 1870. Like the drifting away of the teeing grounds, this new green was in part a response to growing congestion. Prior to this, all play was towards the Road Hole green, or current 17th. The new 1st green removed that play and, more significantly, inspired the development of the 'right hand' course.

When the right-hand course was initially devised however, it was not the preferred direction, and to begin with was only used to spread the wear and tear in defined areas. Preferred play was up the left and back down the left to the newly-extended areas of the widened greens. But this left-hand route had one significant disadvantage to the new right-hand course – players had to 'cross-over' each other twice; once between the first and last hole, and again between the 7th and 11th holes. In competition this extra 'cross' counted against the course and led to the right-hand course being favoured as the 'official' presentation for all tournaments, starting with the first Open Championship, which was played on the Old Course in 1873.

The 1873 Open Championship

Tom Kidd was the first champion golfer at St Andrews, and his score was the highest winning score yet recorded. Twenty-six competitors took part in the event, which was played as the finale to the annual autumn meeting of the Royal and Ancient Club. Driving rain from the Thursday to the Saturday may have reduced the number of competitors, and it definitely affected the scoring, yet local newspapers were at odds regarding the influence of the weather. One paper reported that the putting greens were in fine condition, but another stated: 'New holes had been cut. But pools of water on the greens added considerably to the hazards and militated against good scores.' *The Field* recorded that the course was 'rather damp and in many places covered with water.' At this time, lifting the ball from casual water led to the penalty of one shot.

Reflections on the Old Course in this period were interesting, and one by Mr Ernest Lehmenn published in the *Times*, significantly so. He said, 'When I first commenced the game at St. Andrews in 1876 there were no tin linings to the hole, nor, so far as I can recollect, any marks defining the teeing grounds'. In an article entitled 'A chat with "Old Tom" Morris about St. Andrews' published by *Golf Illustrated* on 12 August 1910, Morris was reported as saying:

The High Hole was... the first on the Links that had a sheet-iron case put in to keep it in a proper shape. I fell on that plan efter a gude deal o'study, an' it suited to a tee. Then, when ither holes got raggit roond their edges, I had them dune up i' the same wye, an' that was the beginnin' o' the modern style o' the hole tin.

It is not clear, however, in what exact year Morris created the first tin cup.

THE 1876 OPEN CHAMPIONSHIP

The 1876 Open Championship was the second held on the Old Course and saw Open competitors sharing the Links with weekend players. This conflict was highlighted when David Strath, on his way 'In' and followed by a huge gallery, hit an upholsterer playing the outward nine on the forehead! Shaken, Strath dropped a shot and another at the next. He got a 5 at the 17th, but his 6 at the 18th put him in a tie with Martin. Normally this would have resulted in a play-off, but a protest had been filed claiming Strath breached etiquette by allegedly playing up to the 17th green before the players on the green had moved away – the inference being a player or a spectator on the green could have stopped the ball going onto the road. Strath refused to take part in the play-off until the protest had been resolved, stating that if he lost the verdict, the play-off would be superfluous. The verdict never came, so Strath didn't show the next day and Martin walked the course to claim the Open.

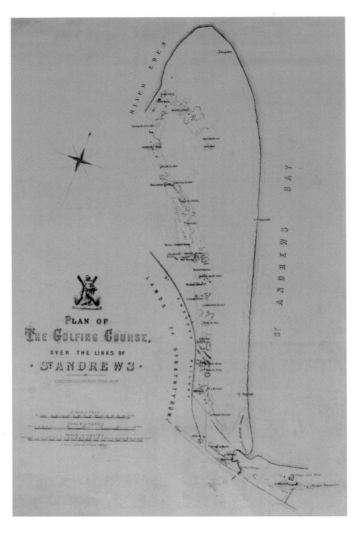

Left: This plan was produced in 1879 by the Kirkcaldy firm of Little and Boothby. The R&A Committee of Management had requested Thomas Hodge to secure this plan. Hodge did this and ultimately the R&A purchased the delicately hand-painted original for £70.

In April 1878 the Green Committee of the R&A, who made most decisions and recommendations regarding the management and running of the links, received instructions that they must submit any proposals to fill up bunkers or materially alter the golf course to the general meeting. They were also instructed to procure a new plan of the links.

Reports suggest the conditioning of the course improved over the next decade, but no other significant changes were reported until 1879. In that year the path of the Swilcan Burn was altered. The Burn was made to curve in a north-west

The 'Old Course' only became known as such in the early 1890s when the 'New Course' was established.

direction, where formerly it had followed further to the south and debouched on a broad sandy channel near the road. Prior to this it had been a much greater hazard. Mr W.T. Linskill, writing in *Chamber's Journal* in 1906, reflected back to the 1870s stating:

> *The historic Swilcan Burn formerly swept almost into the centre of the Links before it turned into the sea, and one often drove into this bed from the first tee. It was then a sandy natural hazard, but now it is a concrete-walled channel.*

Sir Hugh Lyon Playfair initiated the reclamation of the first

fairway. Beginning with such work as the filling-in of Halket's Bunker, he soon moved to considerably larger tasks, most notably the construction of the first sea barrier at the south end of the west sands. However, while Playfair's barrier was backfilled with earth and sown with grass, it was not enough to repel the erosive North Sea swells. It would take the doggedly determined Mr George Bruce to successfully overcome them.

A report in 1893 read:

> *Mr. George Bruce has constructed, at his own expense, a breakwater composed of four old fishing boats, weighted with stones and otherwise secured, at the east end of the West Sands. The object of this is to prevent the tide from washing away the debris deposited at the edge of the links, and so filling up and destroying the utility of the bathing place. It is to be hoped Mr. Bruce's breakwater will stand the winter tides.*

Two months later:

> *It is with much satisfaction that many have observed the great practical utility of the breakwater of old fishing boats formed by Mr. George Bruce. Many experiments of the kind have been tried there before*

Far left & left: These photos show the rebuilding and expansion of the Bruce Embankment in 2004/2005. The wall is set on a giant concrete footing. The 2 inch by 2 inch hollow black plastic pipes allow a small amount of sea water to seep through the stone and concrete wall to a layer of gravel. From here the water can run down behind the wall and back to the sea. It is believed this will relieve pressure on the wall itself.
S.Macpherson

with little success, and when the work was commenced prophecies were rife that the boats would be found some morning at the Swilcan Burn. There have been some heavy seas already, and the boats have not yet set out on their travels towards the setting sun. Of course they have been the means of preventing much of the refuse building material deposited at the edge of the links from being swept away by the sea, and thus have done something towards reclaiming territory from the sea; in addition, in consequence of these boats being where they are, the silt has been kept from filling up the bathing place.

The key to Bruce's design, hatched with the help of his architect son, was to further prevent the movement of the boats. Apart from the stones, on the east side of the boats a sloping barricade of stakes was driven into the foreshore. The council records do not clearly indicate when the dumping of building materials and refuse behind the boats was completed, but soon after the area was sown with a variety of grasses and nitrogen-fixing lupins.

At a town council meeting on 11 January 1897 it was reported that:

A petition was presented from certain inhabitants

praying that a special name be given to the embankment at the back of the Clubhouse. Mr W. Brown moved the motion and it was resolved "that the boat embankment at the back of the Clubhouse be in future named the Bruce Embankment". The main object of the motion was to assert that the embankment was separate from the links, and as there were often complaints of golf balls whizzing through the air to the danger of passers-by, this piece of ground would be an excellent way of getting to the sands without crossing the Links. The passing of the motion would be a compliment to a thoroughly popular and deserving citizen. The motion was agreed to.

Left: Now complete, the new version of the Bruce Embankment gives no hint to its boating beginnings. The marvel of modern engineering, complete with coping stone from China, has improved the access to the West Sands and decreased the risk of tidal erosion.
Iain Lowe

FURTHER ADJUSTMENTS TO THE BRUCE EMBANKMENT

- A plan to have the embankment wall heightened and extended westward at a cost of £150 was resolved by the town council on 13 June 1898. The plan was also for improving the outfall of the Swilcan Burn at the west sands. On 11 December 1899 a further motion was made by the town council, but this time to the 'Roads and Walks Committee' to consider the carrying out of the extension of the Embankment and its details, including walls and surface of the area.
- 30 August 1900 – three old boats to be placed at northwest corner of the Bruce Embankment.
- 9 November 1900 – boats filled with stones gathered from the foreshore, and with bags of sand.
- By December the Bruce Embankment was considered stable enough that sites could be let for use during the Lammas Market, but after consideration, the proposal was declined.
- In September 1904 the wall was raised a further 4 feet 6 inches and backfilled.
- In late 2004 and extending into 2005, new work began to reinforce and extend the western end of the seawall. The new wall is slightly further north and built to widen the well-used road that circles the first and last hole of the Old Course to the north before heading up the West Sands. The design is set at a grade of 2:1 and apart from calming the effect of the sea, the wall allows a small amount of water to seep through the stone and concrete face and drain out towards the sea releasing pressure on the wall itself. It is believed this will reduce the pressure on the wall during heavy seas.

The putting course on the Bruce Embankment was confirmed by councillors on 6 October 1913: 'A plan for a putting course at the Bruce Embankment was submitted. The Property Committee recommended its adoption provided a space of 30 feet is left for a road round the sea margin.' With alterations to the motion, an 18-hole course opened in 1914 and was 665 yards long – the longest hole being 50 yards.

The length of the Old Course had not changed considerably, if at all, during this period. The first known measurements of the holes and course came with Martin's famous plan surveyed in 1821. (See p.15.)

On this plan, the original table showing the 'distances in yards' is not easily legible. However, the chart is accurate and acts as a running tally of the distance played as a golfer moves from one hole to the next. The distance of the course from the 1st to the 10th hole = 1 mile, 6 furlongs and 109 yards;

Distance Table recreated from 1821 Plan of Old Course by A. Martin. (See plan p.15.)

Hole o' Hill								
361	Bridge Hole							
797	436	Cunnen Hole						
1125	764	328	Cartgate Hole					
1503	1142	706	378	Ballfield Hole				
2006	1645	1209	881	503	Hole o' Crofs			
2385	2024	1588	1260	882	379	Muir Hole		
2735	2374	1938	1610	1232	729	350	Eden Hole	
2887	2526	2090	1762	1384	881	502	152	Hole o' Turn

or 3189 yards. A full round = 3 miles, four furlongs, 218 yards or 6378 yards.

In 1821, the first hole in the ground was named the '**Hole o'Hill**', and was cut just west of Granny Clark's Wynd. Players would have their caddies mount their featheries on a small sand cone within a club length of the '**Hole o'Hill**' and play down to the current 17th green – a distance of 361 yards. This was the first hole and known as the '**Bridge Hole**'. The second hole was known as the '**Cunnin Hole**' (Rabbit Hole). It played from the current 17th green to the plateau where the 16th hole is usually cut and measured 436 yards. Play continued in this fashion with players teeing off close to the proceeding hole and playing up a narrow corridor to the next. The 3rd was '**Cartgate**' (328 yards); 4th was '**Ballfield Hole**' (387 yards); 5th '**Hole o'Crofs**' (503 yards); 6th '**Muir Hole**' (329 yards); 7th '**Eden Hole**' (369 yards); 8th '**Hole o'Turn**' (132 yards); 9th '**End Hole**' (302 yards). The '**Hole o'Hill**' hole was played back to as the home or 18th hole. Its length would have been identical to the first hole – 361 yards.

Martin's plan also gives an indication of the width of the Old Course in that period. It appears to have varied from 72 to 193 yards, with the average being 140 yards. However, it is believed that most of this width was taken up by whins, and that the actual playing width was much narrower.

Chalmer's 1836 plan (see p.14) does not specifically list the length of each hole but measurements taken from the original plan indicate the course measures approximately 3166 yards; 23 yards shorter than the total on Martin's 1821 plan. This, while not identical, does verify the chart measurements on Martin's plan.

	1821 Hole Names	1821 Map	1836 Map	1836 Hole Names**
1	Bridge Hole	361	355	Bridge Hole
2	Cunnen Hole	436	440	Hole of Bafield
3	Cartgate Hole	328	325	Hole of Cartgate
4	Ballfield Hole	378	376	Ginger Beer Hole
5	Hole o'Crofs	503	467	Hole o'Cross
6	Muir Hole	379	417	Hole of Shell
7	Eden Hole	350	348	High Hole
8	Hole o'Turn	152	147	Short Hole
9	End Hole	302	291	Last Hole
OUT		3189	3166*	

*   Yardages scaled directly from Chalmer's 1836 plan.
** For hole name variations and descriptions, see Appendix 1.

While hole lengths may be missing, Chalmer's plan offers some notable differences to Martin's earlier plan, not all, some extraordinary rendering detail. Excluding the greater accuracy of what we would term today as fairways, and far greater detail concerning bunkers, Chalmer has surveyed two holes as being cut on the Hole o'Cross. Approximately 60 yards apart– similar to what they may be today between the 5th and 13th – this is the first time a separation of holes on the same green (another term not yet in use) had been illustrated.

Despite the creation of the new 1st and 18th greens, the length of the Old Course did not change significantly before the first Open Championship was held at St. Andrews in

Far left: In 1891 a two-foot putt on the home hole was never a 'gimme' – particularly with the big man bearing down on you! *Cowie Collection, St Andrews University Library*

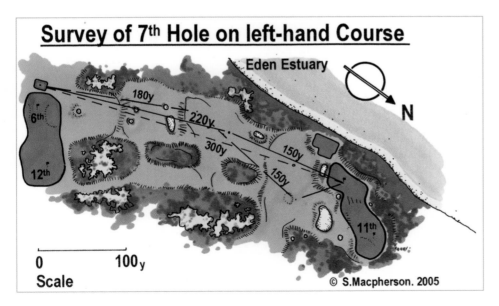

Survey of 2nd Hole on left-hand Course (Reverse Course)

Old Course Hotel

N

OUT-OF-BOUNDS

3rd Tee

2nd

16th

200y

180y

160y

210y

170y

260y

17th Tee

300y

1st

17th 'f'

17th f.

SWILCAN BURN

SCALE

0   100 y

S.Macpherson. 2005 ©

Above: The line off the tee is very important. Few players will be able to attack this pin with two shots because of the down slope on the green and the bunker protecting the front edge. As a result it becomes a very strategic test. Rabbits must tack their way to the green. Tigers may reach it in two shots, but both must exercise confidence in their short game to attain par.

Survey of 7th Hole on left-hand Course

Eden Estuary

N

180y

6th

220y

12th

300y

150y

150y

11th

0   100 y
Scale

© S.Macpherson. 2005

Above: Again, the shot to this hole is very difficult – in spite of its length. The placement of the tee shot is important if one is to avoid bunkers and get close enough to approach the elevated green with a short iron. This green, of course, is the green of the regular 11th hole. The virtues of this putting surface are well documented, so suffice to say, caution is recommended!

1873. The famous Thomas Hodge plan of 1875 (p.32) states the Old Course had a length of 3167 yards for nine holes, or 'when doubled for the full round, gives a total of 3 miles 1154 yards.' Curiously, however, when 3167 is doubled it only equals 6334 yards or 3 miles, 1054 yards – 100 yards less. Was this just the modern version of a typographical error?

Newspaper reports about the length of the Old Course for the early Open Championships are disappointingly vague, as is any reference to which circuit of the Old Course was used. Previous authors and historians have been divided on this topic, but evidence supporting the use of the right-hand course being used can be gleaned from the *St. Andrews Gazette* in October 1879, when a report following the progress of Jamie Anderson said: 'Homeward, Jamie had the worst of his misfortunes going from the heather to the hole across'. *

* In September 1895, *Golf* published the following comment: 'An interesting question has been frequently discussed in St. Andrews as to the proper designation of the fifth hole. It is colloquially described as the "Hole Across" while in the golfing manuals it is given as the "Hole o' Cross." For the local designation it is pointed out that in former days the only road to the hole was "across" the Elysian field and "across" a range of bunkers. What is the argument for calling it "the hole of the cross?"'

Player _____					Hdcp _____		Date _____			
hole	yards	par	str.	score	hole	yards	par	str.	score
1	399	4	1		10	371	4	18	
2	452	4	9		11	162	3	10	
3	356	4	15		12	321	4	14	
4	363	4	11		13	358	4	6	
5	445	5	5		14	525	5	4	
6	345	4	13		15	375	4	2	
7	364	4	3		16	329	4	12	
8	176	3	17		17	375	4	16	
9	276	4	7		18	358	4	8	
out	3176	36			in	3174	36		
					out	3176	36		
					total	6350	72		

Marker's Signature _____

Player's Signature _____

Competition _____

Please repair pitch marks and replace divots.   OR

Basic SSS 72   Handicap _____ Nett Score _____

ALL GOLFERS PLEASE NOTE
If a match fails to keep its place on the course and loses more than one clear hole on the players in front, it should allow the following match to pass.

Above: Card of the reverse course. Once a year in early April the reverse course is set up for play. The 2nd and 7th holes are particularly strong, with the uphill 7th (12th on right-hand course) perhaps playing better in reverse.

This, in modern terms, is the 12th to the 13th holes, and proof the right-hand course was in use that year.

The left-hand course was only used once during a major tournament and that was in the 1886 Amateur Championship won by Horace Hutchinson. It happened by chance when the week of the event coincided with the turn of the left-hand course. The tournament was in progress before the authorities became aware of the situation and so play was allowed to continue.

In terms of length, for the Open in 1882, the Old Course was estimated roughly at 6000 yards. For the same event, *The Field* wrote, '… and as St. Andrews links from tee to 18 holes, is rather under 6000 yards…' This is shorter than accurate measurements of the course around this time indicate. A report by E. Oswald in 1921 looking back at the 1888 Open Championship stated that an accurate measurement of the Old Course in that year was 6434 yards. However it is difficult to know if the course was remeasured in 1888, or if this report is restating the erroneous measurement on Hodge's plan, including the mysterious additional 100 yards.

Fortunately, another plan existed to help clarify matters. Published in 1879, the same year as the Little and Boothby plan, this new plan appears to have been surveyed by J.S. Kemp (see p.40). Entitled 'Plan of the Golfing Course, St. Andrews,' it was published in *Harpers New Monthly Magazine* in 1894 and gives the Old Course a total measurement of 6323 yards.

During this time the 'new ball' went through many phases from being nicked and hand-hammered to being varied in weight. In the mid-1880s a composite India rubber and cork ball called the 'eclipse' joined the pure gutty. This ball tried to alleviate the harsh sound the pure gutty made on contact with the clubface. The famous writer and gifted golfer Horace Hutchinson used one to good effect when winning the British Amateur Championship in 1886 and 1887. He wrote of the ball, 'It goes off the clubface with the silence of a thief in the night'. But the eclipse ball did not carry as far. However, as reported by Martin in *The Curious History of the Golf Ball*, '…being livelier, it made up distance on the run. It bored

Left: View from the tee of the 7th hole in the left-hand course. The red flag can just be seen in the distance off the tee. The best line is often just right of the flag. Care must be taken to avoid the bunkers and the best iron to approach the green with is a short, lofted one.
S.Macpherson

well into the wind but was more difficult to loft on the approach shots. It putted well on greens either slick or slow, seeming by its softness to "creep" over small obstacles that would jar a pure gutty ball off line. But critics so derided the eclipse as "the putty ball" that its makers sought to harden it up, and in so doing ruined it. After about 1892 it was forgotten.'

Greens: Surprisingly, such an important area as the green has only been properly defined in the rules of golf since 1952! In the early days, the word 'green' meant the whole area of the course, similar to the phrase 'through the green' that is still used in the *Rules of Golf*. The first code of rules in 1744 refers to 'the fair green'. The first definition for the green, as restricted to the surface prepared for putting, was in 1851: 'All loose impediments of whatever kind may be lifted from the putting-green or tableland on which the hole is placed, and which is considered not to exceed twenty yards from the hole.' In 1888 the definition was more precise: 'those portions of the links devoid of hazards within twenty yards of the hole'. This with slight variations remained the official definition until the Anglo-American revision of 1952, when the new definition was adopted:

'The putting green' is all ground of the hole being played which is specifically prepared for putting or otherwise defined as such by the Committee.

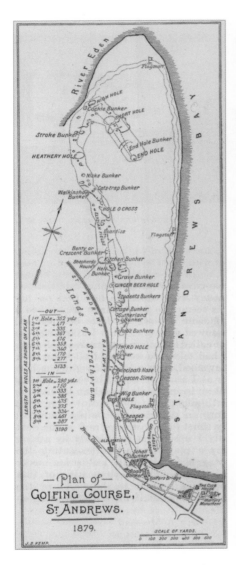

Above: While being slightly mysterious, this plan is of great interest because of its scorecard. Drawn in 1879 and featured in the European edition of the *Harper's New Monthly* magazine, many holes such as the 1st, 2nd, 17th and 18th are essentially the same length today.
Courtesy of the Trustees of the National Library of Scotland.

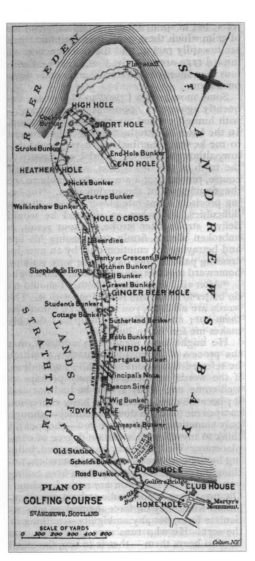

Above: Published in 1892, this plan follows the popular upright format of the day. On it, two variations can be noticed. Firstly, on the 1879 plan the name of the bunker now referred to as 'Scholars' changes from 'Schall' to 'Schold's Bunker'. Secondly 'Cartgate Bunker' is also named for the first time.

DISTANCE A BALL WAS BEING HIT IN 1894

Women golfers	70–100 yards
Average player	120–140 yards
Good player	140–160 yards
Exceptional driver	170–180 yards

As the new ball was being celebrated, a significant change in the rules of teeing grounds started to affect the shape and playing experience of the Old Course. The *Rules* best show the gradual movement of tees away from greens, and are fundamental to all changes to lengthen the Old Course since.

In 1754 the (feathery) ball had to be teed within one club's length from the hole last played. By 1858 this distance had increased to not nearer than six and not farther than eight club lengths. In 1875 the ball was not to be teed nearer than eight and farther than twelve club lengths, except where a teeing ground was provided. And by 1888 all reference to any distance to the hole within which the ball must be teed disappeared from the rules. Instead the rule read:

> *The ball must be teed within the marks laid down by the conservator of the links, which shall be considered the "Teeing Ground." The balls shall not be teed in advance of such marks nor more than two club lengths behind them.*

Sand-boxes were introduced to the Old Course in the early 1880s. This innovation made sand available to players for them, or their caddy, to tee up their ball without having to deface or deepen the previous putting hole; which could often become troublingly deep.

On the Old Course this led to the construction of formalised teeing grounds. One remnant tee, probably constructed by Old Tom Morris, can still be seen just in the approach to the 13th green. (See photos on pp.41 & 42.)

At this time the Links was in the early stages of becoming considerably wider. A description of the course in the 1888 *Golfing Annual* by J.O.F. Morris painted an interesting

picture. Describing the 3rd green, he wrote, 'By the edge of this putting green is a long bunker, which stretches nearly across the green…' The reference is to the bunker now known as 'Cartgate', but today the green is three times as wide as the bunker. Similarly the 11th hole was a much smaller target than currently experienced. 'Leaving the tee you see plenty of bunkers ahead, and if you go too far with your tee shot – say ten yards past the hole – you land into the river Eden; while ten or fifteen yards either right or left drops you into bunkers which are not so easily got out of.' The last bunker that provides a clear indication of the then narrowness of the course is 'Cottage' on the 15th hole. Morris wrote, 'In driving for the next hole there is a bunker which is invisible to the player, and stretches nearly across the course…' Today it sits between the 15th and 4th holes and can be easily avoided to the left or right.

About 1890, golf was embarking on a new voyage. While the gutty had made golf more popular and the new pilgrims wanted places to play, one group in England was about to change the way we looked at golf and our courses forever. On 13 May 1891, the first competition against a hypothetical opponent representing the playing of perfect golf at every hole was played at the Coventry Club. Known as the 'Bogey man' or 'Captain Bogey', he represented the 'ground score' and was the first way of bringing uniformity to the scoring systems employed at varyious courses. This invention would soon shape competitive golf and course architecture.

> While Colonel Bogey was invented first, 'par' was not far behind. Indeed, in the late 1890s and onwards there was much debate about what bogey and par represented. One person commented, 'Bogey presents approximately the number of strokes which ought to be taken to each hole without serious mistakes. The par of a hole or round is defined as the total number of strokes which should be required for them without mistakes… In other words, bogey represents a scratch player's round, whereas par represents absolutely perfect play.'

Golfing terms diverged in America, after the invention of 'birdie' in 1899. Started at Atlantic City, it represented a score of one less than par. The story has it that George Crump put

his second shot inches from the hole on a par 4 after his ball hit a bird in flight. Eagle and double eagle followed, but Britain stuck to bogey until the early 1940s when par superseded Colonel Bogey and 'birdie' officially caught on.

As regards course design, Tom Morris was at the forefront of the new industry and traveled extensively giving advice, often at no cost, to excited clubs, groups and individuals. The change of rules regarding teeing areas had facilitated the laying out of new courses on land that previously may have been impossible. So in *Golf* magazine, Morris responded to one such man anxious to get advice on how to lay out a golf links and made the following points:

1. *As to the length and breadth of links, if you have so many miles of ground you can put holes down at, say, from 100 to 550 yards, vary them accordingly. The breadth may be from 50 to 100 yards.*

2. *Regarding the possible cost of preparing it. If the putting-greens had to be laid out, it would require £5 for each green. Then, if the course had to be cleared of gorse bushes or whins it would likely cost about £200.*

3. *Regarding the third question, the best way to form*

Above: A hand-hammered gutty ball, c.1850–1865.
S. Macpherson

Left: Small and rectangular in size (4 yds by 6 yds) and slightly raised, this tee is representative of most tees on the Old Course and indeed elsewhere. However, it is a rare remaining link in the evolution of teeing grounds between the greens and the modern teeing grounds.
S. Macpherson

Right: The evolution of the teeing grounds can be more clearly seen when viewed from above. The 1875 rules provided for the use of separate teeing grounds and here the tee most likely created by Old Tom Morris can be seen just off the 13th green (as marked in red). Further away to the right are the tees now used for the 14th hole. The general drift is right and back, a drift that affects the play-lines of a hole. This photo was taken prior to the new tee being built for the 2005 Open Championship.
Iain Lowe

Below: The Bramble ball, c. 1898–1902.
S. Macpherson

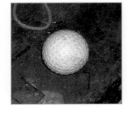

a club would be to get as many friends together as possible, and form a club; then advertise that such a club has been instituted. As to subscription, the scale of club entry money runs from 2s. 6d. to £10.

4. *There is no necessity to have trees on a golf course; large sand pits dug in the course called bunkers or a whin or two serve as a hazard to all players.*

Morris concluded with some remarks about the rental of ground and the best time to lay turf, but it was clear his experiences on the links had defined his ideals as they pertained to golf and the layout of links.

By 1900 the production of gutty balls was in a high state of perfection. The balls were economical in price and the gutta could be melted and remade. Many professionals had their own moulds and made their own balls. As regards to the length to which these gutty balls could be hit, a report in 1896 said:

An average drive is 170-180 yards. A long drive we should take to be 200 yards or over. Taylor's average shot we should say, without actual measurement, is about 180 yards. Mr Tait is a very long driver, and his average shots are 190-200 yards. He has the reputation of having

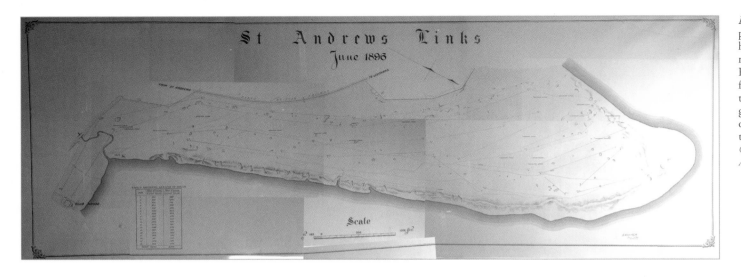

St Andrews Links
June 1896

Scale

driven the longest tee shot on record, namely, 341 yards, 0 feet, 9 inches, on Jan 11th, 1893, at St Andrews...

During the period of the gutty, and the various versions and improvements on this solid ball, few physical changes were made to the Old Course in terms of length. Instead, the most significant change may have been the increase in its width. The causes of this expansion came primarily from two fronts; new irons and more players. With the cheaper gutty ball available, the game became considerably more popular. However, this led to a reported 'trampling' of the Old Course, and its surrounding heather, bunkers and gorse. But more than that, the increasing use of irons brought about a greater physical destruction of the turf and surrounding plant growth than had ever occurred with wooden clubs.

The impact irons had was largely unforeseen. Prior to the gutty, the feathery was played primarily with long wooden clubs. Few divots were taken with these clubs as the ball needed to be struck with a sweeping motion. The combined development of the gutty and the iron club saw a big change in the swing. Players developed a much steeper swing and a 'square stance', as opposed to the open stance employed by the earlier generation. The result was a more downward blow

on the ball, and often thereafter, the turf. The 'sweep' was replaced by a 'hit'. As David Hamilton described in *Golf: Scotland's Game:* 'A bent elbow at the top of the swing appeared with a full pivot, giving the player a full arc of club movement, and the ball was hit with more force. Only later, with the next ball, the Haskell, came the straight left arm, and a shorter swing, and it was commented at the time that the passing of the gutty "took the athleticism out of the game"'. However, while there is some evidence that shows scoring improved after the introduction of the new equipment, history would come to show that compared to the effect golf balls and new clubs in the future would have, the gutty period was perhaps the least dramatic.

TIME TO RESURVEY THE OLD COURSE

Hall Blyth was a civil engineer and chairman of the Rules of Golf Committee. His 1896 plan (above) is interesting for several reasons, the first being that it is in a landscape format, second because it included the new 'New' course and third, for the measurement of the holes documented. In terms of length, the plan states the front nine as being 3015 yards long and the back nine 3132 yards. However, on the scorecard, next to the length of 358 on the 12th hole an anonymous hand has

Hole	Old Course Lineal Yards	New Course Lineal Yards
1	362	287
2	397	380
3	318	301
4	372	356
5	501	206
6	330	425
7	325	333
8	136	490
9	267	265
10	283	447
11	149	267
12	358	366
13	370	129
14	460	383
15	360	292
16	347	447
17	455	289
18	361	406
Total	6097	6189

Above: Detail of scorecard from the 1896 plan above left.

Above: The Royal and Ancient Clubhouse.
S. Macpherson

Far right: Photo from *Guide to St Andrews and Neighbourhood* by Hay Fleming (1897).

written a question mark, and indeed correctly so, for when the hole is remeasured according to the scale of the plan, the hole is approximately only 308 yards, making the back nine 3082 yards, and the course a total length of 6097 yards.

It is possible that the Old Course had developed multiple teeing grounds by this time, and that Hall Blyth's plan only measured from the normal teeing grounds and not the back tees. Especially, according to the official log, as the distance of St. Andrews in 1892, four years earlier, was 3 miles 1028 yards (6308 yards) and the longest of the championship courses – 311 yards longer than the second longest course, Sandwich.

In the case of the back tees, a report about the advent of these could not determine if Sandwich or St Andrews installed the first set of special tees or 'medal tees' to be used on state occasions, but it was thought that this happened about 1890. What is certain is that the rules had been sufficiently relaxed for eight years for this to occur. Additionally, it is not a big leap from this point to having tees constructed for the purpose of lengthening a course to the extreme limit to test the equipment and players of the day.

The first specific measurement found of the championship

tees at St Andrews was made in 1898. Editor and author Garden G. Smith included in his book, *The World of Golf,* an appendix featuring the measurements of the championship courses and the Old Course measured 3133 yards going out, and 3190 yards home for a total yardage of 6323. Perhaps the fact that Smith uses the term 'championship' is the most important aspect of this reference because 6323 yards is the same measurement detailed on Kemp's 1879 plan published in *Harpers New Monthly Magazine* in 1894.

Golfing Crime on the Old Course (*Golfing*, March 1904)

At St Andrews Police Court a couple of labourers pleaded guilty to having, on the links at that part known as the seventeenth teeing ground, without the authority of St Andrews Links, removed for a distance of about 25 yards nearer to the dyke which encloses the ground round the old railway station, the teeing box and the marks placed to indicate the teeing ground.

The Procurator said the teeing ground had been placed pretty well out to give the golfers an opportunity to keep clear of the sheds. On the morning in question, the accused had been seen hanging around in the Stationmaster's garden, and in the evening it was found that the tee had been removed 25 nearer to the dyke, the objective having apparently been to set a trap for the players, as golfers would from this tee have to play right over the corner of the shed, and if the shot was not a particularly good one the ball would fall into the Stationmaster's garden.

Judge Barr said it was diabolical to interfere with the natural course of sport in this way, and in respect that the accused had previously appeared before the court, he imposed the full penalty, namely, a fine of £1, with the alternative of fourteen day's imprisonment.

Definition: A 'Bulger' Club was defined as a club with a convex face.

In pre-championship days Allan Robertson, a man born in 1815 and regarded then in the same awe as Tiger Woods is today, was looked

THE FIRST HOLE IN A GREAT MATCH AT ST ANDREWS (A. KIRKALDY v. W. PARK)

upon as the perfect golfer. His score of 79 (40 out and 39 home) was established in September 1858 and not surpassed till 1869 when young Tommy Morris shot 77 (4,4,4,5,6,4,4,3,3 – 37; 3,3,4,6,5,4,4,5,5,5 – 40) on the Old Course. His score was the St Andrews record until 1888 when the professional Hugh Kirkaldy made it round in 74 (4,4,4,4,4,4,3,2,4 – 33; 4,3,4,4,6,4,5,6,5 – 41). A year later Kirkaldy reduced it to 73 (35, 38) and in February 1894 Freddy Tait broke the course record with 'a marvellous' 72 (36 and 36). Then Andrew Kirkaldy in 1895 equalled this record, going out in 38 and coming home in 34 – a prodigious feat for those days. Finally, Willie Anderson in June 1897 lowered the record to 71 (36 and 35). Now many felt the Links had become at least 5 or 6 shots easier than it had been. For those old stalwarts, who were perhaps denying that the greater width of the course and improved equipment were mostly just making the game more fun, a nasty surprise was around the corner. In the next five years golf would experience a revolution.

It is unknown by whom, but in June 1900, the following assessment of the course was written;

> With the increase of Golf has come a greatly increased labour bill, and the Links are now, despite all the increase of play, in an incomparably better condition than they were when a single old man with primitive ideas on the subject was employed in the upkeep of the Links. Anyone who has had experience of the St Andrews Links for the past 30 or 40 years will tell you that the course is 10 strokes easier than it used to be. Between 1860 and 1870, and even some years subsequent to the latter date, the course was greatly more restricted in its area, being flanked on either side by whins and rough grass. It was altogether rougher, with more bad lies, and the safe line to the hole accounted in not a few instances for an extra stroke being placed on record. Another important factor in the case is the extra hardness of the surface, and the closeness of the turf.
>
> "In times of old" there was nothing like the run got out of the ball that there is now. As an example, take the first hole. Up to and including 1867 the Links east from the Swilcan Burn were regularly let for cattle-grazing. Instead of a smooth, lawn-like surface,
>
> now characteristic nearly of the whole Links, you had rough pasture ground. Cutting obliquely from Clark's Wynd to the burn mouth was the "old road", a trap for many a well-placed ball. This road had been sown out with ryegrass, and the turf consisted of "win'le straes" [tufts of hay] and bare patches cut in every direction with cleek and iron. To traverse the whole course from beginning to end would be to give a repetition of the same story with variations in detail. To the 2nd hole the direct route was to the corner of the dyke. On the one side were the rushes, on the other the whins and the cart-worn hollows, which were rank with vegetation. There was not then, as there is now, any dodging away to the right to approach the green. The bunkers had to be faced boldly, and if any error of judgment was made, you were trapped on one side or the other. The same at the 3rd – straight and narrow was the way, and no backdoor entrance. A weak approach was frequently bunkered, whilst if too strong, with intent to clear the hazard, you were over the green altogether amongst the rough. In the 1900 Open, both Braid and Vardon were reported to have reached the 5th green in 2.
>
> Not to go back to Allen Robertson's time, when the route to the Hole Across was by the Elysian Fields, it is doubtful, even when the low road became practicable, if these long drivers would have attempted this feat. Right along the table in front of the green was a nasty bunker, now filled up. To avoid this hazard Davie Strath and Jamie Morris invariably played short. Going to the Heather Hole, a perfectly straight ball can be got with a certainty on the green in 2. In former times, to have attempted the present line would have resulted in brisk business to the ballmakers. Acres of whin and heather covered that portion of the course, and the only safe road to the hole was away by the left. Generally the long spoon was played from the tee to keep short of the bunkers. Another full shot followed, and very frequently another

quarter stroke was needed to reach the putting green. The High Hole, difficult as it still is, was then even a greater terror. The green was not so spacious, and if you overran it, you had either to play your ball out of the bents or perchance from the sandy bed of the river Eden. Now on the further side good turf is provided, and although over the bank, you may still get down in 4. Passing the Short Hole, we reach the end of the outward journey. Heather on one side, whins on the other, appealed to one's sense of caution, and "sure" rather than "far" was the golfer's motto. Now you may hit all over and not find a bad lying ball to trouble you.

Homeward, the chief difficulties and variations may be briefly sketched. Take the High Hole first. Formerly it was on a steep slope and if you were lucky you might have done the needful in 3, yet miss your putt and a 6 might have been taken. Tom Morris left his mark here on present-day golf. He has got the green nearly flat, and almost eliminated all the "sport" from it. The chief differences in the next two holes lie in the ease with which bunkers may now be avoided, and the more certain approaches to the holes, leaving a good

deal less to be done in the putting. Playing to the Ginger Beer Hole, a little is now gained in the distance, the route being perfectly straight, whilst formerly a couple of obtuse angles were cut out by the golfer. Away to the right of the Elysian Fields, then to the left of Hell Bunker, and then to the right again with a longer and more dangerous approach than is called for now. From the Ginger Beer onward to the home green, whins and rough ground generally were more in evidence. The Mussle Road was in worse condition, and the road from Granny Clark's Wynd to the sea was not macadamised. In winter it was generally a deep puddle; in summer it was scored with deep ruts.

Again, in front of the last green there was an amplitude of heights and hollows, which have been made one uniform level, permitting of a more certain approach. Another feature of St. Andrews Links more easily negotiated are the bunkers themselves. In the procession of wet seasons we had in the 1870s the bunkers were doubly hazardous, in that for nearly whole seasons they stood feet deep in water. In order to prevent a recurrence of this, Tom Morris has raised

PLAYERS VOTES FOR HOLES ON THE OLD COURSE

	2 shot	3 shot	1 shot	3 shot	2 shot	3 shot
	2nd	5th	11th	14th	16th	17th
J.H.Taylor, Open Champ in 1894, '95, 1900		●				
Mr John Low			●	●	●	
Mr H. Hutchinson- Am Champ, 1886, '87	●	●				
Tom Vardon	●		●	●		●
Harry Vardon			●			
James Braid				●		
Leslie Balfour Melville Am. Champ 1895	●		●			●
Herbert Fowler			●			●
Alex Herd			●			

the "level of their foundations", and they are not nearly so deep as they at one time were. Who that has followed a first-class match of former days cannot recall how frequently the players were in difficulties, and how often this factor was the determining influence of the game. Nowadays any player who knows the line may escape every hazard. Let us do justice to those of a former generation, whose reputation was made under conditions eminently less favourable, and so dissimilar as to afford no proper ground for comparison.'

From 1848 to 1902 the gutty ball reigned supreme. Around the world it was the ball of choice for players of all ages and abilities. Golfers at the Old Course had, like many others, taken the wee ball to heart, and the more gifted players had used it to break all existing records set with the feathery.

During the same period, the Old Course had been in a state of constant change. Reviews of the succession of both natural and man-made changes were mixed. Stalwarts were usually aghast, while the more progressive were often supportive. But realists from both groups knew the Old Course could not be frozen in time. It was always going to change, if in no other way than just as a natural response to the wind and rain that constantly shifted the dune sands.

Before all the wind had gone out of the gutty ball the editors of *Golf Illustrated* approached leading golfers and authorities to comment on the best one-, two- and three-shot holes in golf. They wanted to know which courses had held up best in the face of this new technology. Despite all the changes to the hallowed links in St Andrews, the Old Course did very well. (See table p.46.)

It is not the love of something easy which has drawn men like a magnet for hundreds of years to this royal and ancient pastime; on the contrary, it is the maddening difficulty of it.
– Robert Hunter, 1926

THE HASKELL
The three-piece wound ball – 1903–1949

*I think I can say without contradiction that the most significant change made in golf equipment
since the inception of the game was the development of the wound ball, the steel shaft notwithstanding.*
– Bobby Jones

The 'American' ball, as it was snidely referred to in Britain – or the Haskell, as it is properly known – was the second revolution to hit the Old Course, and the biggest yet. The changes this small sphere brought about, and the pace at which they occurred, could not have been predicted at the time, but altered the direction of golf forever.

American Coburn Haskell invented the rubber-cored ball in 1901 with the assistance and expertise of B.F. Goodrich Rubber in Akron, Ohio. Speculation exists about how the balls first came into being, but it seems Haskell, who was a keen sportsman but not the greatest golfer, was looking for a new ball to give him an advantage over his playing partners. He thought that the 'zip' from a ball with a rubber centre would have an advantage over a solid ball.

> Analysis of one of the first modern-rubber-cored Haskell balls showed it used 190 yards of thread that was stretched to eight times its original length!

Horace Hutchinson previewed the new ball in 1901 for *Country Life* magazine and wrote:

Certainly I think they fly better – just a little better, as probably every ball flies – with this pimply exterior. But still I fail to see that they have the distinctly further carry than the "gutty" which is claimed for them in America… They fly further than "gutty" off the iron clubs, are good balls for lofted approaches, and good enough for putting, but are very ill-suited for running over rough ground. I have this fault with them, that out of a dozen or so tested one was distinctly inferior to the rest, which suggests a suspicion that unless special care is taken in the make of this complex article the lots will not come out very even. Also, about one in three or four shows a minute crack after a good deal of play… The ball has merits; it has not every merit.

The best golfers in the land were trying this new ball and in May 1902 *Golf Illustrated* published the response of three leading players, James Braid, Alex Herd and Harry Vardon:

Above: The Haskell ball.
S. Macpherson

Opposite page: A view up the Swilcan Burn to the first green and beyond.
S. Macpherson

Sir, – I have tried three Haskell golf balls and split them all, one at the second shot, another playing the third, and the other at the first hole of the second round. I found very little difference in length of drive between them and the gutta balls; perhaps they run further, but they certainly don't carry as far as the gutta ball. They are also more difficult to stop when approaching, and on the putting green are very liable to jump out of the hole if played firmly.

I am, Sir, etc., Jas Braid.

Sir, – In answer to your letter in regard to the Haskell ball, I think it a very difficult ball to play with. It drives all right, but that is about all I can say about it. As regards putting, especially on hard, bumpy greens, it is simply off altogether; it hasn't got the click to guide you on the putting green, such as the gutty ball has. What one thinks he can gain in the drive he will very soon lose on the putting green. It is too fiery altogether on the green. I hope all the professionals play with it at Hoylake except myself. So much for the Haskell.

I am, Sir, etc., Alex Herd

Sir, – I find with the Haskell ball I can't get as far as with the gutta; they are very difficult to approach and putt with. I don't think they will be much used after a little while. A golfer may play well for a week with them, but he won't be so certain with them as with a gutta; at least that is what I think. I am of the same mind as Herd, that nobody using them will win the Championship.

I am, Sir, etc., H. Vardon

Ironically, when three weeks later the Open Championship at Hoylake came around, in June 1902, better examples of the rubber-cored ball were available and Herd 'cheerfully and unblushingly' played with a Haskell ball, shot 307, beat Vardon by one shot, and won! From that point, the days of the gutta ball were numbered. In 1902, high prices were being paid for the better Haskells, but by 1903 ball production and quality increased and very soon after, the use of the rubber-cored ball became general.

It had not taken those eminent in the golfing field long to speak out about the state of the game and the potential impact of this new ball. At the heart of the issue was the fitness of the courses as a test of championship golf. It was felt there had been a certain state of equilibrium between the power of the ball and the length of the course and that this had been overthrown by the 'clever American invention'.

After the 1902 Open, Vardon commented again:

I have taken some pains to ascertain the opinion of nearly all the leading professionals on the subject, and every one of them holds the view that the game should be kept as it is at present, at the high water-mark of pure skill; and we contend that the rubber-cored ball tends to discount this, and puts a premium on the less skilful player.

The debate may not have been on the merits of the new ball itself, but its suitability as a medium to test golf and the skill of the best golfers on existing courses. John L. Low commented in the *Athletic News* in August 1902 saying,

The mind of the American man is exceedingly cunning, and he has devised a ball which makes it easier for the ordinary mortal to go round a golf course in a low score…We acknowledge that your ball is easier to play with than a golf ball, but you need not make any more, as we don't wish the game made easier, our links being laid out to test the strength and skill of a golfer playing with a ball made out of a certain recognised material.

It was estimated that on courses that were currently a good length, holes would need to be lengthened by about thirty

yards to give good driving its former advantage.

In *Golf Illustrated* in October 1902, John Low commented again about the rapidly changing debate, moving his position from the abolishment of the new ball to the lengthening of holes and increasing the number of hazards,

> *...there can be little doubt that more bunkers, especially in the neighbourhood of the hole, would lessen the ease with which approach shots could be played with the new ball... but the proposal to lengthen the holes is far more important, inasmuch as it involves us in fresh difficulties which must be considered. The chief of these is that the moment we make the distance of the "carries" and the character of the holes suitable for the Haskell, we at the same time standardise the Haskell, for we must never lose sight of the fact that the gutta is, as far as our courses are concerned, the present standard ball. If we speak of St. Andrews as an ideal, a standard course, and the holes as "good," or standard "one," "two," or "three shot" holes, we must allow that we are working on some unit of measurement, and that unit, of course, is the distance a gutta ball can be driven by a good player.*

Ignoring the wind's effect, this is of course true. Any movement of the teeing grounds would standardise the course to the new ball and make play with the old gutta ball difficult, if not obsolete. It was quite a conundrum. With players rapidly taking to the new ball, the Royal and Ancient Golf Club, particularly the Green, Links and Rules Committees, were under pressure. The Club responded by agreeing to tackle the question at the earliest possible opportunity. Indeed, in the old minutes of the Links Committee dated October 1902, there is a note about bunkers stating: 'It was resolved that the members of the Committee should inspect the bunkers on an early day with the view of deciding whether any alterations should be made therein.'

The 'Battle of the Balls' was picking up pace by the end of 1902 and respected English golf architect Herbert Fowler commented,

> *How does the rubber ball affect our standard courses? No doubt it makes them easier, and makes holes less interesting to play... St Andrews is probably three to five shots easier. St Andrews is meant to teem with two-shot holes. With the new balls there are only the fifth, fourteenth, and seventeenth which cannot be reached on a still day by a long driver with an iron club for the second shot. The bunkers and hazards or the course have also apparently shifted their positions, and many old terrors have departed. But they can be brought back to exert their old influence by making new tees at certain holes.'*

In response to Low's comments about standardising the golf courses, Fowler replied,

> *It has been said that to alter our courses to suit these new balls will be to standardise the rubber ball. There is, no doubt, some truth to this, but the question we shall have to face is whether we shall bar the new ball, and play with one in every way its inferior; or so alter our courses as to suit a ball which the vast majority of players of all classes greatly prefer.'*

In 1904 the Royal and Ancient Club was ready to tackle the situation and the decision was made to lengthen the Old Course in the autumn. As the right-hand course had for some time been the medal course, it was acknowledged that carrying out such alterations to bunkers and teeing grounds would render the permanence of this situation.

But first an accurate measurement of the Old Course was required, including the new teeing grounds laid out in 1902. In the old minutes of the Greens Committee on 13 April

The term 'bunker' first came into use in 1812.

that year the following note was found:

It was agreed that the length of the holes on the Links should be remeasured and the chairman was requested to arrange with Hamilton for having this done.

In November the measurements of the holes on the Old Course were certified by Mr Jackson as:

1st Hole	365 yds	10th Hole	312 yds
2nd Hole	402 yds	11th Hole	148 yds
3rd Hole	341 yds	12th Hole	318 yds
4th Hole	385 yds	13th Hole	403 yds
5th Hole	533 yds	14th Hole	516 yds
6th Hole	345 yds	15th Hole	365 yds
7th Hole	333 yds	16th Hole	338 yds
8th Hole	139 yds	17th Hole	456 yds
9th Hole	273 yds	18th Hole	361 yds
	3116 yds		3217 yds
		=	6333 yds

With the Open due to be held in June 1905 on the Old Course, it was expected that the course would have stayed at this length for the Championship. However this was not to be. Changes were afoot!

Golf Illustrated in December 1904 made the following comment on the changes:

Several important alterations in tees have recently been made on the Old Course at St. Andrews with the object of lengthening respective holes. At the Burn hole (1st) the tee has been put fifteen yards back, and now it takes two good shots to reach the corner of the dyke. At the third hole very good play is required now to get a four, as thirty yards have been added to it. The journey to the fourth hole has also been extended by about twenty yards. The long hole has been left

unchanged, but in going to the sixth the tee box has been lifted back nearly thirty yards, so that what use to be an easy four will now be a very good one. It is calculated the length of the out-going journey has been increased by about 140 to 150 yards. There has not been so much alteration on the homeward holes, the most noticeable being at the fourteenth green, where the tee for the fifteenth hole has been put 25 yards back. Speaking generally where par of the hole was four, but modern conditions have made a three probable, it has been the aim to restore the former condition of things.

An article in *The Scotsman* also sheds more light on the position of the new tees:

The tee to the sixth has been placed further back, and well to the right, and by putting the tee further to the left at the ninth some rough country now has to be crossed. Instances of the lengthening process are also found at the thirteenth, fourteenth, and sixteenth holes. In all, about 200 yards have been added to the medal round.

The Field, a very respectable English paper, made additional comments about the new tees in June 1905: 'Before the lengthening of the tees took place in view of the present Open Championship St. Andrews was the longest of all the championship courses. Its measurement up to today was 6333 yards, and by lengthening the tees... another 200 yards [have been gained]'.

Indeed, the extended course length was exactly 200 yards longer. The front nine had been stretched 150 yards and the homeward journey 50 yards, making a total yardage of 6533 yards.

	1900 OC	1905 OC	
Hole	June 6,7	June 7,8,9	
1	365	365	Burn
2	402	416	Dyke
3	341	353	Cartgate
4	385	417	Ginger Beer
5	533	533	Hole o' Cross
6	345	370	Heathery
7	333	345	High
8	139	164	Short
9	273	303	End
	3116	3266	
10	312	312	Tenth
11	148	148	High
12	318	318	Heathery
13	403	413	Hole o' Cross
14	516	516	Long
15	365	405	Cartgate
16	338	338	Corner of the Dyke
17	456	456	Road
18	361	361	Home
	3217	3267	
Total	6333 yds	6533 yds	

Official yardage of the 1905 Open layout as compared with distances from the previous measurements in 1900.

The Royal and Ancient Club did not settle for just lengthening the course: after the new tees had been completed a plan showing suggested bunker locations was drawn up and put on view in the Clubhouse for members to discuss. Soon after, at the spring meeting of the R&A, it was agreed, on the recommendation of the Greens Committee, to introduce several new bunkers to the course.

While sadly the plan showing the proposed locations of the bunkers is no longer thought to exist, H.S.C. Everard described the situation on 12 May 1905 in *Golf Illustrated*:

[In the Spring meeting] the convener next brought up

Left: A view down the 15th hole shows the three bunkers known collectively as 'Rob's Bunkers', and hiding up in the distance on the left, the 'new' bunker.
Iain Lowe

Left: This 'new' bunker was added just prior to the 1905 Open to catch a pulled second stroke to the fifteenth hole. Due to the undulations that surround it, rarely will it ever catch an over-hit shot to the third hole. It is believed that this bunker was originally called 'Fowler's' when first cut. See p.70.
S. Macpherson

the subject of the new bunkers, divided into two classes, those on the course and those off it. A plan of these new hazards has been on view for some weeks past in the club. The bunkers off the course have been introduced in the interests of the long but erratic drivers, who will no doubt appreciate this consideration for their welfare. It has been the object of the committee charged with the delimitation of these bunkers to restore the course as far as may be to its former condition, to render it more similar in character to what it was in years gone by. In the meantime the bunkers are being opened up, to be ready, if possible, for the Open Championship in June.

The location of these new bunkers was further described in *The Scotsman* in June 1905:

At many points the tees have been put back to give greater length to the holes, and placed to the side of the fairway so as to introduce new hazards. Including the sand bunkers which have been made, in all thirteen

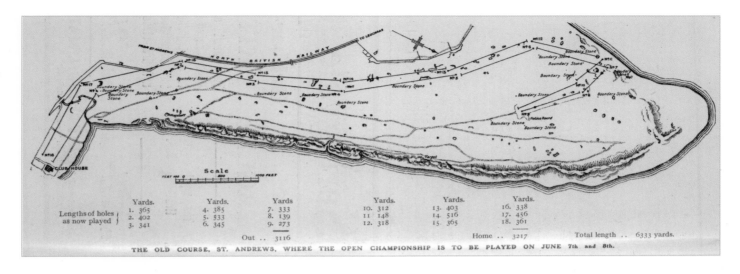

	Yards.		Yards.		Yards		Yards.		Yards.		Yards.
Lengths of holes as now played	1. 365	4.	385	7.	333	10.	312	13.	403	16.	338
	2. 402	5.	533	8.	139	11.	148	14.	516	17.	456
	3. 341	6.	345	9.	273	12.	318	15.	365	18.	361

Out .. 3116   Home .. 3217   Total length .. 6333 yards.

THE OLD COURSE, ST. ANDREWS, WHERE THE OPEN CHAMPIONSHIP IS TO BE PLAYED ON JUNE 7th and 8th.

additional hazards will test the skill of the golfer. The bunkers have been cut on the right of the fairway to the second, third and fourth holes, and a new bunker has been introduced beyond the third green to trap the strong approach and to catch a pulled second stroke to the fifteenth hole.' (See photos p.53.)

Horace Hutchinson described the 'Recent Changes in the Old St. Andrews Course' in an article published in *Golf Illustrated* in May 1905:

The first is unchanged; of course the tee will be kept as far back as possible. The tee for the second is kept right back almost at the burn; bunkers are cut at intervals right along the right hand of the fairway. It will be remembered that for the medal days the custom was for the tees to be placed in front of the holes and almost on the putting greens. This is no longer done. The tees are kept back. The description of the second hole fits the third and fourth also, with the addition that a bunker has been made just beyond the green of the third… Little has been done to the fifth, the long hole, and the tee shot may be sliced far to the right

without any greater disaster happening.

The sixth and seventh are the two holes at which the destruction of the whins has made the greatest difference. At the former the space between the bunkers in the fairway and the whins on the right used to be so narrow that it was a most dangerous line to take. The whins there vanished, and the straight line to the hole became the right and obvious one. Now a few bunkers have inadequately replaced the whins, but still the hole is far easier than it was. At the seventh everybody now plays his tee shot to the right of the big hill straight on the hole. Not many years ago this was an impossible line owing to the whins. Nothing in the way of bunker cutting has been done to take their place, and the hole is consequently a good deal easier than it was, but at both this hole and the preceding one much is to be said for allowing play along the right hand side, because it takes the players out of the way of those home-coming. Of the Short hole, there is nothing to say. There is a back tee but it makes little difference. Some bunkers are cut on the left side of the course to the ninth, and there is one on the right that comes in as a hazard for a short and pulled tee shot to

the tenth. There is a back tee, too, for the ninth, and some cross bunkers to catch a topped tee shot, and these also catch a sliced tee shot to the tenth. The eleventh is practically the same, though there is a levelled green at the head of the old sloping green which is dangerous because there is no rise to stop the ball going into the Eden. The twelfth is just the same as ever, always a catchy hole, though the course both left and right for the tee shot is wider than it used to be. The tee to the thirteenth is rather back, and both here and at the next hole, where the tee is far away back from its old position– behind the hole on the right– this lengthening of the tee shot brings an added element of danger. At the former hole it is difficult to steer beside the bunker, whether the right hand or left hand line is chosen, so closely as to give a good chance of getting home in two. It has to be said, however, that both the tee shot and the second may be sliced off the line with an impunity that was not known in olden times. At the fourteenth hole the lengthening of the tee shot has the effect of making the horrible little "Beardie" bunkers very dangerous hazards. If the wind is at all against it is not possible to carry them and the wall of the field. For the rest of the hole is much as it has been for twenty years– always difficult enough. At the fifteenth hole bunkers are badly wanted, and the want is to be supplied, to catch a sliced drive. A sliced second, too, goes without penalty here as it never used to, but a bunker, as said when talking of the third hole, makes a bad hazard for a pulled approach.

The sixteenth is a hole at which taking back the tee has added very much to the difficult of the tee shot. It may be possible to carry the Principal's Nose; it is not possible to carry the little pot beyond it. If you go to the left you are among the ditches and furrows and a long way from home. The heroic course between the Nose and the railway is the right one, but it is mighty

narrow. The seventeenth is as it always was, except that sloping down the bank from the green to the road has made the latter a less desperate hazard than it use to be. And the last is quite unchanged.

Hutchinson felt compelled to also mention that a 'modern engine' was changing the playing conditions of the Old Course. While the first small mower had been introduced in 1882 and could replace sheep and scythes, the larger 'horse-mower' – widely known as 'Shanks' Pony' (because they were widely manufactured by Shanks) – was now available. Drawn by horse or pony but powered by a petrol motor, it was significantly better at cutting grass. It was advertised in 1905 as being 'specifically designed for golf courses'. Hutchinson wrote that its use meant 'you do not any longer get the hopelessly smothered lies in the long grass that you used to get,' meaning, on the fairway, as Mr W.T. Linskell had earlier described, 'all the grassy hollows were overgrown with long, rank, benty grass or rushes'. But even with the new bunkers and added length, the course was, in his modest opinion, four or five shots easier with a gutty ball, and more with the rubber-cored ball than twenty years earlier.

Never before had such widespread improvements been made, even when the gutta percha ball had emerged. Previously bunkers had been regularly changing, often without any formal notice. One report in *Golf Illustrated* in November 1901 stated:

Left: On the 9th hole, what was originally one bunker is now two, but still just named Kruger after the South African president Paul Kruger, who held power during the Boer War 1899–1902. Another bunker called Mrs Kruger can be seen in the distance.
S. Macpherson

One of the new bunkers recently made on the Old Course at St. Andrews, viz., that in front of the tee at the last hole out, has already received a sobriquet; it goes by the name of "Kruger," perhaps on account of its hidden and treacherous nature.

These were comprehensive and unparalleled changes to the Old Course. They were believed necessary for three chief reasons.

1. The course had grown wider than it had ever been.
2. The ground was becoming harder with the trampling of the 'multitudinous feet, seldom of the smallest size, of the golfer.'
3. The American rubber-cored ball.

Additional inventions such as the Bulger club and improving turf had also reduced the sternness of Old Course examination. After the Open, reactions from the players and press were varied, but this cartoon (below) which featured in *Golf Illustrated*, 23 June 1905, summed up the feeling of some.

Below: Cartoon of 'Spittoon's' – *Golf Illustrated*, 23 June 1905, published after the Open Championship.

THE LATEST IMPROVEMENTS AT ST. ANDREWS, AS DESCRIBED TO OUR ARTIST BY A COMPETITOR.

To be truly admirable, a course will probably incur in the general opinion the accusation of being unfair.
– H.N. Wethered 1931

THE 1905 OPEN CHAMPIONSHIP

Prior to the alterations, there was much speculation about what the winning score would be for the 1905 Open. Many expected it to be, with the new ball, four to five shots lower per round than J.H. Taylor had scored with a gutty ball in 1900. Considering Taylor's total was 309, his best round being a 75, sixteen to twenty shots lower would put the winning total in the low 290s – a remarkable total indeed!

However, a report in *The Field* read:

Even with the 200 yards added to St Andrews the winning scores would be found to average 73 or 74. This concession in low scoring, as compared with earlier years of the Open Championship, is made not only on the ground that the new ball has made the game generally easier, but also because the leading professionals have attained a higher level of scientific skill…

As it turned out, James Braid won using a Spalding 'White' ball with a total of 318 – incomparable to Taylor's 309. The *Times* on 10 June 1905 reported:

It was generally agreed, however, by those present at this meeting that the course used this week was much more difficult than any previous course over which the championship had been played at St Andrews. The greens, which were exceedingly keen, were very difficult, and in addition a strong cold wind blew during the first two days, making low scoring almost impossible.

While the strong cold winds adversely affected the projected winning score, they also prevented an accurate analysis as to the value of the renovation works. It was commented that the wind led to the punishment of many well played shots. Rumblings from the players included: 'The bunkers are badly placed'; 'the course is too narrow at the sixth and thirteenth holes'; 'the greens are like skating rinks'; 'it is no test of golf at all.'

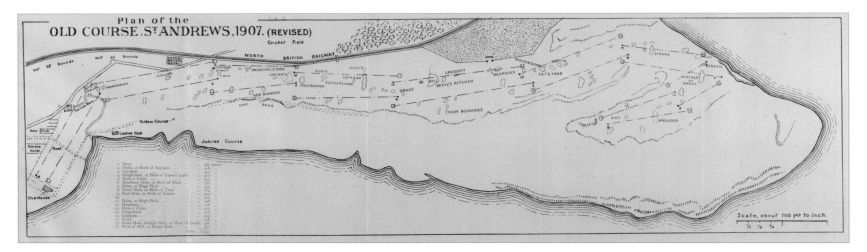

Plan of the
OLD COURSE, St ANDREWS, 1907. (REVISED)

Scale, about 160 yds to inch.

A report in *The World* read:

There were very few competitors in the open champion-
ship who did not find occasion most heartedly [sic]
to abuse the putting greens on the old course at St
Andrews. The bunkers also came in for their full share
of disparagement. "They were far too numerous",
"badly placed", "unfair"– such were the opinions
expressed by those whose scores were higher than they
should have been. Doubtless the authorities will take
cognisance of these complaints and arrange matters
differently when the chief event of the season falls
again to be decided at St Andrews. The putting greens,
needless to say, must be returfed forthwith, unnecessary
bunkers filled up or levelled to the ground and the
way of all competitors by all means made easy. But,
after all, the test was the same for everyone, and it is
only fitting that it should be a severe test for those who
aspire to win the highest honours of the game. Although
undoubtable keen to a degree, the putting greens were
true, and the perils of the hazards were to be avoided
by a nice union of skill with judgment.

A report in *The Scotsman* soon after the event read:

1. Burn	...	365 yards
2. Dyke, or Hole of Bayfield	...	416 ,,
3. Cartgate	...	353 ,,
4. Gingerbeer, or Hole of Cunnin Links	...	417 ,,
5. Hole o' Cross	...	533 ,,
6. Heathery Hole, or Hole of Shell	...	370 ,,
7. Eden, or High Hole	...	345 ,,
8. Short Hole, or Hole of Turn	...	164 ,,
9. End Hole, or Hole of Return	...	303 ,,
10.	...	312 ,,
11. Eden, or High Hole	...	148 ,,
12. Heathery	...	318 ,,
13. Hole o' Cross	...	413 ,,
14. Gingerbeer	...	516 ,,
15. Cartgate	...	405 ,,
16. Dyke	...	338 ,,
17. Road Hole, Bridge Hole, or Hole of Leslie		456 ,,
18. Hole of Hill, or Home Hole	...	361 ,,
	Total	6,533

To our mind the professionals seemed to forget alto-
gether that the course was not layed out to suit the
weather conditions such as prevailed on the first and
second days of the championship… The fact remains
that the alterations in the course were made by a body
of gentlemen well qualified to speak with authority,
and while there is not the slightest doubt that the
weather conditions led to undue punishments, many

Above: Nisbet's plan
shows the changes made
to the Old Course for
the 1905 Open. The
lengthening of the tees
and the new bunkers
were a deliberate effort
to maintain a status quo
when it came to scoring.
Nisbet's Plan 1907 (revised),
published in 1908 Yearbook,
p.476.

Above middle: A close-up
of the plan reveals some
of the revisions. Some of
the new bunkers have
been labelled.
Plan courtesy of the trustees
of the National Library of
Scotland

Above left: Hole names
and lengths as described
on Nisbet's 1908 plan.

Above: Now commonly referred to as the 'Seven Sisters', these seven bunkers catch many shots that leak to the right off the 5th tee. The penalty is almost always a dropped shot – and sometimes more!
Iain Lowe

of the new hazards did their work well. In spite of all that was said, the Green Committee of the Royal and Ancient Club have no intention of taking their instructions as to how to lay out a course from young English professionals.

Although tough but timely words, it was generally felt that the judicious changes had proved successful in counteracting the effects of the rubber-cored ball. The added length had done something to restore the proper proportion of the course and the new hazards had re-emphasised the importance of accuracy on an ever-widening course. And if there was still an issue remaining, it was the width of the course. A continuous trench down the middle was one solution, as was having the railway fields categorised the same as the Stationmaster's garden, i.e., out-of-bounds (this happened in 1911), or continuous bunkers down the sides of the holes. A more sensible and practical idea brewing was the notion of increasing the rough around the course. This was thought to perhaps improve the beauty of the

course without the danger of having it periodically overblown with sand.

In late July, Horace Hutchinson offered his experienced position firmly, but with diplomacy, in the *Westminster Gazette*:

> They [new bunkers] *were made primarily to act as substitutes for the whins that the massive feet and niblicks of the golfer have worn away; they are an attempt to revert to the old classic conditions; and accordingly as they succeed in restoring that golden age shall we who knew that age and loved it appreciate them.*

Before all talk of the 1905 Championship faded, H.S.C. Everard speculated about the par value of the renovated links. During the event proper, he did not think it difficult:

Out	4	4	4	4	5	4	4	3	4	=	36
Home	4	3	4	4	5	4	4	5	4	=	37
										=	73

All the holes given a 4 were being reached with a drive and an iron, except the 13th, which played exceptionally long due to its length – even Braid required two long raking shots with wooden clubs to reach the flag. But Everard did wonder if this rating would hold up under all circumstances. As it turned out, though par had been invented in 1891, the R&A finally recognised bogey in 1910 and Everard's approximation was adopted sometime after.

Definition of the Day – Bogey represented a scratch player's round, whereas par represented absolutely perfect play.

In 1905 Tom Morris acted for the last time as official starter for the Open at St Andrews.

Numerous things were to happen before the next Open would be held at St. Andrews, but perhaps nothing brought more sadness to the town than the sudden death of Old Tom

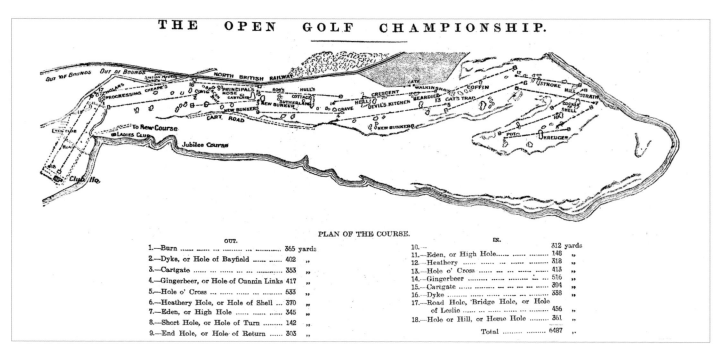

THE OPEN GOLF CHAMPIONSHIP.

PLAN OF THE COURSE.

OUT.		IN.	
1.—Burn	365 yards	10.—	312 yards
2.—Dyke, or Hole of Bayfield	402 „	11.—Eden, or High Hole	148 „
3.—Cartgate	353 „	12.—Heathery	318 „
4.—Gingerbeer, or Hole of Cunnin Links	417 „	13.—Hole o' Cross	413 „
5.—Hole o' Cross	533 „	14.—Gingerbeer	516 „
6.—Heathery Hole, or Hole of Shell	370 „	15.—Cartgate	394 „
7.—Eden, or High Hole	345 „	16.—Dyke	338 „
8.—Short Hole, or Hole of Turn	142 „	17.—Road Hole, 'Bridge Hole, or Hole of Leslie	456 „
9.—End Hole, or Hole of Return	303 „	18.—Hole or Hill, or Home Hole	361 „
		Total	6487 „

Left: This plan of the Old Course seems identical to that printed in Nisbet's *Golf Yearbook,* (see page 57) but was printed in *The Scotsman* during the 1910 Open and features a scorecard showing that the course had been shortened.
Courtesy of The Scotsman

Morris. An unsuspicious accident in the New Golf Club on 24 May 1908 saw the end of a man who had contributed an enormous amount to both the town and the Links – not the least being the design and construction of the 18th green. Appropriately, the Royal and Ancient Club paid tribute to his life by renaming the 18th hole after him on 29 September 1908.

September 1908: 'Willie Auchterlonie accomplished a very unusual thing the other day. All golfers know the 4th Hole at St. Andrews. It is 417 yards and quite a good 5. Auchterlonie holed it in 2, a great swipe with his brassie running home. There are not many recorded instances of long holes being done in 2.'

Prior to the 1910 Open Championship, plans and guides of the course indicate approximately ten new bunkers may have been cut over the 3rd, 5th, 6th and 10th holes, probably between 1905 and 1908. As well, in about 1907 the turf either side of the Swilcan Burn, which frequently held its 'poachiness' long after the autumn rains, was heavily sanded. With this work done, word regarding the course set-up for

the upcoming Open was eagerly awaited. When it came, the notice read 'to all intents and purposes the holes will be the same, as regards the positions of teeing grounds and putting greens, as they were on the last occasion the event was at St. Andrews.' The lengths of the holes given however, gave an overall course length 44 yards shorter than in 1905.

1st Hole	365 yds		10th Hole	312 yds		
2nd Hole	402 yds		11th Hole	148 yds		
3rd Hole	353 yds		12th Hole	318 yds		
4th Hole	417 yds		13th Hole	413 yds		
5th Hole	533 yds		14th Hole	516 yds		
6th Hole	370 yds		15th Hole	395 yds		
7th Hole	347 yds		16th Hole	338 yds		
8th Hole	142 yds		17th Hole	456 yds		
9th Hole	303 yds		18th Hole	361 yds		
	3232yds			3257 yds	=	6489 yds

The report mentioned that 'last time the greens were very fiery, owing to a prolonged spell of dry weather; on this

April 1910: 'Last week Mr. A.B. Mc-Intyre, St Andrews Liberal Golf Club, actually holed the 9th from the tee; this is a par 4 and a good 3. There was a following wind at the time; although extensive inquiries have been made, there is no record of this feat ever having been accomplished before. The hole is about 277 yards in length.'

occasion Hugh Hamilton, the greenkeeper, is taking measures to prevent a repetition of this by having them all copiously watered in the evenings.'

What would be the effect on scoring of softer greens and a shorter course, with an improved Haskell ball, including new smaller, heavier models introduced in 1909 such as the 'Baby Kite', 'Midget Dimple' and the 'Heavy Colonel'? Regardless of the new bunkers, with the skills of top golfers also advancing it seemed obvious that the winning score in 1910 would be lower than 1905, and so it proved.

THE 1910 OPEN CHAMPIONSHIP

Oddly, while the course actually ended up measuring 6487 yards after the 7th hole became shortened by 2 yards, in June James Braid averaged 74.75 in achieving his winning total of 299. A storm cancelled the first round and softened the greens further, but the long-hitting Braid with his well-trained aluminium putter played well to demolish his previous winning score at St. Andrews by nineteen shots.

A humorous story regarding the sodden conditions in the first round involved this ultimate champion. While his excellent score of 76 ultimately never counted, he managed to play the conditions better than most because he was using a ball that sank. In an age when some balls were 'floaters', Braid had a denser model that fell to the bottom of the hole when reaching it. Others playing the floating ball may have had an easier shot from flooded bunkers, but when they reached the top of the hole, were seen jabbing it down with a mashie. Down it went, only to bob back up. 'Was that holed out?' the man would ask.

Comedic situations aside, however, the new Haskell had seen a great number of scoring records being broken. The Old Course had held out bravely for a long time but Mr N.F. Hunter shot 74 in 1904, prior to the course being made more difficult for the 1905 Open. In that Open the best round was 77 by Rowland Jones. But in 1910, George Duncan and Willie Smith both shot 71!

Many of the new scoring records were to be made with a new, smaller rubber-cored Haskell that came into being around 1909. The first Haskell was a light, floating ball, but the new small ball offered less wind resistance. Being much heavier, it ran further along hard ground and did not require the same skill to control, especially in the wind.

Golf, for the first time, was becoming a game that was played more in the air than along the ground. The change was mainly in response to the new balls that now had dimple patterns to diminish friction, add length and ensure steadiness of flight. Now, lofted shots could be played with greater control and more spin. Under these circumstances, the 'pitch and run' shot was required less often. Those at the Royal and Ancient Club favoured the limitation of the ball, but the degree of this limitation, and the methods by which it could be best achieved, caused much debate.

In 1912 Garden G. Smith wrote an interesting article entitled 'Some facts for Anti-Standardisers'. It reflected on the differences of the gutta ball versus the new smaller Haskell. In the article Harold Hinton is quoted as saying the difference 'in all conditions of weather and all conditions of ground, would be about sixty or sixty-five yards'. Using this math, the claim is that 'if the balance of the game and its old character is to be preserved, that the modern two-shot hole should be 120 yards longer than the old.' A chart was then provided showing the lengths of old and modern courses.

Course	Yardages in 1898	Yardages in 1912	Difference
St. Andrews	6323	6487	+164
Sandwich	6012	6143	+131
Hoylake	5955	6455	+ 500
Muirfield	5890	5952	+ 62
Prestwick	5732	5918	+186

Obviously the total course yardages in 1912 had not kept up proportionally with the distance the new ball could be hit.

Indeed, allowing for two short holes, the others had only increased on average, 19 yards. Smith concluded that 'rubber-cored apologists' had some pretty maths 'to compute' before they could make good their assertion that 'the advocates for standardisation [of the ball] have no grounds for saying that the rubber-cored balls have altered the balance of the game and destroyed its character.' There was no doubt that the longer Haskell ball had altered the balance, but had it destroyed its character?

The character of golf was constantly changing. Whilst the new ball was affecting the golfer's experience on the course, on a global scale the more user-friendly ball was enticing people to the sport. So with a growing demand for new courses, the profession of 'Golf Course Architect', which had only existed in a minor capacity, was given a giant boost, especially in the United Kingdom and the United States. The growth and popularity of golf was almost certainly a response to the improving equipment.

But there was rebellion in the ranks. A report in the *Manchester Courier* said:

The first sign of a revolt against the principal of making a course to suit the ball has occurred at Hythe, where the members agreed that the alterations carried out last

Left: This is a famous picture of Hell Bunker, published by Horace Hutchinson in his remarkable book *British Golf Links* in 1897.

year had made the course too long and too difficult for the majority of members and for the average player. The course is to be again re-constructed: all the best features of the new alterations will be retained, but one or two holes will be closed.

The decision of the Hythe golfers will strike many sympathetic chords all over the country. No club which seeks to keep its place among the foremost in its district can do so unless it as a course not less than 6,000 yards, and if it does not measure that distance it may be safely assumed there are people plotting to stretch it out at least to that length. This contest between the

Below left & far left: The rebuilding of Hell Bunker took on new proportions in late 1998. It took five men a month to revet Hell Bunker using 10,000 turfs. It is the largest bunker at 600 square metres and at its highest point it is 3 metres (10ft). The face of the bunker was also reinforced. Railway sleepers were sunk into a concrete base beneath the turf wall. Furthermore, as one of the most common causes of revetting failure is dryness, irrigation was installed into the sod face. Time is a greater cause of revetting failure, however. And when it came time to rebuild Hell bunker in March 2007 (for the second time since 1998), the Links Authorities decided to remove the sleepers and their concrete bases. This change brought great relief to many Old Course traditionalists. Golfers who visit 'Hell' are unlikely to feel the same relief however.
Iain Lowe

Above: A postcard showing Hell Bunker in the 1920s. It was a frequently visited hazard for golfers playing in both directions… and not a rake in sight!

Below: Photo of Horace Hutchinson, Amateur Champion at St Andrews in 1886.

ball and the ground cannot go on indefinitely. The ingenuity of man cannot make 60 yards into 70, though it is quite likely it will invent another ball that will travel ten yards further. Apart from the expense and inconvenience of annual alterations, the game is losing its appeal to many people. Courses are too long, too exhausting, and too difficult, but, unless something is done to set up a standard ball, there is nothing left but to extend the holes, and cut more bunkers.

Some concern was being shown for the famous hazards. It was felt that the length the new ball could be hit was making hazards like the Cardinal at Prestwick and Hell Bunker at St Andrews obsolete.

Hell Bunker, from 1882 onwards, was regarded as losing some of its former terror anyway. In the old days when golfers played out and back on the same course it was necessary to cross the bunker twice, but now, with the whins pushed back, it could be avoided on either side. Also, about the turn of the century, photos clearly show the face of the bunker was not as steep or as high as it is today.

In a story written around the turn of the twentieth century, Horace Hutchinson narrated an incident in which Hell Bunker was not as formidable as it sounded, and indeed, was

predisposed to having a bottom in which grass grew after the rains. In the story as it was told, a golfer had fallen into this bunker but been able to play 'a long spoon' out:

Coming in from a round of Golf in a season when the lies through the green were not all that they should have been, [the player] gravely [told] Old Tom Morris that the only decent lie he had had all day was at the bottom of Hell Bunker. Whereupon that sage custodian of the green was aroused to drastic action and sent out Honeyman [his assistant]… with picks and hoes to delve in the bottom of the parlously-named place till no man could possibly boast that he came out of it with a long spoon.

In 1908, Horace Hutchinson became the first Englishman to Captain the Royal and Ancient Golf Club.

The placement of hazards and their condition was always a talking point at St. Andrews. In 1913, a budding golf course architect named Dr Alister MacKenzie delivered a lecture to the Golf Greenkeepers' Association about the Old Course:

The great object in placing hazards is to give the players as many thrills as possible. On many inland courses there is not a thrill on the whole round, and yet on most of the championship courses one rarely takes a club out of the bag without having an interesting shot to play. This particularly applies to the Old Course at St Andrews, and is one of the chief reasons why it always retains its popularity with all classes of players. It is quite true that even this course is condemned by some players, but this is usually due to the fact that they have not brains enough, or have not played on it long enough to appreciate its many virtues. I do not pretend that the Old Course at St Andrews is perfect; it has many disadvantages particularly in the absence

of long carries from the tee, and in its blind bunkers, but there is no doubt about this that no course in the world grows upon all classes of players in the same manner. The longer one plays there the keener one gets, and this is a much truer test of a good course than the one which pleases one at first, and bores one later on. St Andrews is a standing example of the possibility of making a course which is pleasurable to all classes of players…

These were wise and timely words to the greenkeepers, who were rapidly gaining new tools and equipment. However, while the power mower was a great step forward from the horse-mower, the application of sand was still important at St Andrews. Tom Morris had made an edict about it in the late 1860s, and everyone had followed it. Sand, Morris thought, was the best restorer of an exhausted green. Hugh Hamilton, the greenkeeper during the extensive course extensions, followed Morris's practice but also included a compost of black earth and an admixture of nitrogen and phosphatic manures when top-dressing his greens. While early comments about the effects of the manure were good, by 1906 this mixture was no longer used. Ordinary sand blown up from the seashore had taken its place, 'with the result that the greens look less like those of a suburban inland course than has lately been the case,' it was reported.

However, Hamilton read the report and replied,

The only green on which seashore sand has been used as a top dressing is the home green, the soil of which is of a heavy nature and requires toning. All the other greens continue to be dressed with sand and loam in equal proportions, or when it can be had, the top spit of the natural soil and my mixture of manure for putting greens. This treatment yields the utmost success, and I shall be only too glad to hear of something that will give better results. I only wish the writer of the article

referred to would take a walk around the links with me and I would show him the mischief done to the greens by sand when blown across the links by a strong gale, such as that we had last week. It simply cuts through the fine grass leaving bare patches here and there. In my opinion, the proper place for seashore sand, so far as worn out greens are concerned, is the beach.'

Above: Hell Bunker full of water in 1912.
D. Smyth

As regards the quality of the greens, they were in a far improved state than how they had been. Dr J.G. McPherson, who played his best golf in the middle of the nineteenth

Left: Here men fan out with buckets of sand gathered from the local beaches and repair divoted areas on the Old Course.
While modern top-dressing methods have improved, repairing divots is still mostly done by hand.
Cowie Collection, St Andrews University Library

Right: The 1913 plan of St Andrews Links. Though from well after the 1905 changes, this scorecard still reflects the earlier course length. A notable alteration on the plan, however, is the 11th hole which shows the green in a location only currently used in the winter. (See close-up below.)
Plan courtesy of the Trustees of the National Library of Scotland

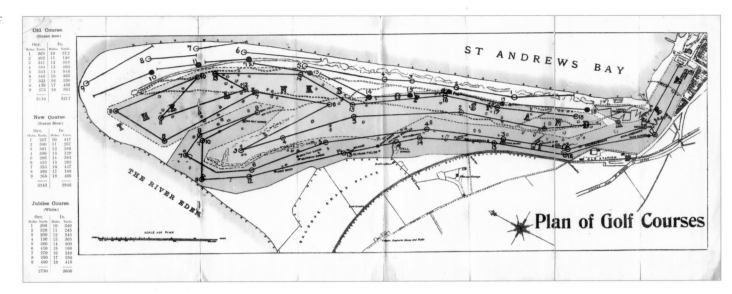

Plan of Golf Courses

Right & far right: Close-up of scorecard and 11th hole from above plan.

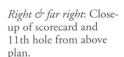

Old Course.
(Tinted Red.)

Out.		In.	
Holes.	Yards.	Holes.	Yards.
1	365	10	312
2	402	11	148
3	341	12	318
4	385	13	403
5	533	14	516
6	345	15	365
7	333	16	338
8	139	17	456
9	273	18	361
	3116		3217

century, estimated the Old Course had become six shots easier before the 1890s. And while he put this down to the gutty ball, the widening of the course and the reduction in size of the bunkers, he thought the most serious change of all was the uniformity of the greens. In earlier days, Dr McPherson wrote, 'There was a variety of surface which brought out the greater skill; now all are nicely turfed over and artificially dressed like billiard tables. The Sandy Hole puzzled the uninitiated with its heavy putting surface; now it is a stroke easier.'

Since 1908 water had been available at all greens via a system of wells. Only the 1st, 17th and 18th lacked their own well, but were instead fed by water hand-pumped from the burn. Occasionally the greens benefited from an extra-long soak when the local fire brigade practiced their monthly drill on the links, using the engine to pump from the burn.

The condition of the links was unstable, with both dry and wet conditions causing consternation. During the dry periods measures taken to improve the Old Course involved decreasing the amount of play on it. To ensure this, flags were removed from the greens on the Old Course and temporary greens employed. The tariff was also taken off the New Course. In early August 1912, after good rains, the greens and turf had significantly improved so the ordinary putting greens on the 1st, 2nd, 16th, 17th and 18th holes were reopened, and several more the week after. Similarly, the flags were reinstalled.

Casual water through the greens and in the bunkers often caused issues. Pumping operations out of the bunkers were common and in 1913 Garden G. Smith commented in *Golf Illustrated*,

The Old Course has been going from bad to worse for the last fifteen of twenty years, and of late, it has been evident to competent observers that a crisis in its history

Far left: Looking across the front of the 6th green and the back of the 12th green when the sun is setting gives the overwhelming impression that the form of these greens has been modified. Over the long period that the Old Course has been maintained, some of this is undoubtably from the aerification and top-dressing processes, but these slopes could have been 'created by the hand of man' also.
Iain Lowe

was rapidly approaching. The deterioration of the course is due to several causes. The fine old seaside turf got completely worn out with the increased traffic which followed the great golf boom that began about 1890…the authorities took no steps to restrict play on [the Old Course]. *Instead they endeavoured by the use of top-dressings and the sowing of strong grass to enable the course to stand the extra strain on its constitution. To a certain extent, for a certain period, they succeeded, but it was at the sacrifice of the kind of turf that gave the St. Andrews course its special and superlative quality. The course gradually took on a grassy, inland aspect, and the whole character of the golf was altered.*

…The course has become water logged. In other words, either the level of the links has sunk, or the water level has risen, so that the rain-water, which used to disappear very quickly, now remains for long periods, and in the deeper bunkers is more or less present continuously, except in a dry summer.

Measures were taken to drain some areas, but little if any substantial work was completed. Instead, it had been noticed that many of the bunkers had become deeper, and

Top left: More apparent from the back of the 4th green (and the back of the 14th) is the possibility that this green may have been artificially levelled. The longer slopes and flatter areas indicate that some degree of slope-smoothing may have taken place, most likely when the greens were expanded.
Iain Lowe

it thought that raising the bottom of the bunkers by adding sand might help. It did. Additionally, to control water flow through the Swilcan burn, in late 1913 the last section of the burn was piped.

December 1913: 'Playing in a foursome, Mr Edward King, M.A., ex-captain of the New Golf Club, holed at the 13th hole of the Old Course in 2. This is a record for the 13th, par play for which is 5.'

The year 1914 seemed to be a reasonably quiet year, perhaps because the nation was preparing for war. One event that was of note however, concerned Mr H.S. Colt, the designer of the new Eden course. He had suggested some alterations to the

Above left: For its size, Boase's bunker gets more customers than it deserves. Acting like a catcher's mitt, balls that land in it on the full do not bounce out and the ground around the bunker funnels many other shots into it. If players can reach it, they must aim left or right.
Iain Lowe

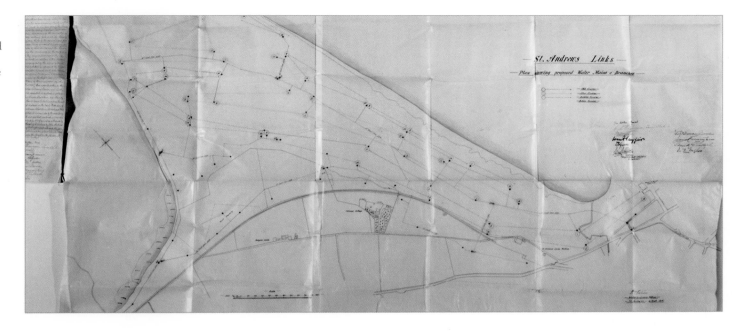

Old Course, and the St. Andrews Town Council had taken the matter up. Sadly, no records attributed to him directly have been found, but in August of that year, one suggestion was found. The sub-committee appointed to consider changes reported that apart from the improvement of the shape of a few bunkers nothing was revolutionary,

till the sixth green is reached. Here, where it will be remembered there is a very great deal of room on the left, a bunker is suggested to be cut in the left-hand part of the green. While in this neighbourhood it may be added that a new bunker is also proposed to be cut on the left in the face of the twelfth green. Thus anybody taking the safe and wide line to the left to this twelfth hole, would have to pitch his second right home over a bunker, a feat of considerable nicety. Something like a radicle [sic] alteration is proposed in the case of the ninth hole., the one hole at St. Andrews which even patriotic persons will admit is not a very good one. Here the suggestion is to carry the green some 80 yds

further on and to the left, where there is a fine natural site for a green. On the way home, except for the twelfth before mentioned, there is nothing very exciting. A belt of grass to be left purposely rough under the wall on the Elysian Fields is one small alteration, and another is the filling up of a little bunker on the way to the fifteenth, which is sometimes, I believe, known by the name of Mr Hull [see photo p.84]. Some people have desired also to fill up Deacon Sime, the famous, or infamous, little bunker beyond the Principal's Nose at the sixteenth hole, but iconoclasm did not get quite so far as this.

Were these Colt's ideas?

Speaking of changes to the Old Course, one feature that is rarely mentioned but is referred to by James Balfour in his 1887 book *Reminiscences of Golf on St. Andrews Links* (and followed up by Hutchinson in his 1913 article called 'Milestones' in *St Andrews Golf*; see Chapter 8), is the levelling of putting greens by the terracing up of their lower edges. Golfers at St Andrews

Length of Holes on the Old Course					
HoleNo.	Name	Yards	HoleNo.	Name	Yards
1	Burn	370	10	Cenh	312
2	Dyke	401	11	High coming home	164
3	Cartgate going out	350	12	Heathery going home	314
4	Ginger Beer	427	13	Hole o'Cross	410
5	Hole o'Cross going out	530	14	Long	527
6	Heathery	367	15	Cartgate coming home	400
7	High going out	352	16	Corner of the Dyke	348
8	Short	150	17	Road	467
9	End	306	18	Tom Morris	364

This famous plan is by renowned architect Alister MacKenzie. The original (*above left*) hangs above the desk of the secretary of the R&A in St Andrews. A copy of the original (*below left*) is published in more vibrant colours than the original and often with a slightly changed scorecard (*enlarged at bottom of page*). It is not known who altered some yardages on the reprints, but because the new card features 'Bobby Jones' as the name of the 10th hole, it must have been done after 1972 – and possibly in 1981 when the plan was reprinted. Other slight alterations on the reprint include the identification of the march stones and less accurate colouring demarcation of the green and tee areas.

Top plan (1924) courtesy of the Royal and Ancient Golf Club

Bottom plan (1981) courtesy of Auchterlonies of St. Andrews

Length of Holes on the Old Course.					
Hole Nº	Name	Yards	Hole Nº	Name	Yards
1	Burn	370	10	Bobby Jones	318
2	Dyke	411	11	High coming home	172
3	Cartgate going out	352	12	Heathery coming home	316
4	Ginger Beer	419	13	Hole o'Cross	398
5	Hole o'Cross going out	514	14	Long	523
6	Heathery	374	15	Cartgate coming home	401
7	High going out	359	16	Corner of the Dyke	351
8	Short	178	17	Road	461
9	End	307	18	Tom Morris	364

have often regarded the angles and gradients that adorn the greens as being provided by the gods, and because of their beauty and effectiveness it's hard to believe they were not, but some were actually created by the hand of man. As an article in the *St. Andrews Citizen* in 1913 concurs, the greens almost certainly artificially levelled are the 4th and the 6th, 'and of course the corresponding holes coming home'. One additional change made between 1901 and 1907 was on the 17th hole. According to a report, the green was 'enlarged or banked up on the side nearest the road.'

Right: The double greens and widening of the putting surfaces preceded the gradual widening of the course, but there was a direct relationship; function determined form. For greater safety bigger greens were required. Here, the only direction for expansion was right, and as a result the green now has a lower section.

Right: The intriguing 2nd and 16th green has baffled players for centuries. In the two photos on the right, the top photo shows the flags are located in their traditional positions with the 2nd hole located on the right side. It is more common now for the 2nd hole to be located on the lower plateau to the right, but for important competitions it is always returned back to the original green area where it is protected by the large undulations.
Iain Lowe

Above right: The bottom photo is a view from behind the green looking back down the fairway with the flag on the lower level.
S. Macpherson

The Evolution and Extension of the 2nd Hole Green

© S.Macpherson. 2005

In 1915, during World War I, the water supply became an issue and the work of laying down pipes to supply water from the town to the links commenced. This supply made the job of hand-watering the greens from the wells obsolete and it also provided a better water source during any drought periods. (See irrigation plan p.66.)

Around this time, at least one change appeared. Sometime between 1913 and 1920, on the 9th hole a little bunker known as Boase's (since at least 1932) came into being. Rarely documented and presumably named after chairman of the Greens Committee of the R&A, Norman Boase, this bunker sits 30 yards tee-side of End Hole bunker and causes much havoc to those travelling up the middle of the fairway to reach the green.

THE 1921 OPEN CHAMPIONSHIP

For the 1921 Open Championship, no changes were made to the course. The course length was the same as it was in 1910. Little had happened since the end of the war. With the world still licking its wounds, money was held on to tightly and golf had suffered. The most dramatic move had been the standardisation of the '1.62' ball by the Royal and Ancient Club. For the first time a limitation on size and weight was placed on a ball, and the United States Golf Association (USGA) followed suit. The standard ball would weigh 1.62 ounces and have a diameter of 1.62 inches. In practical terms this meant a ball that was a little smaller and a little heavier, and travelled a bit further. The result was predictable. In excellent conditions, on a course running hard and fast, the winning score was lower.

The only controversy created by the 1921 Open had been the deeply grooved clubs used by the champion Jock Hutchison, a man born in St Andrews, but who had emigrated to America. The spin he could create concerned the implement controllers and in 1924 new regulations were introduced governing such markings.

11th May 1922: 'This tournament will always be memorable for the fact that 70 has been beaten in a competition over the Old Course in full dress order. George Duncan produced such golf as has never been seen and finished in 68, a tremendous effort, one long sustained brilliant spurt… His 12 foot putt at the 18th went in without a waver, and the crowd, now going mad in earnest, carried him off the green and up the stone steps in triumph. His figures were 3, 4, 4, 4, 5, 5, 4, 3, 3 = 35; 3, 4, 3, 4, 5, 4, 4, 3, 3 = 33.'

During this period, work continued on the Old Course, and this work cost money. In 1922 the Greens Committee of the R&A, chaired by Mr Norman Boase, allocated £3000 to the task. The details of the budget were as follows;

Wages	£1850
Cartages	£350
Ballot	£25
Seeds and Manure	£150
Printing	£30
Tools, Repairs	£150
Rents, Taxes, Insurance	£60
Miscellaneous	£35
Water Supply for Links	£70
Links Curator	£200
	£2920
Say	**£3000**

In 1924, the now renowned golf course architect, Dr Alister MacKenzie, made one of the most popular plans of the course (see plan p.67). MacKenzie had done a great deal of study of the Old Course and wanted to map the course. He approached the R&A in 1923 and a price of not more than thirty guineas was agreed. In his book, *The Spirit of St Andrews*, posthumously published, MacKenzie wrote, 'It took me a full year to complete the task, notwithstanding the fact that I thought I knew the course thoroughly. In actual fact I found that my knowledge was of the slightest, and the subtleties which I discovered have always been a source of amazement to me.'

The accuracy of the plan was extraordinary, even though MacKenzie later admitted 'after I had made the plan and it had appeared in printed form, I discovered several mistakes and omissions which have, so far, fortunately been overlooked by anyone else'. But the plan was applauded: one R&A member even attributed his victory in the spring and autumn medals to it.

In tracing the changes to the course, MacKenzie's plan helps. Of particular interest is the 2nd green. In MacKenzie's plan the putting surface is only on top of the plateau. It did not seemed to be extend down to the right as it is often played

now. His plan also shows only three pot bunkers around the 3rd tee, but by 1932 there were four.

On the 4th hole, the plan shows a new bunker was added to the left of the 'Students' between 1920 and 1924. In the same period an extra bunker was added down the right side of the sixth hole, closer to the green, and a bunker which existed in front of the 7th tee in 1920, had become a grass hollow by 1924.

On the back nine, the two bunkers which feature just forward and left of the 13th tee on MacKenzie's plan are gone by 1932. The plan also shows the change in size of some of the bunkers. One bunker to be noticeably decreased in size is the one to the right or west of 'Hell', sometimes known as the 'Pulpit' (because from it you can see Hell).

Norman Boase, a man MacKenzie described as 'a stalwart', chaired the Greens Committee of the Royal and Ancient Club at this time, and believed like many others, including John L. Low, that the Old Course was too sacred to be touched. But while he may have been a protectionist, he and the Greens Committee were constantly working with the greenkeepers to maintain the strength of the Old Course. A note in the minutes of 17 January 1923 said:

Work on Links; The Committee discussed with the curator work requiring to be done on certain bunkers and

Left: This interesting photo is of Bobby Jones putting out as he wins the 1927 Open Championship, but it also shows a rare view of the unsealed road that became the battle ground for the Links Road War. Those familiar with this area today will also note Granny Clark's Wynd – that Jones was forced to play off of – and the absence of the fence up the right side of the 18th hole.

also as to altering some of the tees on the Old Course.

On 3 October of the same year, the minutes stated:

Work on Links; In the absence of the curator on account of illness, the Committee had a general discussion as to top dressing certain greens. They considered that it was not necessary to use Weed Killer on the Old Course greens.

Old Course 5th Hole; It was agreed that the bad parts at the 5th hole should be graiped, raked and sown with grass seeds and be roped off and out of play.
Seventh Hole; It was agreed that the new tee should be got into readiness for play later on.
Swilcan Burn; The Committee agreed that the burn should be cleaned out as soon as possible and as the Town Council had offered to give help, it should be accepted.

On 6 February 1924:

Work on Links; It was agreed that the new back tees at the seventh and thirteenth holes on the old Course should be proceeded with as soon as possible.

On 5 March 1924:

Fifth Hole Old Course; It was reported that the Committee had recently decided that turfing from about 180 to 220 yards from the tee at the 5th hole should be done and that this work had now been completed.
Sixteenth Green Old Course; It was agreed that the 'Wig' Bunker at the 16th green should be trimmed but that this should not be done until the Committee had had an opportunity of seeing it along with the Curator.

* It is believed Fowler's bunker was the bunker cut in 1905. There is no information describing the origin of this name, or equally, why it has not been retained. However, one man with the surname Fowler who was active at the time of its construction was Herbert Fowler the golf architect. Was Boase attributing the bunker to him?

1 October 1924:

Work on Links; The Committee discussed with the curator the work requiring to be done on the links and it was resolved that the following turfing should be carried out;
On the Old Course
1. Second half of fairway at fifth hole with special attention to any part of that fairway at the end of the drive.
2. Sixth hole drive.
3. The hollow at the seventh hole and round the hill to the westwards.
4. The foot of the hill at the end of the drive at the thirteenth hole.
5. The ground to the east of Kitchen bunker.
6. The approach to the fourteenth hole.
7. The approach to the fifteenth hole.

12 November 1924:

The Greens Committee requested additional turfing;
a Round the edges of the Burn Green and especially between the Green and the burn and the Green and the tee.
b A patch of about eight by twelve yards at the back of the third green beside Fowler's* bunker.
c A rectangular piece of ground between the 4th and the 14th greens and between the bunker.
d A rectangular piece between the 6th and 12th greens from the slopes to the North and the South between the two hand-weeded portions.
e A rectangular portion between the 7th and 11th greens stretching between the hand-weeded portions of those greens.
f A piece 20 yards wide running north and south between the 8th and 10th greens measured from the

hand-weeded portion of the 8th green.

g   A piece at the southern side of the 9th green between the rough and the hand-weeded portion of the green.

It was also decided to make a new Championship Tee of about five yards square at the 9th hole about fifteen yards northwest of the present back tee.

These minutes show a deliberate effort by the Greens Committee to improve the course and prepare it for upcoming championships. By the time the 1927 Open had arrived, the Old Course had undergone much needed and significant extensions. Skills and technology developed during the World War I were being reapplied, and golf became a benefactor. In the United States the most significant development was the acceptance of the steel shaft for championship play. The move reportedly came only after extensive experimentation, where it was proved that no additional distance came from the use of a steel shaft, and that having a choice between hickory and steel would result in a greater conservation of the hickory.

Plentiful supplies of hickory in the UK was one reason the Royal and Ancient Club did not approve the use of steel shafts at the same time, but another reason was because of representations made by the executive of the Professional Golfers Association – many of whom were clubmakers. Steel shafts were however permitted in countries where there was an insufficiency of hickory and where the climate was such that wooden shafts could not retain their condition.

When first advertised for sale in 1891, steel shafts were only in a relatively embryonic stage of development. Around 1905 experiments with tubular shafts were carried out in the United States, but shafts really only became reliable in the 1920s. It was in November 1929 that the R&A approved steel shafts for use.

The date of the championship was moved back to July so players coming from the United States had time to travel after playing in the US Open. The course was made 82 yards longer, and it measured a total of 6569 yards, after significant changes were made to the 11th, 14th, 15th and 17th holes. Interestingly, not all holes were lengthened. Some holes actually measured shorter than they had in 1921. The 5th hole was 6 yards shorter, the 6th 3 yards less, the 12th 4 yards less and the 13th 3 yards shorter. Whether these were just measurement variances or if the tees were intentionally moved closer to the green is unknown, but it does indicate an ongoing elasticity in the authority's attitude to course set-up.

Bobby Jones's victory in 1927 was remarkable for many reasons, including from a scoring perspective. Though he had good weather and was at the top of his game, the course was also set up in his favour. A report in *The Field* noted:

Unfortunately circumstances throughout [Mr Jones] visit combined to rob the Old Course of its peculiar distinction. There was no wind, and the links was thoroughly sodden by recent and persistent rainfall. Mr Jones who had come three thousand miles to play certain well remembered shots found himself constrained to take his lofted clubs and hit the ball high to the pin, just as if he were golfing on an ordinary course. The green committee had assisted nature by cultivating a thick velvety nap on the putting-greens, and cutting the holes in easy places.

Jones commented: 'Those greens used to be so crisp that you could hear the crunch of your spikes made when they cut into the turf. Oh they were fast!'

Another report that followed his course record-breaking 68 on the third day was in *The Scotsman* on 14 July:

With the exception of three shots he played like a

Bobby Jones savours winning the Claret Jug at the 1927 Open Championship.
Cowie Collection, St Andrews University Library

machine, and put, at one spell, as fine an exhibition of what Americans call "birdie" golf, as I have seen since the American invasions became a familiar feature of our big event. His approaches might not in every case have passed the strictest criterion of "pin splitters," but his putting was positively inspired. On five of the first nine greens he used only one putt. Here are the details of his card, with the putts indicated in the brackets:

Right: Bobby Jones's record-breaking scorecard from his third round. His putts are indicated in brackets.

1	368 yds	4	10	312 yds	4
2	401 yds	5 (10 yds)	11	164 yds	3
3	356 yds	4	12	314 yds	4
4	427 yds	4	13	410 yds	4
5	527 yds	3 (32 yds)	14	527 yds	5
6	367 yds	3 (2 yds)	15	409 yds	4
7	352 yds	4	16	348 yds	4
8	150 yds	2 (6 yds)	17	467 yds	4
9	306 yds	3 (2 yds)	18	364 yds	4
		32			**36**

What also makes Jones's scoring achievement so extraordinary is that this was the first time the winner's average score was below par. Jones averaged 71.25, 1.75 shots below par.

When Jones left St. Andrews, he took more with him than the trophy. On the 72nd hole of the tournament, he hit his ball onto Granny Clark's Wynd, which had been tarred in 1923. A bit of the tar stuck to his ball, and some blades of cut grass clung to the tar when the ball dropped into the hole. As a report concluded, 'Ball, tar and grass are his memento of his St. Andrews championship – and of that last rather ticklish approach, with 10,000 spectators to watch it.'

Calamity Jane: Bobby Jones was given a rusty blade putter by Jimmy Maiden, brother of his teacher Stewart, after missing too many putts in a heavy defeat by Francis Ouimet in the 1921 US Amateur Championship. Jones at once began to sink everything with his new putter, so much so that Jimmy nicknamed it 'Calamity Jane'. Since Jones's form was anything but a calamity, the humour of the situation appealed to everyone, and the name stuck.

Years after the event, Bobby Jones wrote about his experiences at St Andrews in his book *On Golf*. He wrote:

In my humble opinion, St Andrews is the most fascinating golf course I have ever played. When I first played there in 1921, I was unable to understand the reverence with which the place was regarded by our British friends. I considered St Andrews among the very worst courses I had ever seen, and I'm afraid I was even disrespectful of its difficulties. The maddening part of the whole thing was, that while I was certain the course was easy, I simply could not make a good score. Self complacently, I excused myself by thinking the course was unfair, that the little mounds and undulations should not be there, and because my shots were deflected continually away from the hole, I regarded myself as unlucky. Yet I did begin to think a little when a course so unprepossessing forced me to take 43 to the turn in the third round of the Tournament, and finally goaded me into the disgraceful act of picking up my ball after taking a pair of sixes at the tenth and eleventh holes. I must, however, give myself the credit to say that even then I was beginning to know St Andrews — at least to realise that the Old Course was not to be taken lightly. In the interim between 1921 and my next visit to Britain in 1926, I heard such a great deal of St Andrews from Tommy Armour and other Scotsmen, who seemed to be convinced that Divine Providence had had a part in the construction of the course, that I went there determined to make an effort to like it. I really did not have to try very hard. Before I had played two rounds, I loved it, and I love it now......... There is always a way at St Andrews although it is not always the obvious way, and in trying to find it, there is more to be learned on this British course than in playing a hundred ordinary American Golf Courses.

A notable feature of the 1927 championship that was of concern to many was the repeated driving of many two-shot, or par 4 holes. The 9th, 10th, 12th and 18th holes were driven consistently and the two par 5's often reached in two. The power of the ball was becoming an issue. It was carrying, reportedly, 15 yards further than the ball used in 1913.

Course architect Herbert Fowler thought that while the Old Course was 'nearly 600 yards longer than it was in the eighties, it is many strokes easier. Of course it is wider than it was...To make a course now which would compare in length with the St Andrews of old would require some 8000 yards (or more).'

Limiting the power of the golf ball was a burning issue. Charles Ambrose wrote an article called 'A Question of the Ball' in 1927, published in *Golf Illustrated*, in which he summarised the only people he thought wanted a change in the ball. They were:

1. Champions who drive so far and so straight that they get no variety of stroke; and champions who drive too far, but not too straight.
2. Elderly ex-champions who do not like being out-driven by 100 yards or more.
3. Owners of courses laid out for the gutty ball.
4. Golf architects who don't like seeing their most subtle 'two- shotters' played with a drive and a niblick pitch.
5. 'Handicap' players who model their opinions on those of their golfing betters.
6. Journalists who want something to write about.

He thought these people were 'certainly not more than one in a hundred, perhaps not one in a thousand.'

The editors of *Golf Illustrated* were slightly more pragmatic and wanted greater studies to be conducted and if changes were to be made, for the golf-ball manufacturers to be consulted. In 1927 in a column entitled 'What We Think', they wrote,

Left: Here, in front of the green, the Swilcan Burn is being widened approximately two to three feet. It was also reported that stones replaced the wooden sleepers that previously supported the sides of the burn.
Published in Golf Illustrated, *April, 1933*

Left: Standing on top of the Swilcan Burn Bridge, this is the view towards the 1st green. The Burn is regularly dredged and maintained now and rarely overflows. The route the burn takes can catch many long hitters out off the first tee.
S. Macpherson

They [golf ball manufacturers] *have always been willing to help, and apart from any financial consideration that a change must involve, they, through their technical experience and skill are possessed of the power to negative any desire of the authorities to limit length. It would be fatuous to introduce a new ball for the manufacturers to commence immediately to utilise their technical skill upon increasing its flight whilst remaining within legal specifications.*

The Americans had taken measures to limit the distance a ball could be hit in 1931 by moving away from the R&A and standardising a larger, lighter ball. The ball was 1.68

Right: "Bogey" series of cigarette cards. These cards were produced in 1933 with the approval of the St Andrews town council and the R&A by the Imperial Tobacco Company. They serve as an interesting and accurate record of the Old Course in that era. The descriptions by Mr Bernard Darwin feature three types of players – Mr Rabbit, Mr Everyman and Mr Tiger and provide some entertaining reading. For some it may come as a surprise that the term for a good player is tiger, but this is an old term for an accomplished player.

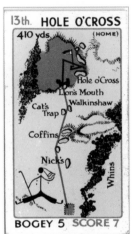

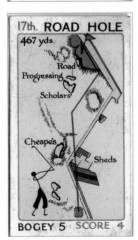

inches and 1.55 ounces. Studies published in a report in 1924 by A.E. Penfold, technical adviser for the Dunlop Rubber Company and inventor of the 'MaxFli' ball in 1922, said,

> *The scientist present at these tests advocated the adoption of a ball not less than 1.71 in. diameter, and weighing not more than 1.55 ounces, adding a rider to the effect that these conclusions must be recognised as being free from all considerations of playing qualities as they appeal to a golfer, and must be taken as intended solely as a means to reduce abnormal length.' The tests had proven that a larger, lighter ball would have greater wind resistance and less specific gravity, and therefore not fly as far, or 'run' along the ground as far and the 1.62 ball. Penfold concluded, '...the total representing a shortening of five or six yards on the average and introducing no detrimental effects.'*

In a subsequent article entitled, 'The Modern Ball; Changes that make for increased length', Penfold reviewed the changes in the structure of golf balls since the introduction of the Haskell ball, and assigned where the probable increase in length had come from. He thought it to be from:

> *1. CENTRE – Substitution of 'plastic' centre for paste centre, three to four yards: but no increase in distance has resulted from centre changes for the past twelve years.*
> *2. CORE – Improved tensioning devices and modified winding machines together with improved rubber quality, ten to twelve yards, the gain having been made during the past three of four years.*
> *3. COVER – Improved methods of preparation and application, four or five yards gained during the past two or three years.*
> *4. MARKING – Markings replacing Bramble marking, five or six yards, probably not more than a*

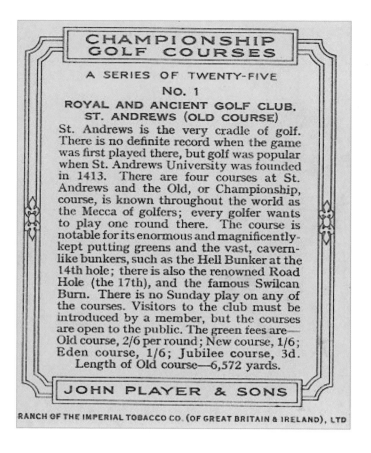

CHAMPIONSHIP GOLF COURSES

A SERIES OF TWENTY-FIVE

NO. 1

**ROYAL AND ANCIENT GOLF CLUB.
ST. ANDREWS (OLD COURSE)**

St. Andrews is the very cradle of golf. There is no definite record when the game was first played there, but golf was popular when St. Andrews University was founded in 1413. There are four courses at St. Andrews and the Old, or Championship, course, is known throughout the world as the Mecca of golfers; every golfer wants to play one round there. The course is notable for its enormous and magnificently-kept putting greens and the vast, cavern-like bunkers, such as the Hell Bunker at the 14th hole; there is also the renowned Road Hole (the 17th), and the famous Swilcan Burn. There is no Sunday play on any of the courses. Visitors to the club must be introduced by a member, but the courses are open to the public. The green fees are— Old course, 2/6 per round; New course, 1/6; Eden course, 1/6; Jubilee course, 3d. Length of Old course—6,572 yards.

JOHN PLAYER & SONS

RANCH OF THE IMPERIAL TOBACCO CO. (OF GREAT BRITAIN & IRELAND), LTD

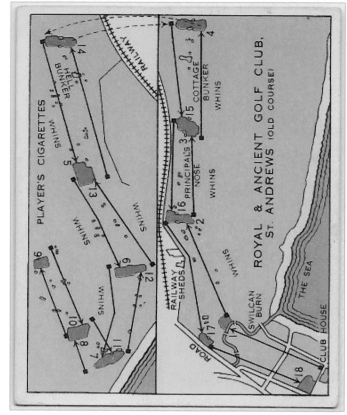

Far left & left: This plan of the Old Course is from a different series of cigarette cards showing twenty-five championship golf courses. The card cleverly delineates the Old Course – in two halves – as it stood in 1933. It is interesting to note that the card indicates no bunkers on the right of the 3rd and 4th holes. Additionally, some bunkers are featured that no longer exist!

single yard gained during the past three or four years.

5. REDUCTION – in size and INCREASE in weight.

...These changes in themselves are responsible for an increase in length during the past quarter of a century of not more than seven or eight yards, and there has been no advantage gained by these changes for the past twelve years.'

...Golf has given renewed youth and vigour to thousands of business men who spend a large proportion of their lives in city offices. They are induced to play golf not only for reasons of health, but because of the

pleasure in hitting the ball. Take that pleasure away and you lose many golfers who are, after all, the backbone of the game and on whom its future development and success depends.

As it turned out, the 1.68 inches by 1.55-ounce ball 'ballooned' when hit and so the USGA abolished it in 1932 and changed the specification to 1.68 inches and 1.62 ounces – this remains today's standard. The R&A however, did not move with the Americans, instead keeping to the 'small' ball. Indeed, the R&A did not change the ball for British PGA events until 1968, and not for the Open Championship until 1974. Until then the 0.06-inch diameter discrepancy was a thorny issue between the two ruling bodies, an inconvenience

Far right & right: Plans by J. Crane featured in *Golf Illustrated* in January 1934 outlining an alternative design for the first hole on the Old Course. The notable features are the rerouting of the Swilcan Burn, the reorientation of the green and the addition of a bunker behind the green.
Courtesy of Golf Illustrated

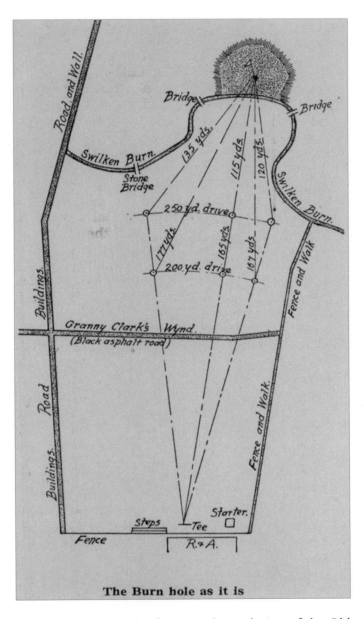

The Burn hole as it is

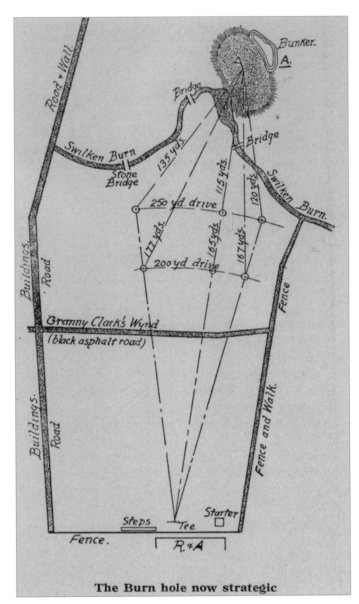

The Burn hole now strategic

for professionals, and a factor in the evolution of the Old Course.

Prior to the 1933 Open Championship, the Silvertown Ball Company carried out an interesting trial. Being in possession of moulds dating back to 1888, it had old-style balls made to original specifications and hit by its mechanical

driving machine to prove the inferiority of their performance in comparison the new balls.

The longest recorded drive by a US standard ball, which was at the time the same weight as the British ball but slightly larger, was 285 yards by the machine, with a carry of 241 yards. In the same test, the British ball recorded a distance

of 276 yards, with a carry of 246 yards. In other words, the US ball in calm conditions had very similar distance characteristics to the British ball of the day.

Ball	Carry	Total length
1888 ball	174 yds	
1913–1922 ball	220 yds	
1932 British standard ball	244 yds	
1932 British standard ball, no dimples	115 yds	180 yds
US ball (1.62 by 1.68)	241 yds	285 yds

Silvertown's 'no dimple' test is also interesting as it shows the increasing importance of this development in ball technology. A similar test was done by Dunlop on their Maxfli 65 with the results being:

Dimple Depth	Carry	Carry + Roll
.001 in	117 yds	146 yds
.004 in	187 yds	212 yds
.007 in	212 yds	232 yds
.010 in	223 yds	238 yds
.013 in	238 yds	261 yds
.016 in	225 yds	240 yds

Further experiments proved that the optimum dimple depth for the 1.62-inch ball was 0.012–0.0125 inches.

In 1923, Roger Wethered, the newly crowned British Amateur Champion competed in a long-driving competition at the Troon Open. Each entrant had four drives with three to count. Despite competition from many professionals, Wethered won with an average of 266 yards, 4.5 inches. His longest drive was 276 yards, 8 inches.

THE 1933 OPEN CHAMPIONSHIP

When the 1933 Open came around, the length of the Old Course was all but identical to that in 1927, a rather surprising fact considering all the developments of the golf ball in the interim. Apart from the widening of the Swilcan Burn (see photo p.73) the only change was 3 yards extra length on the 5th hole, but this may only have been a remeasuring correction.

Danny Shute won the Open with a score of 292, seven higher than that of Bobby Jones six years earlier. It was a mildly surprising victory because many expected the winning total to be lower, owing to the improved ball, steel shafts, the course being in good condition and the weather fine.

One incident, however, that shook those concerned about the distance a ball could be hit involved Craig Wood. Wood, who tied Shute in the championship but lost in a playoff, hit a drive on the 5th hole of the final round that finished in a bunker known as the 'left-hand spectacle'. Though downwind and at the end of a hard, glassy fairway, this bunker, which normally caught a mortal's second shot, was measured at about 430 yards from the tee – just under quarter of a mile!

An extremely interesting study came out following the Open. Compiled by Brownlow Wilson, it was an analysis of the average score per hole. He took the cards of the fifty-eight players who completed the 72-hole event and calculated the average number of shots taken hole-by-hole for their 232 rounds. The average score was 75.28 with an average per hole of 4.16 as against the 4.055 allowed in a par score of 73. The hardest hole was the 13th, while the easiest – as Woods's drive indicated – was the 5th. This study provided an excellent means for comparing the difficulty of holes in Opens to come.

After the Open, the condition of the Old Course was again a hot subject. Though the hand mowers were now state of the art, and not too dissimilar to modern hand mowers, respected golfer, golf course architect and writer Guy C. Campbell felt it necessary to discuss the prevalence of coarse

grasses on the Old Course and compare them to the New Course:

There are several reasons for the difference in texture in the greens of these two links. To begin with the Old Course has far more play. It has also suffered in the past – after "old Tom's" death – from faulty treatment. Its top-dressings were of unsatisfactory soil, which brought in weeds and coarse grasses. These have never been completely eradicated and, nor can we hope that they will be, so long as heavy mowers are employed to cut the greens, for these gradually but progressively "bind" the top spit and produce a soil condition in which the roots of the fine grasses cannot "breathe" properly and so cannot flourish.

In 1939, another article appeared, this time in *Golf Monthly*, questioned why St Andrews had changed, and it provided an interesting agronomical history of how they thought the links were transformed. First it was rabbits that trimmed the grasses, producing the close-cropped turf dear to a golfer's heart; their scrapings scattering sand across the turf and maintaining the natural bristle-leaved hardy grasses. Then man came along and lent a hand:

Mowers were brought in to crop the turf. They left in their wake a trail of raw grass remains that settled on the soil and clogged the porous surface. The modern mowers, by their very weight, compacted and bound the matted surface. Worms, which were absent from the dunes, as there was poor feeding for them in the open sand, made their appearance with the increasing organic matter in the soil. They would tend to keep the surface open, but the greenkeeper dosed them with iron salts. The iron salts permanently cemented the surface particles, giving a concrete basin which held every drop of rain as casual water on the greens. The heavier soil was now a choice site for daisies. To rid the links of their summer mantle of white, artificial manures were applied to assist the vanishing grass plants in their losing fight. These artificial manures assisted the growth of the more responsive broad-leaved grasses, which finally ousted the typical seaside grasses with their hard bristle leaves. These soft broad-leaved grasses would not stand up to the wear of modern conditions. The course must be closed to allow these grasses to recover; they were artificially fostered grasses that required watering to keep them green in the summer.

Right & far right: Supposedly named after the principal of St Mary's College in the early nineteenth century, these three bunkers form the Principal's Nose and can be quite an obstacle. However, they are generally easily avoided and elite players usually play short and slightly left. John Daly, however, plays over them.
Photo on left: Iain Lowe

Bunkers between 15th and 16th Holes ("Principal's Nose,") Old Golf Course, St. Andrews

The Old Course often came under attack, and most commonly from those who misunderstood its virtues. To quote Alister MacKenzie, the course 'escaped destruction by vandals' only because the majority of golfers loved and respected the features of the Old Course. The revolutionaries still found the time to outline their desired attacks on paper. The 9th hole was an easy target. Many thought it was a poor hole and suggested pushing the green back at least twenty or thirty yards and raising the back by a few feet. But in 1934 an American by the name of Joshua Crane completed a series of articles outlining the changes he wanted to make to the Old Course. The first of these was probably the most interesting, and perhaps meritorious: 'How simple it would be to introduce strategy into the playing of the first hole, without changing any of its apparent features, and thus induce players to keep to the right so as not to interfere with those playing the last hole.' (See plan p.76.)

Max Behr, an associate of MacKenzies and Crane, editor of the magazine *Golf*, and a finalist in the 1908 US Amateur Championship had concerns also, but his related to the power of the ball. In 1937 he completed a yardage analysis that shows the distance that needed to be added to the Old Course to meet and balance the ever-growing power of the rubber-cored ball.

Distance of Drive from the Tee (yds)	Equivalent length of Old Course (yds)
200	6200
220	6790
240	7380
250	7675
260	7970
270	8265
280	8560
290	8855
300	9150

In summary: If the ball could be driven 300 yards with a new golf ball, to experience the same distance relationship players using the old gutty balls had from the tee to hazards and the green, the Old Course would need to measure 9150 yards!

To reach these extraordinary figures Behr based his calculations on the length of the Old Course when the gutty was the ball available; namely 6200 yards. From here he subtracted 300 yards, the sum of the lengths of the two short holes, and was left with 5900 for the remaining sixteen holes. He explained:

> *Since in the days of the gutta the reasonable expectancy of the tiger was 200 yards off the tee, we multiply 200 by 16 to arrive at 3200 yards... this leaves us with 2700 yards to be covered otherwise.' The remaining 2,700 yards is increased by the percentage increase. i.e., 10%, 20%, 25% off the tee etc, with finally the par 3's yardage (300 yards) added back.*

Harold Hinton talked about how the length of the ball had destroyed the character of some holes on the Old Course, most notably the 12th and the 16th. In 1927 he wrote,

> *With the "gutty" (the 16th) was a five, and a somewhat terrifying hole – particularly in a score-play event. More often than not, the "Principal's Nose" group of bunkers could not be carried by the good-class average driver, and he therefore had to work out some scheme of his own. He could, for one thing, attempt to hug the railway line, and play into the narrow valley between the railway and the bunkers, but that shot required very accurate placing. Then there was the alternative of playing well to the left. That was certainly a safe line, but it left the player with a longish second and a difficult one. It was a very testing hole then. How is it played nowadays? Well to the long*

CHAPTER THREE | THE HASKELL – THE THREE-PIECE WOUND BALL

hitter who can pitch with a "spade" club. This sixteenth hole in the present era is more a test for good-class women's golf than anything else. It may still have character, but not to the degree that it had. Another hole which has suffered is the twelfth. In the "gutty" days it was a most difficult two-shotter, and the majority of players had to steer a course either to right or left, leaving them a comparatively long second to play. Nowdays the bunkers in the centre of the course do not disturb Abe Mitchell and his kind. They can afford to have a real "go" at the tee-shot, and if it comes off the ball will finish quite near the green.

Alister MacKenzie had been an advocate of limiting the flight of the ball. In *The Spirit of St. Andrews* he said:

> *Pleasure in obtaining length is only a matter of relativity. One got quite as much fun in driving the old Haskell ball twenty yards further than one's opponent as today one gets in hitting a small heavy ball twenty yards further.*
>
> *One of the difficulties with which we have to contend is that any marked limitation of the flight of the ball is certain to be unpopular for some time after its inauguration. Golfers would dislike to find that they were unable to carry a bunker they were formerly able to do. They would feel as though they had suddenly grown old.*
>
> *Something drastic ought to have been done years and years ago. Golf courses are becoming far too long. Twenty years ago we played three rounds of golf a day and considered we had taken an interminably long time if we took more than two hours to play a round. Today it not infrequently takes over three hours.*

Bernard Darwin, grandson of Charles Darwin, captain of the R&A in 1934, a prolific golf writer and talented golfer, wrote about the ball in his 1946 book *British Golf*,

> *I think it may be said, though the statement is a controversial one, that in the first few years of its existence the (rubber-cored) ball gave much innocent pleasure without irretrievably hurting the game. Scores grew lower but there is not necessarily any harm in that; the ball went farther but not far enough to make fools of the courses by rendering negligible many of their natural features. It was rather when golf began again after the 1914 war that the harm became apparent. The ball-makers concentrated more and more on one point, power; the new heavier ball they produced bored its way too easily through the wind and went too far. In particular some devil within its jerkin was so amenable to hard hitting that the difference between the medium and the long driver was vastly emphasised and the long hitter became so long that there remained for him hardly such a thing as a good two-shot hole… More and more lengthening, more and more space and so more and more money were wanted and even so the old balance of the game was gravely impaired.*
>
> *There was no hope of reform as far as the man in the street was concerned, for he thought only of the length of his own drive. At last, however, the authoritative bodies all over the world were canvassed; their verdict was in favour of a reduction of power and the matter would have been considered at St. Andrews in September 1939, but for the war.*

Aware of the issues relating to the ball, but prior to an consensus regarding the best way to proceed, in November 1935 the Links Committee of the R&A was preparing for moderate changes to the Old Course – possibly with the 1936 Amateur Championship in mind. One set of minutes signed off by Mr Norman Boase make specific reference of their intent:

NEW COURSE

BEARDIES

THE ELYSIAN FIELD'

HOLE O'CROSS BUNKER

HOLE O'CROSS GREEN

6th Tee

LION'S MOUTH

CATS TRAP BUNKER

14th Tee

Below: Hickory-shafted clubs are still available at Auchterlonies Golf Shop in St Andrews, but serve mostly as a reminder of the history of the game.
S. Macphereson

Sixth hole: *It was agreed that a wide path be made northwards at the east of the Sixth Teeing Ground to facilitate the control of spectators.*

Mound at Eleventh Teeing Ground: *It was agreed that the mound to the West of the 11th Teeing Ground be heightened and increased in size. (Note- several hundreds of tons of sand deposited on it to raise it by some 18 inches).*

Bridge over Swilcan Burn: *It was agreed that the line of the North most bridge over Swilcan Burn be altered so as to permit an extension of the Second Teeing Ground.*

Tenth Teeing Ground: *It was suggested that the Club Green Committee should take into consideration the formation of a new Teeing Ground for the 10th hole, by the removal of a large patch of whins behind the 9th Putting Green.*

By 1938, the R&A Greens Committee had firmly turned their attentions to the upcoming Open Championship and were planning the greatest extension since 1905. It was an interesting time because in the matter of pure length, St Andrews was on surface value, considerably longer than it had ever been. But even with this extra yardage the course

played infinitely shorter with the ball of the day compared to the gutty.

An article in the *St Andrews Times* in March 1939 entitled 'Old Course Prepares for Open' read:

Improvements being effected at the Old Course, St Andrews, for the Open Championship in July are calculated to bring several dangerous bunkers in to play, which could previously be avoided by long hitters. The tee at the long fifth hole has been taken back, the idea being, not to lengthen the hole, but to bring into play the cluster of bunkers on the right of the fairway. This also has the effect of making the approach to the fifth green more difficult because of the two bunkers

that guard it. In previous years it was an easy matter for professionals to get to the green with a drive and a pitch. It will now require two good shots to reach the green with a good chance of the second being trapped.

Improvements effected at the long fourteenth hole are calculated to have the same effect. The tee in this case, also has been constructed 60 yards further back, so as to bring the "Beardies," the bunkers on the left of the fairway, into play.

This gives an extremely difficult second shot, as it will require two exceptionally long shots to carry "Hell" bunker. Those who are in doubt will either have to play short or go out to the left of the bunker.

Right: After a request from a reader the *St Andrews Times* compared the yardage of the Old Course in 1939 with that of 1933, the last time the championship was held at St. Andrews. *Published in* St. Andrews Times, *July 1939*

Hole.	Yds.	Yds.	Diff in Yds.		Par.
1.	368	374	increase	6	4
2.	301	411	,,	10	4
3.	356	367	,,	11	4
4.	427	424	decrease	3	4
5.	530	576	increase	46	5
6.	367	377	,,	10	4
7.	352	354	,,	2	4
8.	150	163	,,	13	3
9.	306	359	,,	53	4
	3257	3405	Increase	148	
Hole.	Yds.	Yds.	Diff in Yds.		Par.
10.	312	314	increase	2	4
11.	164	170	,,	6	3
12.	314	316	,,	2	4
13.	410	422	,,	12	4
14.	527	564	,,	37	5
15.	409	424	,,	15	4
16.	348	380	,,	32	4
17.	467	466	decrease	1	5
18.	364	381	increase	17	4
	3315	3437		122	73
	3257	3405		148	
Totals	6572	6842	Increase	270	

A follow-up article in the *St Andrews Times* published after the Open 'by request', showed the new length of the Championship course, but interestingly, also compared it to the previous Open course noting all the increases or decreases in distance.

Contrary to the information in the March article in the *St Andrews Times*, the 5th and 14th holes were not lengthened by 60 yards each, but nine holes were significantly lengthened; four on the front and five on the back nine. Additionally, while this chart (left) indicates the 7th hole was almost untouched in this extensive reconstruction, it was altered. One report said the tee was just raised to give 'the player a full view of the fairway which is at present partially hidden by a defiant lump of whins. He may even be able to see the hungry jaws of "shelly" bunker, though he may not relish the sight.' At this time, in late 1938, the road through the whins at the 7th hole was also cut for the convenience of spectators.

This lengthening was excessive to some, but had the R&A sought to calibrate the Old Course to the power of the 1939 ball according to Behr's chart, the Old Course would need to be stretched to 7500 yards– an all but unobtainable length in 1939, and perhaps even now.

One other change was put in place for the 1939 Open, but this related to the rules. The '14 Club Rule' was in the statute book, and the players would need to negotiate the Old Course under this limitation. This was not a number small enough for some. While most professionals were carrying over twenty clubs, Alister MacKenzie had wanted them to be restricted to a set of six, claiming 'In the old days Johnny Ball, eight-time British Amateur Champion, frequently played with two clubs only and played as well as anyone else with a bagful of ironmongery.' However, Mr Henry Gullen, the secretary of the R&A at the time confirmed the rule: 'If a player begins with 14 clubs, he cannot add to them in any way during a round.'

Shafts had continued to improve and most professionals had moved away from hickory, realising that golf was, as Henry Cotton wrote in *The Complete Golfer*, 'a more simple game with this new standard link between the hands and the clubhead'. Older golfers brought up with hickory were looking for a steel shaft with a similar torque to hickory, but all experiments were failures. It was realised that a shaft with whip was satisfactory, but one with no torsion was nearer to the ideal.

The steel shaft had another effect. While play with hickory shafts was more of a sweeping action, no strain on a steel shaft was too much... if a player's wrists could handle it. This caused divots to become longer and deeper, and powerful players like Craig Wood, Lawson Little and Sam Snead could, when they desired, attack the ball with a steep, downward motion and get maximum pressure and grip on the ball. With improved grooves on the clubface, this new swing action created enormous spin on the ball, and adept players could pitch the ball to the hole and stop it on the spot or even spin it back!

Thomas Horsburgh, an amateur golfer and Midlothian blacksmith, forged himself a set of steel shafts in the 1890s and played with them at the Barberton Golf Club, of which he was a founding member in 1893. He found them so good he took out a patent in 1894 claiming, 'the use of steel shafts for golf clubs for the purpose of giving strength and elasticity'. They proved popular with players but were banned. When they were finally permitted for use, Horsburgh had let his patent lapse – possibly costing him a fortune. However several of Horsburgh's clubs can still be seen in the Barberton clubhouse near Edinburgh, Scotland.

American Arthur F. Knight is credited for inventing steel shafts in the USA.

Right: There is quite a degree of elasticity in the tee of the Old Course. The general drift of the tees back and right has occasionally been countered by the movement of some tees forward.
Illustration ©
S. Macpherson

The Movement of Championship Teeing Grounds

16th

2nd

15th

3rd

19y 1946 Open Tee 348y

1939 Open Tee 367y

45y 1939 Open Tee 424y

1946 Open Tee 469y

THE 1939 OPEN CHAMPIONSHIP

The course extensions almost certainly contributed to higher average scores during the Open, but for the second time, the winner's average score was below par. In variable weather conditions and on a firm course, Dick Burton averaged 72.5, one clear shot below the average of the other golfers making

up the top ten. The best rounds of 69 were those of Peter Alliss and James Bruen's in qualifying.

In the ten years before World War I, golf course architects had made great strides to regain parity between ball and course. After the war this continued, with courses extended, hazards remodelled, and features such as trees, whins, lakes and doglegs incorporated. A real improvement was seen and golf courses became strategic. A psychological aspect was also introduced, of hazards often looking more threatening than they actually were. However by the 1930s, with the power of the ball still increasing and a balanced set of steel shafts becoming standard, the money spent on renovations was often seen as a waste. The solution was the return to centrally-placed hazards and specific landing areas such as on the Old Course. Unfortunately, the outbreak of World War II interrupted both these changes to the course and the holding of the Opens. And after the war a new issue faced golf – a threefold rise in maintenance costs.

Right: Located next to Cottage bunker on the 15th hole was the Hull bunker. Filled in in 1949 it sat where the two golfers are seen walking and the hollow still remains. This bunker was the last bunker filled in on the Old Course. For the location of the Hull bunker see the Nisbet plan on p.57.
S. Macpherson

Left: Looking at the 6th tees, the regular teeing ground sits out prominently in the foreground. Back to the left is the current championship tee. The tee used in the 1946 Open sits off to the right on the small spur of green (and apron) east of the front of the 5th green. Here it is seen sticking out directly above the small white stake. Though the 'small ball' in use during this period bore through the wind better than the larger American ball, it would still have been a very big carry (possibly 230 yards) to reach the fairway into the wind.
Iain Lowe

In a *History of Golf in Britain*, the now knighted Sir Guy Campbell, wrote:

> *...a bunker that in 1939 averaged £10 to make and £5 to maintain, now runs well into £30 and £15 respectively. One of the first priorities for clubs now confronted with the task of closing, or at least of stabilizing, financial "gaps" is therefore, the reduction of bunkers... Unnecessary flanking bunkers are being turned into natural grass features, that become integral parts of the fairways, and centrally positioned bunkers are being reintroduced – sparingly – at strategic points.*

The first Open Championship after the war was scheduled to be back again at St. Andrews in 1946. With the 1939 decision on reducing the power of the ball postponed, and no new decision on the horizon, the weather and the set-up of the course were the two factors critical in determining the

winning score. Many prophesied that the Old Course would be torn apart, with one article in the *Golf Monthly* entitled 'Will Americans Atomise St. Andrews?'

Careful planning went into the course arrangement, particularly as for the first time coordinated and comprehensive spectator controls were put in place. Access to the players and the centre of the course were roped off. Evidence that Open Championship matters were of increasing importance is to be found in a note in the Links Committee minutes on 21 December 1945. It was entitled 'Sheep On The Courses':

> *It was unanimously decided that the Town Council be approached with a view to its making representation in the proper quarters for a non-renewal of the grazing lease on the Links; the Links Committee being strongly of the opinion that the sheep should not be allowed back on the Courses, more especially in view of the fact*

Below: This plan featured in the 1946 Open Championship programme and showed the spectators the whereabouts of important features such as the car park and crossing points. Interestingly, if font size corresponds to importance, it seems pointing patrons in the direction of the beer tent was also paramount!

that The Open Championship and a Professional Tournament are being held in 1946.

It was pointed out that the damage to the bunkers was enormous and that it took the green-keeping staff several hours per day keeping the greens free from manure. If the Town Council could give the Links Committee an indication as to whether the sheep would not return it would be possible to proceed with certain work. In this respect, the Chairman reported that the German labour was being used to repair the damage done by the sheep.

Sheep or no sheep, the 1946 Open was a serious affair, yet also a celebration. The end of the war was an opportunity for the nation to reclaim one of its favourite past-times. And with expectations of spectator turnout high, this was probably the first time the course set-up and tee locations were influenced by the location of spectator crossings. As a result,

with some tees brought forward and others moved back, the front nine was longer by 81 yards, but the back nine becoming shorter by 40 yards. The holes most notably shortened were the 3rd, 13th and 17th, which between them lost 59 yards. Surprisingly, the 17th hole was played from where the regular tee now sits, and measured only 446 yards.

THE 1946 OPEN CHAMPIONSHIP

The holes significantly lengthened for this Open were the 4th and 6th. Both gained an enormous 45 yards, pushing the 4th to the limits of par 4 length, and making the 6th 422 yards, the longest it has ever been before or since!

One headline at the conclusion of the Open read,
BRITISH "OPEN" GOLF TITLE
AMERICAN WINS FIRST TIME ON
OLD COURSE
Sam Snead had come to St. Andrews, and after 71 holes got to the last requiring only a seven to win. The article

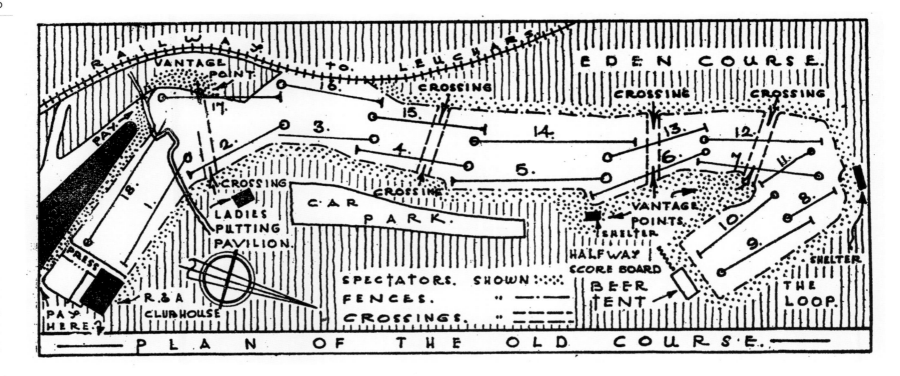

described his victory: 'He holed out in an orthodox four, which gave him a winning margin of four strokes.' The article also gave praise to the spectator arrangements, which, it claimed, were a 'triumph for the R and A' and 'a complete and outstanding success.'

Snead had played well during the Open, and years afterwards he commented on his performance: 'I especially remember driving the ball very well. In fact, I drove the 10th hole three out of four rounds.' This was the first and last time Snead ever played the Old Course.

In 1891 when bogey and par were devised, par was to be 'the ideal score for the scratch golfer'. Snead had beaten par, but only by the small and identical margin Burton had pipped it by seven years earlier. Meanwhile, the other golfers who made up the top ten in both 1939 and 1946 averaged higher than par. Could this be the perfect balance? One that in which, for the first time, the ideal relationship had been

Left: After hitting his ball dangerously close to the out-of-bounds fence on the first hole, Sam Snead plays to the green.
Cowie Collection, St Andrews University Library

Forget your opponents; always play against par.
– Sam Snead

arrived at where equipment, length of course and skill of the golfers produced scoring that balanced with the strategy of the Old Course and its par?

87

It is possible to say, not without reason, that some of the glory of golf departed for ever with the gutty ball. But it is not possible honestly to deny that the rubber-ball was, through its resilient quality, a pleasanter ball to play with and this not merely because it was less exacting in point of accuracy and more merciful to the half-hit shot. The sensation of first hitting one and the sweetness with which it flew away can never fade wholly from the mind. It was perhaps a pity that the ball was ever invented but, save in the minds of a few die-hards, there never could be any question of going back. Beyond all doubt the Haskell made the game more enjoyable for the great mass of players.

– Bernard Darwin, *British Golf*, 1946

CHAPTER FOUR

THE HIGH-TECH TWO-, THREE- and FOUR-PIECE BALLS
– 1950–1999

Many are coming to the view that the 'open' ought always to be played at St. Andrews... Others, mainly professionals, are equally certain that the Old Course should be painlessly destroyed.
– Byron Nelson, 1955

With course length, the power of equipment, and player skill all delicately balanced and providing winning scores at par on the Old Course for the first time, a new ball again tipped the scales. The refinement of golf ball manufacturing techniques and development of a high-tech performance model reignited the debate about limiting the ball, and sent course owners, managers and Club committees scuttling away to find new ways to extend their courses. The Old Course was not exempt. Within five years the R&A sought locations for new tees to extend the links.

The storm had been brewing prior to 1950. Many players had been dissatisfied with the 1946 Open course set-up. The 4th hole had caused particular discussion. In a report in *Golf Illustrated* Graham Cant wrote,

> At the fourth hole it used to be possible, and still is off the ordinary tees, to drive up the gully on the right. It was a fairly narrow shot, with rough and bunkers on the right, and the steep hillside on the left, but it was the shortest way to the hole, and left a fairly

straightforward second. The new tiger tee has made this shot almost impossible, because one is playing into the gully from an angle and the ball is almost sure to finish in a horrible lie on the hillside on the left. The only safe line is away across to the fifteenth fairway, and involves a long, carrying second shot to the green. [see the plan on p.90]

The angle of the back tee on the 14th hole was introduced for the 1939 Open and also created some discussion. In his article entitled 'Limiting the Ball', Cant felt the challenge of this hole had also been diminished:

> The fourteenth hole is even worse. There used to be at least four different ways of playing this hole. You could drive to the left of the Beardies on to the fifth fairway, which gave a safe, but longish passage to the green. The longer drivers carried the Beardies and continued round the left of Hell bunker. Shorter players followed much of the same route by skirting the Beardies on the

Opposite page: A late August afternoon view of St Andrews and the Road Hole.
S. Macpherson

Right: As technology has changed, and as players have improved, teeing grounds on the Old Course have evolved. The degree of these changes has impacted on the playing experience by bringing certain features into play. Here, shifting the teeing grounds back in 1946 without a correlating improvement in the distance provided by equipment, brought the strong central landforms back into play. Players could no longer easily carry the hillocks as they could in 1939. This meant the character of the hole played more as it did in 1895. For the 2005 Open, the carry was about 285 yards. For the longer hitters this was achievable, particularly in the south-westerly wind conditions – but those shorter off the tee found it difficult to reach the main fairway, and the other options were treacherous and unappealing. As a result, the hole played third hardest.

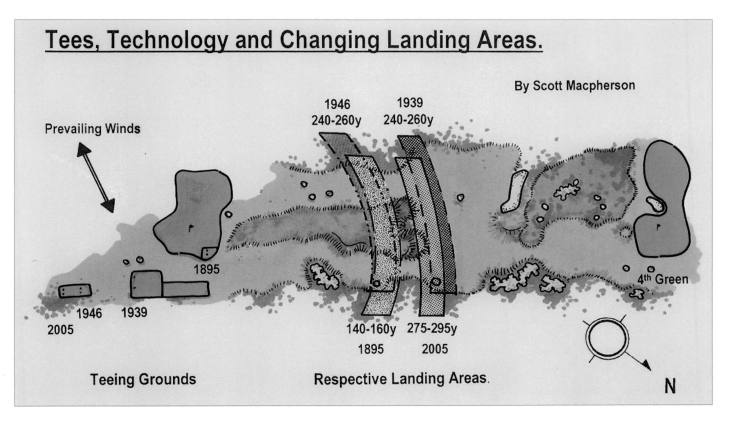

Tees, Technology and Changing Landing Areas.

By Scott Macpherson

Prevailing Winds

1946
240-260y

1939
240-260y

1895

1946   1939
2005

4th Green

140-160y   275-295y
1895   2005

Teeing Grounds

Respective Landing Areas.

N

right. The safest and easiest shot of all was straight down the Elysian Fields, followed by a shortish second to the near side of Hell, but it left a very awkward approach to the green sloping away from the player. The out-of-bounds on the right scarcely came into the picture, which was both right and proper, for out-of-bounds has no place on a natural course.

With the new back tee, which is really set on the Eden course, most of these routes are gone forever. The angle has altered to such an extent that it is fatally easy to finish in the rough on the far side of the fifth fairway. The route over the Beardies leads nowhere except to peculiar lies behind the spurs of the Elysian Fields that run out into the fifth...Most players carry the corner of the out-of-bounds dyke and try to finish somewhere in the middle of the Elysian Fields. It is not an

attacking shot, but a defensive one, and the out-of-bounds has become the main danger. The Beardies, while they still claim many victims, do so, I think, rather unfairly. The new angle of the drive has made them cross bunkers rather than lateral ones. You no longer flirt with them for the benefit to be received from a bold shot...

The Evolution of the Teeing Grounds

The evolution of the tees on the Old Course requires some greater examination, and the 14th hole provides a good study. Permitted by the changing rules, as described in Chapter Two, greater flexibility was available for all teeing grounds. To add extra yardage, and to enhance safety, which might also result in an improvement in the speed of play, most tees on the Old Course – particularly the 14th – have moved

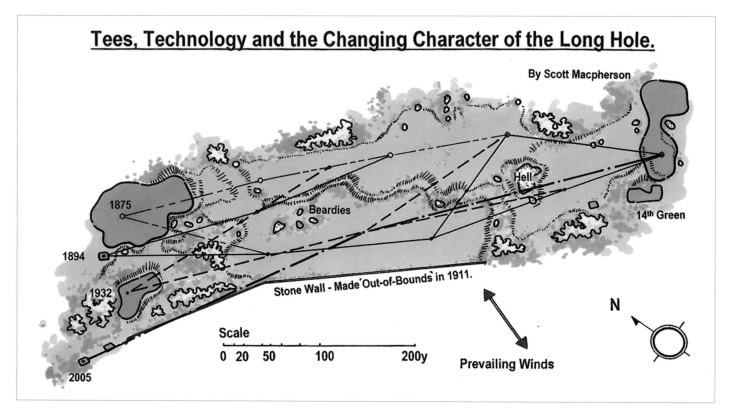

Tees, Technology and the Changing Character of the Long Hole.

By Scott Macpherson

1875

1894

1932

2005

Beardies

Hell

14th Green

Stone Wall - Made Out-of-Bounds in 1911.

Scale

0 20 50 100 200y

Prevailing Winds

N

Left: This diagram shows the movement of the tees and effect on likely play-lines from each tee. The distance of the drives corresponds with the average for a good golfer of that period. For the 2005 Open, the distance for players to carry past the Beardies is 290 yards. Due to the set-up of the course very few competitors will choose to play down what used to be the safer but longer route, and for good reasons: thick rough separates the Elysian Fields (14th fairway) from the 5th fairway; there's a carry of 270-280 yards to reach the 5th fairway; only a narrow gap exists between the Beardies and the left-hand spectacle; and now there is the added hazard of a lurking television tower. The target line on the tee is at the large clock tower in St Andrews (see bottom far right photo on p.92).

further right and back. Each successive move has been to keep pace with powerful new technology, and to a position that was thought would improve the length, lack of difficulty or strategy of the hole. Each time the tee was moved, however, there was a significant impact on how the hole played, especially from the tee.

In the case of the Long Hole (In), the 14th, it perhaps started with the creation of the old tee that can still be seen in front of the 13th green (see photo on p.42). Off the greens, this changed the angle a golfer could take. For example, where once the golfer aiming for the Elysian Fields was required to play over the heathery, bunker-infested hollows and 'Beardies' before finding salvation on the relative splendour of the Elysian Fields, the movement of the tees right reduced the distance required to be carried and turned the Beardies into a lateral hazard for most golfers. Also, when the tee was on

or near the 13th green, it was easier for a golfer – even armed with hickory shafts and a gutty ball – to play an alternative route down the now much wider area known as the 5th fairway. Perhaps the most significant difference however is the effect the stone dyke that divides the Elysian Fields from the Eden Course now has on play.

Before the teeing ground's great shift right, hitting a ball over the wall would have been more difficult due to its angle and distance from the tee. Only golfers veering sharply away from the Beardies may have found this stony hazard. However, even if they did, because hitting over the wall was not considered out-of-bounds until 1911, it would have been an unorthodox but legitimate alterative longer route to the green. But since 1900, when documents show the hole was extended from 475 yards to 516 yards – and it is almost certainly where the 'new' teeing ground in the location of

Top right: View from the 13th green – most likely used up to 1894.
S. *Macpherson*

Top far right: View from the tee most likely built by Old Tom Morris and used in 1894.
S. *Macpherson*

Bottom right: View from 1932 Championship tee, still in frequent use today.
S. *Macpherson*

Bottom far right: View from 2005 Championship tee.
S. *Macpherson*

Tee views above: As the teeing ground for the 14th hole has moved to the right and back, the view from the tee has changed markedly. Here the photos show the views from the tees (as shown on the plan p.91). It is interesting to note how in the early teeing grounds, the white end of the small house was a good target for those aiming to reaching the Elysian Fields, but as the tee moves, this target becomes replaced by the large clock tower in St Andrews. Previously, this target may only have been used by those golfers choosing to play their way back down the 'Long Hole Out' (5th hole).

the current 14th 'forward' tee was built – hitting the ball over the wall was much more straightforward – in more ways than one! The wall was closer and almost parallel to the line of play. Also, in a desire to stay clear of the threatening Beardies, the wall appeared even closer.

The latest change has seen the championship tee pushed further back, but on the same line as the previous Open Championship tee. Built in 2003/2004, this tee incorporated the wall as the primary danger. The extra distance put the Beardies in-play for a pulled drive, and into the wind making even reaching the fairway a test for the shortest hitters, but there was no doubt that this latest change was a significant departure from the original set-up of this hole. Indeed, from the tee, the options were reduced to one – hit the fairway. While accuracy is a legitimate test, a feature that made this hole so famous and respected was the various options a player could take. Now it appears the unfortunate trade-off to compensate for the more powerful ball has been a reduction in these choices and challenges.

The placement of new tees has always been conducted with great thought by the Royal and Ancient Club and the Old Course curator, and with the ball travelling further, nobody

wanted the strategic merit of the Old Course to be lost. The 8 January 1954 minutes of the Joint Links Committee stated:

Open Championship and Walker Cup of 1955. The Committee considered whether any additional preparation should be undertaken in view of the Championship Committee's decision to hold the Open Championship and the Walker Cup Match in 1955 at St. Andrews. The Chairman suggested that the Championship Committee should be consulted as soon as possible with regard to the tees to be used on the Old Course. He (Air Commodore Farmer) had made an inspection and recommended as follows:

(1) That the following holes be played from the medal tees, viz: – Numbers 1,2,8,11,17 and 18.

(2) That the special Championship tees already provided at the following holes should be brought into playing condition viz: – Nos. 4,5,6,7,9,14,15 and 16.

(3) That new special tees be constructed at the following holes: –

3rd hole: – In the rough about 50 yards behind and to the right of the medal tee.

10th hole: – About 20 yards behind the medal tee. The tee is already built, but requires the whins to be cleared out to allow spectators to circulate.

12th hole: – New Medal and Championship tees at the rear of the 11th green. The existing tee to be removed and the ground landscaped to open up a view of the fairway from proposed tees.

13th hole: – New tee about 25-30 yards behind the medal tee.

After discussion the said recommendations were approved, subject to the following provisos, viz: –

That the 4th hole be inspected to see whether a tee could be provided at a position not so far back as the

present Championship tee.

That the Committee make a visit of inspection to consider the suggested alterations at the 12th tee.

Detailing more about the proposed changes to the 12th tee, a letter from the Joint Links Committee on 12 January 1954 stated:

The present position here is unsatisfactory because the teeing ground is so small that it is impossible to keep it in reasonably good order. An attempt has been made to provide a new tee on the lower ground at the rear of the 11th green, but this does not appear to have been used presumably because it does not command a view of the fairway. It also has a very artificial appearance, and does not fit into the landscape. It is, however, situated in the only position where an

improved tee can be made, and my Committee's proposal is that it should be enlarged, raised and improved, and that the existing tee should be removed entirely in order to open up a view of the fairway, the whole area being landscaped so as to give as natural an appearance as possible. In addition a Championship tee would be built a short distance further back.

In the February minutes of the Joint Links Committee, a decision regarding the suggested alteration to the 12th tee can be found:

The Committee inspected and approved the new Championship tee at the 12th hole. The proposal to improve the ordinary tee by removing the existing high level tee and building a much larger tee at the lower was also examined and approved, and it was resolved

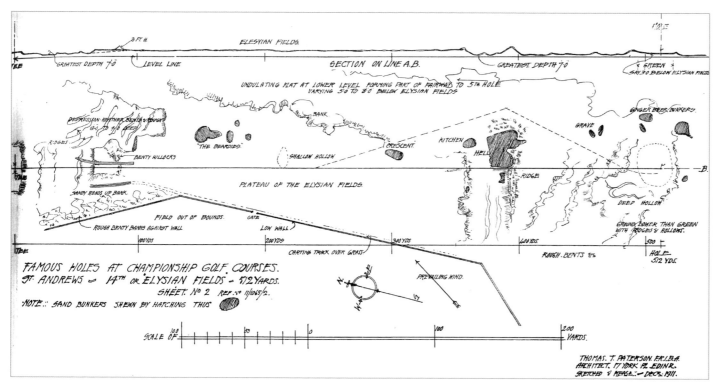

Left: This plan of the 14th hole was surveyed by Edinburgh architect Thomas Paterson in 1911. It nicely shows the elevation change of the hole, tee position, hole features, play-line and hole length (512 yards). It also mentions the newly defined out-of-bounds wall.
Plan Courtesy of Golf Monthly

Right: This plan shows the movement of the Championship tees over four periods 1900-2005. The movement has been somewhat elastic: while the general trend has been back and right, during certain periods the tees have also been brought forward. The teeing ground on some holes has remained unchanged for over a hundred years, such as the 1st and the 17th, while others, for example, the 2nd, 13th, and 15th, have moved back in a more conventional fashion. But the most curious are the tees which have been used twice by Open Championships separated by many years – the 3rd, 5th and 11th – or those that have come forward, such as the 12th and 18th.

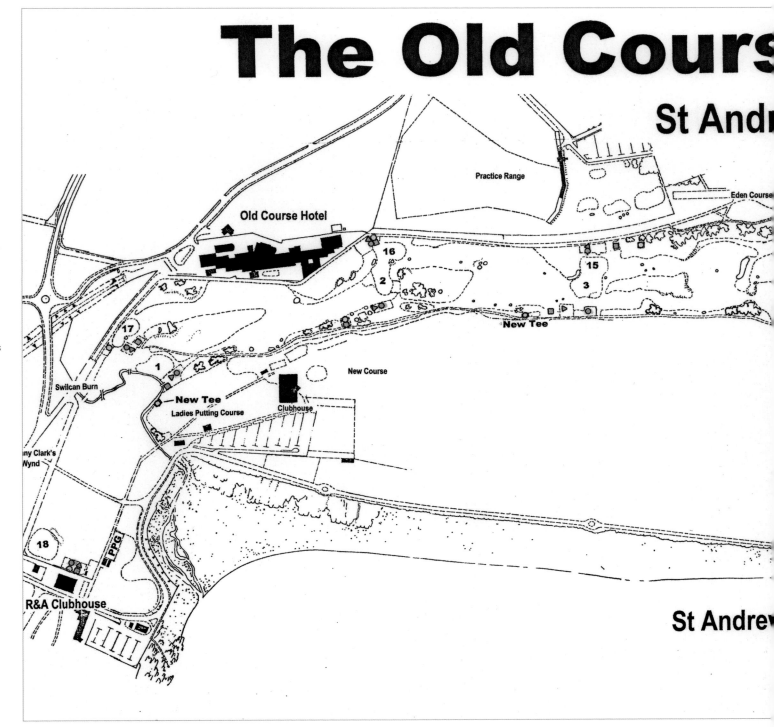

The Old Cours

St Andr

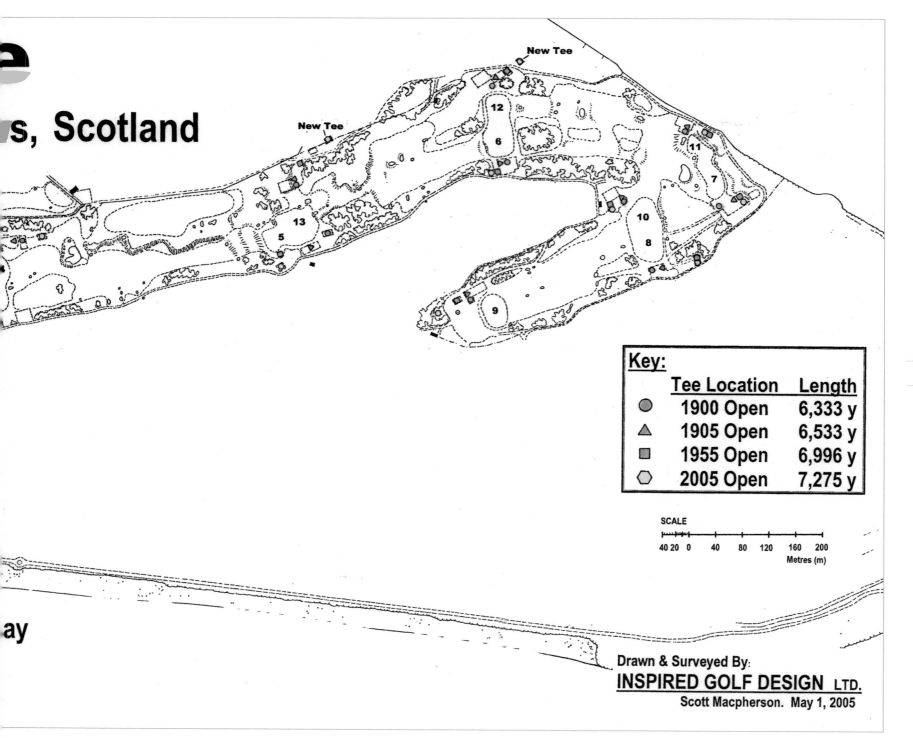

s, Scotland

New Tee

New Tee

12

6

11

13

7

5

10

8

9

Key:

	Tee Location	Length
●	1900 Open	6,333 y
▲	1905 Open	6,533 y
■	1955 Open	6,996 y
⬡	2005 Open	7,275 y

SCALE

40 20 0   40   80   120   160 200
                                Metres (m)

Drawn & Surveyed By:

INSPIRED GOLF DESIGN LTD.

Scott Macpherson. May 1, 2005

ay

that this proposal be submitted to the General Committee of the R&A and subject to their approval that the work be put in hand next winter.

Soon after, the Committee's proposal for the 12th tee was pegged out so that the members of the R&A might view the proposal. One fine amateur golfer, Mr G.H. Micklem, who had also captained the Great Britain team in the Commonwealth tournament on the Old Course in May 1954, made his views known about it:

12th hole: – I am very opposed to the new Championship tee; this seems to take all the brain work out of the hole. The Tee parallel to the present one can well be used in the ordinary way, but I suggest the present Tee be used for (the) Championship.

It was soon reported that the opinion of the R&A 'appeared to be against any change being made in the 12th tee. It was resolved to take no further action'.

At that time a measurement of the Old Course from the medal markers was made. The measurements were as follows:

Hole	Length	Hole	Length	
1st	367	10th	314	
2nd	403	11th	163	
3rd	342	12th	316	
4th	424	13th	409	
5th	522	14th	513	
6th	370	15th	404	
7th	354	16th	351	
8th	161	17th	466	
9th	310	18th	356	
	3253		3292	= 6545 yds

This decision was later reversed however, and it was decided that the Old Course would be lengthened for the 1955 Open

Championship and five notable changes were made.

Hole	1946 Yardage	1955 Yardage	Length Increased
3	348	400	52 yds
7	364	380	16 yds
10	314	338	24 yds
12	316	360	44 yds
13	402	427	25 yds

While many holes were stretched to the longest they had ever been in St Andrews Open Championship history, it was the changes to the 3rd and 12th holes that stood out. The 3rd was 33 yards longer than it had been in 1939, its previous all-time record, and the 12th tee was relocated on top of a mound behind the 11th green – 12 yards further

back than it was for the 2005 Open!

These changes made for a total increase of 161 yards, but the actual overall increase in the length of the Old Course from 1946 was only 113 yards because several tees were also moved forward. The most notable of these being:

Hole	1946 Yardage	1955 Yardage	Length Decreased
4	469	439	30 yds
6	422	405	17 yds
15	424	413	11 yds

(For the 1955 Open, the Old Course measured 6996 yards.)

THE 1955 OPEN CHAMPIONSHIP

This year saw Peter Thomson, the defending champion from Australia, win his second Open Championship with a record low total of 281 strokes. Comments about the course after the Open Championship were mixed, as usual. One article in the *St Andrews Citizen* remarked:

Of the competitors, the winner and the leaders were loud in their praise of the course, but others, notably Eric Brown, the Scottish player, condemned the Old as being unfair because of the element of luck that entered. At the same time he stated that Thomson was a lucky winner of the Title.

Byron Nelson, the great American, quoted Bobby Jones, Gene Sarazen, Walter Hagen and Sam Snead as all telling him "You've never played on a real course until you have played over Scotland's Old Course," He continued: "And what about the Grand Old Lady of St Andrews herself? Well, my play in the championship did not give me a true picture of the Old Course. The rainy conditions of the practice days and the warm sunshine of last week made the grass on the greens and fairways grow. Leading American amateurs and professionals told me the St Andrews greens were keener,

the wind blew harder and the fairways faster than another course in the world. My second shots were consistently short and I found the greens actually slow.

About the most difficult holes, Nelson had said,

I know the old story; "A good player can adapt himself to any conditions." But I was unable to school myself to the point of hitting the ball up to the hole. The most difficult holes on the Old Course are the 4th and the 14th. The danger at the 4th is the championship position of the pin. At the 14th the drive is very important. Your worries start when you cannot decide which side of 'Hell' Bunker to pass.

But it when it came to the renowned 17th hole:

I do not think the Road hole is particularly difficult if you play for a five. Watching Peter Thomson playing this notorious hole in the round, I described to a friend how I would play it. Without appearing bombastic I must tell you that Peter played it precisely my way. And my way is a low running second to the left half of the green and then a good pitch for your 4. If the pitch doesn't finish dead, you are always sure of a 5 — and that was the Bobby Jones method 25 years ago.

Frankly I was surprised to find so many easy holes. The 1st, 3rd, 8th, 9th and 18th are holes where you cannot go wrong if you can hit the ball 200 yards. Probably the best hole on the course is the 170-yard "High" 11th. The "Strath" bunker that caught Johnny Fallon's tee shot makes the hole. Cerda had two 2s on Friday, while Brown had two 5s... when you take a 5 at a Par 3 hole, your mental poise goes. That cleverly placed little bunker can break the strongest of hearts.

I have never seen a course that is so favourably

Above: Peter Thomson.
Cowie Collection,
St Andrews University
Library

Right: American Herb Kohler bought the newly-extended Old Course Hotel and gave it a face-lift in time for the 2005 Open Championship.
S. Macpherson

Far right: Still very much a hazard for the casual golfer, the old railway sheds loom in front of golfers… and the brave feel compelled to take on the challenge!
S. Macpherson

designed for the "hooker", yet the more you hook the more awkward are the second shots. It is a first class championship test. If we Americans had the Old Course we would level out the bumps and mounds on the fairways with a bulldozer. But then if you did that you would have just another municipal course.

to stress that 'the character of this famous hole would remain unchanged' by the presence of the building. The truth of that statement is debatable now. Apart from the hotel being the cause of swirling and unpredictable winds on the course, recent extensions to the north by new owners have limited the number of shots a player can employ to hit the fairway, especially for the Championship tee. No longer can a player hit a 'draw on the wind' as Roberto di Vicenzo liked to do.

Just as Peter Thomson was not 'a lucky winner of the Title', the Old Course was not 'just another municipal course'. The officials at British Transport Hotel (BTH) recognised it importance when they released plans to build a 'super luxury hotel' next to the 17th fairway, just before the 1957 Open Championship. As part of the launch, the officials were keen

The entrance of the hotel was originally built on the east side of the building, on the golf course side, where the conservatory now stands – a very dangerous situation for arriving and departing hotel guests. Also of interest is the timing of the project. BTH had not built a new hotel since 1938 and when they announced this facility, they were considering closing the branch line between Leuchars and St Andrews!

Below far right: This photo was taken about 1912 and is looking back towards the 17th tee. It shows the well-worn area around the dyke, and the original railway sheds.
Courtesy of D. Smyth

Right: This postcard is of the 17th hole showing the tee shot. When taken, fewer golfers than today could hit over the sheds. Most satisfied themselves by playing around the dyke.

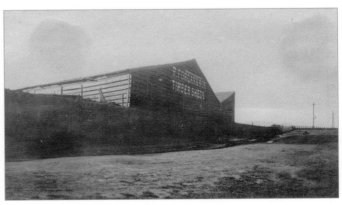

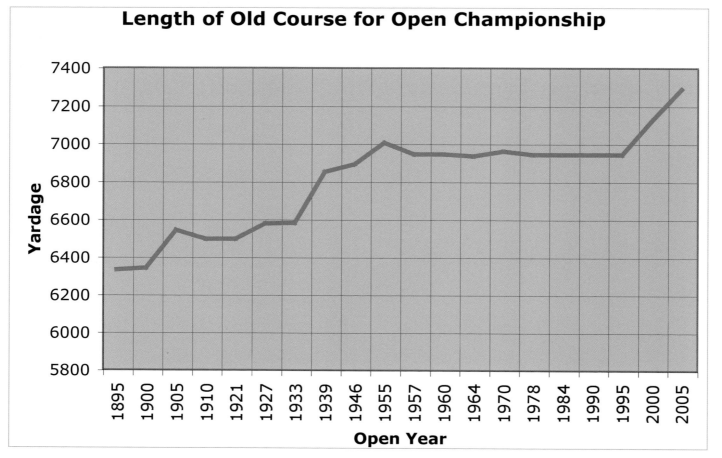

Length of Old Course for Open Championship

Yardage (y-axis): 5800, 6000, 6200, 6400, 6600, 6800, 7000, 7200, 7400

Open Year (x-axis): 1895, 1900, 1905, 1910, 1921, 1927, 1933, 1939, 1946, 1955, 1957, 1960, 1964, 1970, 1978, 1984, 1990, 1995, 2000, 2005

At the same launch, BTH were keen to state that the Old railway sheds were to be kept, but as history records, they had been demolished for many years before being rebuilt in 1983/84.

THE 1957 OPEN CHAMPIONSHIP

In 1957 the Open Championship returned to St Andrews – and sooner than expected. The political crisis involving the Suez Canal and petrol rationing (imposed on 17 December 1956, and which limited private motoring to 200 miles a month), saw the Open moved from the relatively isolated Muirfield to the Old Course at short notice. St Andrews was

seen as being easier for R&A officials, contractors and the public to get to. But as a result, even if it was desired, there was no opportunity to construct any new tees. The only changes were at the 6th and 7th holes, which were shortened to 377 and 364 yards from 405 and 380 yards respectively. These were the same two tees used in the 1947 Walker Cup.

This meant that the Old Course, for the second time in Open Championship history, was shortened from its previous length. The first time, between 1905 and 1910, the course played 46 yards shorter; this time the difference was 60 yards.

Many predicted the effect this reduction in length would have on scoring. Bobby Locke won the Open with a record

low total of 279, and he did it in variable weather conditions. Locke's victory broke another scoring record too. For the first time the average score of the Open Champion was below 70. He averaged 69.75. The top ten golfers had all scored well. As in the 1955 Open, and for only the second time, the average of the top ten finishers was below par.

> The 1957 Open Championship was the first time there was television coverage of the Open.

It would be harsh to describe what happened for the 1958 Eisenhower Trophy as a knee-jerk reaction, but the following year, those in charge of the course set-up in the Royal and Ancient Club immediately restored the course to the length it had been for the 1955 Open – 6996 yards. This would be the second and last time the Old Course was played at this length until, in 2000, the course exceeded the magical 7000 yards barrier for the first time.

THE 1960 OPEN CHAMPIONSHIP

For the highly planned Centenary Open in 1960, the Old Course was rested for five months without a single ball being struck on the much-used and much-loved fairways. When the event started, the Old Course length was re-set to the 1957 length of 6936 yards. The reason given for this return was that it allowed better spectator access through the course. However, the trade-off would be an even lower winning score... and so it proved. This time Australian Kel Nagle took home the Claret Jug with a new Open record of 278 – 14 under par.

Winning-score records were not the only ones being broken. The lowest round was also dropping. In 1960, the best round was reduced to 66, bettering the previous best score of 67, which had stood since 1946.

Arnold Palmer came second at the 1960 Open, and as he described it, 'suffered one of the biggest disappointments of my entire career'. Summing up the defeat he wrote,

Mostly, the fault was in my putting or my inability to read the greens. Tip Anderson may have misread a few, too. We kept seeing breaks – or "borrows," as the Scots called them – that did not exist. And there was the 17th, a hole which I dislike to this day. Mind you I love the Old Course, but I have never come to terms with the Road Hole, as the 17th has always been known. I keep trying to play it as a par 4 on the card, rather than a par 5, which is more the way it plays.

In the aftermath of the 1960 Open, renewed voices called for the championship to be held at St Andrews every four years due to the huge success of the event. Sadly not all enjoyed the Open, and one article published in the *New Zealand Herald* was entitled, 'Americans Don't Like St Andrews'. The article quoted some comments from Americans competing in the Open. One player, Stan Dundan from Philadelphia, was quoted as saying, 'Give me two bulldozers for about a week and I'll give them a golf course...' adding, 'There are humps all over the fairway as if Marilyn Monroe had the hives. In front of the greens there are dips such as the one on the 18th hole known as the Valley of Sin, where a man can be on the green facing a putt where the cup is on a level with his eyes.'

A professional from Virginia in the same article said, 'This is an outmoded and completely unfair course. You are at the mercy of the knolls in front of the green. So it's a pitch and putt course. But the knolls make it so unfair that you can hit a perfect pitch-and-run shot and an unfair bounce puts you in the boondocks. It's kind of like playing Russian roulette.'

While these views were in the minority, a report in the *St Andrews Citizen* said there was 'an increasing volume of opinion that the deeply-shelved bunkers are unfair and that some of them should be re-shaped. As to the hillocks, they are less of a hazard than many people think, and any attempt to interfere with them would result in an endless and world-wide controversy.'

Left: The right-hand Spectacle bunker at the 5th hole being revetted. The greenkeeper standing in the bunker is holding a device that checks that the angle of the bunker face is built at 65 degrees. Many bunkers in recent years have actually had faces much closer to 90 degrees.
S. Macpherson

Left: Returfing around bunkers left of the 5th green in 2006.
S. Macpherson

Bunker Revetting: Revetting is a process whereby small turf sods are stacked upon one another – usually slightly offset – to prevent a bunker face collapsing. This style has become a look closely associated with the links. It is not known exactly when it started, nor when it started on the Old Course, but old photos show bunkers on the Old Course were not always revetted as they are today. (See, for example, photo on p. 61.)

Along with the new balls and new clubs, a new attitude had been borne. Modern golfers had a different attitude to golf than their predecessors – the spirit of adventure had gone from the game. Golf was no longer an imitation of life where the player had to thread his or her way between unexpected dangers and bad lies. It was now a highly coordinated eye and muscle target sport, far removed from its cross-country roots. As a result, and in the name of fair play, many have been keen to remove the element of luck.

Luck is crucial to golf, however. As John L. Low had written in 1903 in *Concerning Golf*, 'A course should never pretend to be, nor is it intended to be, an infallible tribunal of skill alone. The element of chance is the very essence of the game, part of the fun of the game.' And C.B. Macdonald wrote in 1928,

> *Many people preach equity in golf. Does any human receive equity in life? He has to take the bitter with the sweet, and as he forges through all the intricacies and inequalities which life presents, he proves his mettle. Equity has nothing to do with golf. If founded on eternal justice the game would be deadly dull to watch or play. The essence of the game is inequality. Take your medicine where you find it and don't cry… If there were not more or less luck in the game it would not be worthy.*

Far left above: Perhaps the most treacherous bunker on the Old Course, deep and unforgiving, Hill bunker saw the end of Bobby Jones in the 1921 Open, and remains as merciless today. Here it is being prepared for the 2005 Open.
Iain Lowe

Robert Browning's diagnosis in *A History of Golf* was,

> *...we have been so anxious, in the sacred name of fair play, to take all the elements of luck out of the game, that we have to a proportionate extent destroyed its value as a test of each man's ability to stand up to bad luck. Modern golf is a stiffer test of a player's skill, but it has robbed the game of something of its charm as an adventure of the spirit.*

If the modern golf in the 1960s was a stiffer test, it wasn't being reflected in the scoring on the Old Course. But like knights in shining armour to the rescue of a fair princess, some of the old school fought to reverse, or at least slow, the onslaught. Henry Cotton, who had shot an incredible 65 in the 1934 Open at Sandwich – a feat that inspired Dunlop to issue a new ball called the Dunlop 65 (see photo on p.105) – shared his views vociferously. He was looking for ways to toughen up the Old Course. It was somewhat ironic because the record scores set by Thomson and Locke in 1955 and 1957 were with a Dunlop 65. Cotton's sentiments lay with the Old Course, however. He wanted holes to be placed in more difficult locations and he also said, 'perhaps my old idea of tilted tees would help!' His great disappointment was that the magnificent courses were not playing to their real length because of the new golf balls. He complained that the '"tigers" of today ignore tradition and bunkers set for erring drives 25 years ago'.

Cotton made several suggestions in *Golf Illustrated*. One was for the Road Hole, which was no longer played over the sheds. He wrote, 'this spoils the drive to the hole completely… I would make a tee just beyond the railway line on the other course [He was referring to the Eden Course which is now the practice range]. It would restore this drive to its former value and make the course a shot harder and still cater for crowds… A dream maybe, but a solution.'

Interestingly, the back tee at the Road Hole had not been used since the 1939 Open Championship. The change had come due to crowd control, but Cotton wanted the spectators to be led over the railway (west of the hotel) and for the hole not to be spoilt. The back tee was not used in 1964, however. As with the preceding five Opens, the hole played at 446 or 453 yards, allowing golfers the option to avoid playing over the sheds and the station-master's garden.

Cotton seemed particularly aggrieved by the ease with which the Road Hole played and he blamed the authorities in charge of the course. In a later comment, but before the Open, he wrote,

> *The terrors of the road have gone; there are no pot-holes in the macadam road surface, there is no steep step up to the grass kerb and the bank of the green is smooth. It used to be foot-holds and holes, making a run-up a matter of chance. So since the war it was possible to ignore the road as a "death trap", it was just – well, a road! – with nicely trimmed wide grassy strips on it, from which it was not difficult to get back on the green, whether pitching the ball or running it, and players went unpunished many times.*

Good news was in store for Cotton. The Links supervisor, J.K. Campbell, was intending to make some effort to toughen up the back of the green. The main intent was to steepen the slope of the grass bank down to the road.

The second main suggestion Cotton had to toughen up the Old Course before the 1964 Open was: 'How about a chain of bunkers down the middle of the ground marking the 1st and 18th fairways?' This was an interesting idea, but one sure to receive scorn from those inside the R&A. Before signing off, Cotton took his last shot, 'I could place a few more "puzzling pots" too. There is little room left for more back tees.'

Cotton was correct, in that there was little obvious space to place new back tees. It would take some radical ideas and

forty years before any length was added to the Old Course.

In the meantime, the ball did not stand still. The most significant changes were in the 'feel' of the ball. Golf professionals with fast swings preferred the way certain balls felt and sounded off the clubface, flew though the air, and reacted when they hit the ground. In the United States, a young engineer by the name of James Bartsch had been investing enormous amounts of time and personal money into developing a better golf ball. His journey had taken him everywhere, including, in 1963, a submission for a patent for a solid one-piece golf ball. While this patented ball was not a great success, his work eventually helped turn the golf ball industry away from the wound ball and towards the modern ball.

At the heart of all Cotton's issues was that he hated seeing the Old Course being disregarded by the new generation of golfers as a formidable test of golf. He had seen all the top players play the course since the 1920s, including the last playing years of 'The Great Triumvirate' of Taylor, Braid and Vardon, and believed few of the 'new boys' could compete under the same conditions of play as the previous generation, when St Andrews was a fearsome test of golf.

While this debate was still going on, St Andrews had to host the 1964 Open Championship. Perhaps aware of Cotton's comments regarding the famous Road Hole and almost certainly aware of the wealth of statistics indicating that it was not playing as a par 5, the hole was reduced to a par 4 for the Open. The R&A also made another concession; competitors could use either the 1.68 or 1.62-inch ball.

As for the course itself, changes were made but changes that again, for the third time, made the course shorter than it had been from the previous Open. The course only lost an overall distance of 10 yards, but four holes were significantly altered:

Hole	1960 Yardage	1964 Yardage	Length Increased	Length Decreased
3	400	370		30 yds
4	439	470	31 yds	
6	377	414	37 yds	
12	360	312		48 yds
		Total Change	68 yds	78 yds

THE 1964 OPEN CHAMPIONSHIP

Only the weather could save the Old Course from receiving its sixth successive record low score. Fortunately for those concerned with such matters the gods were smiling. Windy conditions and a comparatively firm course conspired to make scoring difficult. The eventual champion, 'Champagne' Tony Lema, who had only had time for twenty-five holes of practice, shot 279, one shot higher than Nagle in 1960.

Far left top & bottom: Here the change to the back of the Road Hole green relates to how much the road can be seen. Originally the path sat higher than the road and the bank up to the green was rough and relatively unmaintained. For the 2005 Open Championship (*bottom*) Vijay Singh chips to the same green but, while it is still dangerous, it has less of the 'terrors' behind it that it once had.
Top photo: St Andrews University Library
Bottom photo: Iain Lowe

Above: Tony Lema teeing off in 1964. Tip Anderson can be seen holding Lema's dark-coloured bag on the first tee.

* Tip Anderson died in St Andrews in January 2004, aged 71.

Although more players used the 1.68 American-sized ball, Lema choose to play with a smaller British ball made by Slazenger. It was one of many good decisions he made. A second critical decision was employing local caddy Tip Anderson. Arnold Palmer had decided not to come to St Andrews in 1964 due to a hectic schedule in the States, but lent his putter and Tip to Lema. Tip guided Lema around the Old Course with deft accuracy. Tip's inside knowledge was that he knew that the Old Course, despite its dramatic width, was a driver's course. A copy of his caddy notes show the how simple and accurate his directions for Lema off the tee were:

1st	About 20 per cent to left of the flag, with a 3 wood.
2nd	25 yards to the right of Cheape's bunker, on left.
3rd	Slightly to the right of bunker nearest tee.
4th	Best line is straight on flag.
5th	Aim for the hill coming from bunkers to left.
6th	Aim slightly left, on buildings in distance over river.
7th	Skirt whins on right to land right of hill.
8th	Short hole; don't run off.
9th	Line on flag, directly over left of two bunkers.
10th	Aim for white flag of 8th hole.
11th	Short (170 yards) hole. Slopes towards you. Trouble if you overshoot.
12th	Keep left. Aim to stop on flattish hill.
13th	Drive tight on whins to right, playing hole narrow dog-leg to left.
14th	Sight on church spire to right of town.
15th	Just to right of large bunker on right. Direction church spire.
16th	Bear to left of bunker group, playing hole as dog-leg. Don't attempt straighter line between bunker group and railway.
17th	Care needed. Only tackle short cut (over corner) if driver really working.
18th	Straight on monument back right of clubhouse. A big one puts you on the apron.

> **"Teeing Off"**
>
> *'The Old Course is the hardest I know on which to align yourself correctly for both drives and approach shots. Its legendary undulations make the majority of its landing areas invisible as the ball is addressed, and there are no trees and relatively few other landmarks to serve as guideposts… I began on every shot to draw an imaginary line back from it (the target) through the ball, then to look for a bit of debris or grass discolouration on that line three or four feet ahead of the ball, and to use that as my key set-up reference point. This system, which is followed today by many tour players, helped enormously not only in that championship but for the rest of my career.'*
>
> Jack Nicklaus, commenting on his difficulty in correctly targeting himself in 1964.

After the Open, Cotton praised Lema's victory, and Tip Anderson*, who carried Lema's three woods, ten irons and blade putter with ease: 'Lema often used a No. 3 wood off the tee, even a No.2 iron, and then all his clubs from a No. 6 iron downwards, except at holes Nos. 4, 5 and 14 and the short 11th, He once used a No. 4 wood and a No. 4 iron – this was in his final round.'

But Cotton thought the course played too short. He wrote after the event, 'For a start the 18th tee must go back against the wall of the railway yard, so that it can be treated with more respect – it is only good as a two shot hole! This would make it quite a big second shot… but we must stop St Andrews becoming a drive-and-pitch course.'

Lema was driving the ball consistently long at the 1964 Open Championship, possibly averaging about 280 yards, as twice he drove the 359-yard 9th hole. Using the chart Behr calculated in 1937 to preserve the integrity of the Old Course as it was played with a gutta percha, this driving length would require the Old Course to measure over 8000 yards to ensure

the same shot values to modern golfers. It was little wonder Cotton was searching every nook and cranny for possible new tee locations.

Nevertheless, extending a golf course is not a cheap or one-off cost. Since 1953 the increased cost of running the links had hit the R&A and Town Council hard and it was known that any decision to construct new tees would also increase the cost of maintaining a course. In *Golf Illustrated* an article written by J.K. Robertson, 'Economy at St. Andrews', stated, 'Their headache is the steeply mounting upkeep of the courses. Even "natural" circuits require maintenance, in this case to the costly tune, nowadays, of £16,000 a year.' It had been obvious for years that something needed to be done to reduce expenditure but the excessive deliberation had become debilitating. The decision was made that all four courses (Old, New, Jubilee and Eden) and their staff and equipment would be amalgamated. There was also an increase in the tariff charged to visiting and local golfers. Up until 1946, such golf had been free.

Golf's popularity grew in the 1960s. The interest came from many areas. Some people just had more leisure time, some interest was corporate, and others were attracted to the game by better, user-friendlier equipment. The positive effect of this on the Open Championship was greater spectator interest. With gate takings increasing but spectator vantage points few, St Andrews embarked on a programme of improvements to make the Old Course better equipped to handle the huge crowds and offer them better facilities to follow the progress of their favourite players. *Golf Weekly* reported,

> *Huge mounds were built using hundreds of tonnes of soil at selected points for good viewing. Spectator routes were improved and widened, and new pathways were constructed by clearing a way through dense gorse to allow the crowds free movement at all parts of the links.*

This 'improvement' would help spectators for many years, and provide access and viewing areas never before on offer. But was it enough?

The 1970 Open saw some significant new developments in the golf industry, St Andrews and the Open Championship. For the golf industry in particular, equipment development continued its relentless march forward. Bartsch's one-piece ball had received its patent in 1967, but the ball was inferior to the wound ball in that it lacked distance and feel, and it was also brittle. But the invention still led to the ball of the future.

Far left: Vantage points had first been recommended by the Championship Committee in August 1957, just after the 1957 Open. A note in the minutes of the Joint Links Committee reads, 'Suggestion that provision be made for additional points for viewing play on the Old Course. It was resolved that the committee would be opposed to anything which would alter the appearance of the Course, but it would be interested to have detailed suggestions.'
Iain Lowe

Above: The once-celebrated Dunlop 65 is now a collector's item.
S. Macpherson

Left: A far cry from the silence demanded by today's professionals, here the train steams its way past the 16th green on it way to Leuchars as Open competitors putt out.
Cowie Collection, St Andrews University Library

Right: The back tee being used on the last practice day before the 2005 Open Championship. The 17th green can be seen just over the old railway sheds in the distance. For players seeking the middle of the fairway, the direct line off the tee is generally over the letter 'H' in the Old Course Hotel sign on the old railway sheds.
Iain Lowe

Note: Surlyn replaced balata, but it was not introduced until 1968 when 'Ram' brought out the three-piece wound rubber-core covered with surlyn.

Spalding, a company that had been at the cutting edge of golf technology since 1907, found the solution in 1967. A researcher at the company, Bob Molitor (whom the Molitor ball was later named after), took Bartsch's ball and covered it in a polyurethane plastic. This reduced the chance of the ball chipping, and increased feel. The ball was the first two-piece ball since the feathery, and it swept the market.

As John Hotchkiss summarised in *500 Years of Golf Balls*, the two-piece ball would be the 'Fourth Revolution of the golf ball', following the feathery, the gutty and the wound rubber-core ball. The major factors that led to a successful two-piece ball were:

1. The Bartsch research and introduction of a solid core.
2. Spalding's addition of a cover material.
3. The advent of surlyn in 1966.

However, by the time the Open Championship started in June 1970, most touring professionals still preferred the balata-covered, wound ball. They felt it gave greater spin, greater directional control and better trajectory.

THE 1970 OPEN CHAMPIONSHIP

The 1970 Open was the first championship to be held when the train did not rumble past the 15th and 16th holes – though the out-of-bounds stayed in place. More importantly, the Links Trust was on the verge of being set up. In 1970, local clubs had joined with the R&A to retain control and management of the Links within the town, but in 1971, the R&A issued a memorandum outlining their proposals for control and management by establishing a Links Trust. The town council agreed to seek power to set up the trust and in 1974 the Links Act received royal assent.

The Royal and Ancient Club had also made decisions about their championship. Television coverage was increased

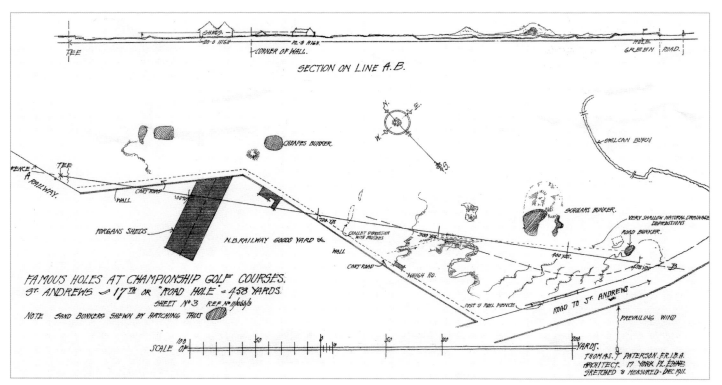

SECTION ON LINE A.B.

FAMOUS HOLES AT CHAMPIONSHIP GOLF COURSES.
ST. ANDREWS — 17TH OR "ROAD HOLE" = 458 YARDS.
SHEET No 3 REF No. 11/166/3
NOTE SAND BUNKERS SHEWN BY HATCHING THUS

THOMAS J. PATERSON, F.R.I.B.A.
ARCHITECT. 17 YORK PL. EDINR.
SKETCHED & MEASURED. DEC. 1911.

Left: This survey of the 17th hole was done by Edinburgh-based architect Thomas Paterson in December 1911. It was part of a series that examined 'Famous Holes at Championship Golf Courses'. The hole measures the same distance as it does today, though the bunkers have changed in shape and size. But the path that now exists between the road and the green is not shown here. *Plan courtesy of* Golf Monthly.

to twelve holes, the first six and last six, and it would be in colour. To encourage people to come to the course, spectator stands were enlarged (for a seated capacity of over 14,000), and had their vantage improved. Additionally, the Open was to be played over four days for the first time, with play starting on the Wednesday and finishing on Saturday, with, (as it turned out that year), the play-off between Nicklaus and Sanders taking place on Sunday.

The last significant change was to the course itself. It was extended, possibly to counteract the effect of the high-tech three-piece ball. The 3rd hole was pushed to its longest ever – 405 yards – and the 17th tee put back to 466 yards, where it had last been in 1939. One hole, however, was shortened – the 18th. This year the tee was to be located just off the back of the 17th green.

Hole	1964 Yardage	1970 Yardage	Length Increased	Length Decreased
3	370	405	35 yds	
17	453	466	13 yds	
18	381	358		23 yds
Front Nine	3492	3527	35 yds	
Back Nine	3434	3424		10 yds
Total	6926	6951	25 yds	

Remarkably, the result of these changes, combined with some stormy conditions – winds gusted at a gale force 53 knots during Nicklaus's play-off with Sanders – was a winning total that for the second consecutive event, proved higher than the previous winning total. Old stalwarts and officials rejoiced.

Nevertheless, a closer look at the statistics indicated some

Above: Dr. Alister Mackenzie's sketch of 17th Hole as featured in *The Links* by Robert Hunter in 1926.

Right: **17th green area:**

Size-wise, the green it-self is deceptively large at 660 sq m (789 sq yds). However because of the shape of certain landforms – particularly the 'corner' that juts out at the front edge – and the way the bunker pinches into the left side of the green, hit-ting it is a stern test. The diagonal of the road behind the green adds considerably to the anxiety and difficul-ty, particularly for those approaching it with long irons. As for the bunker itself, it is only 9 sq m (11 sq yds) in size, but has a much greater collection area – possible five or six times its size. Balls on the green and shots missing the bunker left can all be funnelled into the sand. For those think-ing this is all by chance, you may be disillu-sioned to discover that the authorities have in recent times conspired to make this bunker the way it is. The latest re-construction occurred in February 2005, and was with the deliberate aim of making it catch *more* shots.

Slope Analysis:

The putting surface itself should be separated into the elevated component and the small lower portion at the front – this varies in size depending on the greenkeeper's whim and the season. The elevated section is the most important. Of this, the Open pin placement area (the area where the slope is between one and three per cent) is shaped like a 'dogs-bone' and angles away from the centre line of the hole, and is generally slightly less than half the area of the green. The slopes on the surface are interesting in that the majority of the green slopes away from the line of play. As well, while most of the green slopes right to left (away from the road), small sections slope the other way making putting in these areas particularly tricky.

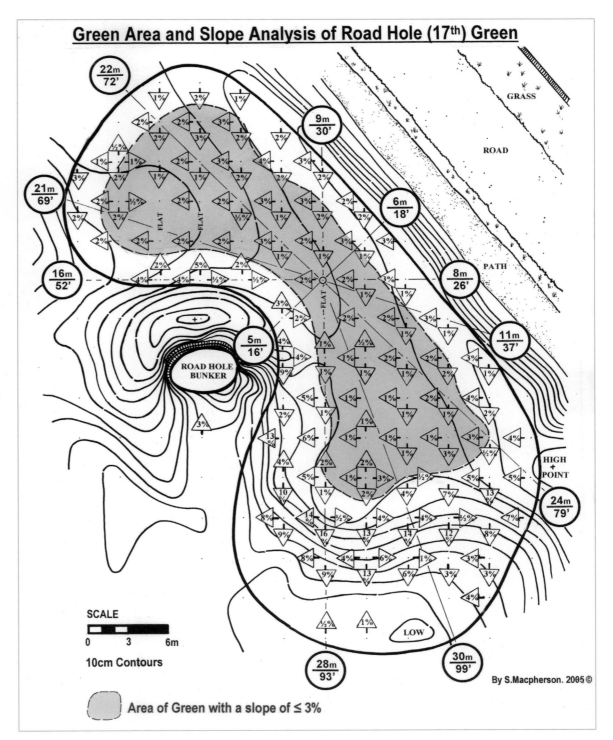

Green Area and Slope Analysis of Road Hole (17th) Green

SCALE
0   3   6m
10cm Contours

By S.Macpherson. 2005 ©

Area of Green with a slope of ≤ 3%

BUNKERED AT THE ROAD HOLE, ST. ANDREWS

gloomy news for those wishing for a stabilisation in the scoring. In the first round, played in very good weather conditions, the average score for all 134 competitors was 72.9, that is, under one stroke more than par (72) for the course. This was the same difference from par that the top ten golfers achieved in 1927.

Looking at the stroke averages for the holes, the 17th hole (which was made less intimidating by the removal of the railway sheds in 1967), was the most difficult hole on the course. Indeed, only five birdies were scored on the hole out of 404 rounds played. The hole with the next fewest birdies was the 4th hole where only fifteen were registered. The 18th hole had the greatest number of birdies with eighty-seven, beating the 12th by one.

American golf course architect Pete Dye once described the 17th hole in this way:

> [It] *may very well be the best par-four in the world. Whether that's true or not, the legend of the Road Hole befits its image, for in my opinion the design is textbook perfect… Every time I played the seventeenth, I appreciated the strategy for the hole more.*
>
> *'I was so impressed with the design of the green… [my wife] Alice and I rented a tripod in the city to measure the dimensions. We were amazed to see that*

the green was in fact a perfect rectangular shape even though it appears oval from the fairway.

'The distinctiveness of the Road Hole comes from the positioning of the pot bunker, the severe slope of the green down into the swale, and the close proximity of the wall.'

Driving from the back tee validated the 17th's stroke difficulty as a par 4, but perhaps the opposite was true of the 18th hole. It is unusual for the last hole to be the easiest on the course. Was making it reachable – Nicklaus drove it once, and famously through it in the play-off * – a concession to the golfers for difficulty they were forced to endure on the preceding hole? Or was it a strategic move whereby having the tees forward, more golfers would be tempted to drive the green?

In 1970 *Golf Monthly* explained,

> *Comparisons with the 1964 championship are not easy, because of the strong gale which blew during part of the first and second days six years ago. But in one respect there was a sharp improvement in scoring in this year's championship, compared with the 1964 event. This year no fewer than 14 eagles were scored during the championship; in 1964 the total was eight.*

* In 1964, in similar wind conditions, Nicklaus had driven the 18th hole three times with his 3-wood!

Right: This photo of the 17th hole was taken about 1910. It is interesting to note the orientation of the Road Hole bunker and the distinct lack of rough grasses (or perhaps, lack of a modern fairway).

Above far right: The Road Hole green, seen from side on, shows the shadows of the green and bunker. The trough that funnels balls into the right-hand bunker can clearly be seen.
S. Macpherson

Right: Arnold Palmer started strongly with a 68 in the first round of the 1970 Open, but a 72 and 76 in the second and third rounds pushed him back. This round of 74 resulted in a 12th place finish.
Score card courtesy of the British Golf Museum

Hole	Par	Eagles
5	5	4
7	4	1
9	4	1
10	4	2
12	4	3
14	5	1
18	4	2

Individual scoring improved in the Open as well. The course record of 68 by Jones in 1927 was beaten by one shot in

THE OPEN CHAMPIONSHIP
OLD COURSE, ST. ANDREWS
Game No 21
Competitor   Arnold Palmer   Saturday

Hole	Length in Yards	Par	Score		Hole	Length in Yards	Par	Score
1	374	4	5		10	338	4	4
2	411	4	4		11	170	3	3
3	405	4	3		12	312	4	4
4	470	4	5		13	427	4	4
5	567	5	5		14	560	5	5
6	414	4	4		15	413	4	4
7	364	4	4		16	380	4	4
8	163	3	4		17	466	4	5
9	359	4	4		18	358	4	3
Out	3527	36	38		In	3424	36	36
					Out	3527	36	38
					Total	6951	72	74

Signature of Competitor   *Arnold Palmer*
Signature of Marker   *M. Bembridge.*

(290)

1933. The low score of 67 for an Open Championship at St Andrews remained until 1960, when it was lowered to 66. Nicklaus shot another 66 in 1964 but relatively unknown golfer Neil Coles shot a remarkable 65 in his first round in 1970.

The 1970 Open: Privately, the Open officials had fretted about a hot player tearing up the Old Course in this year, and in hindsight, with good reason. In the first round 23-year-old Tony Jacklin, the current US Open champion, had teed off late and was caught in the storm that blew in late on Wednesday afternoon. Jacklin had to mark his ball and complete his round the next morning. Sadly, the weather and time delay extinguished the fire from Jacklin's round. Up until that point he had a record-tying outward nine of 29 including an eagle two at the driveable par 9th, and was eight under par looking to shoot 62 or 63! With the magic gone, Jacklin bogeyed three of his remaining five holes to shoot 67.

After the 1970 Open Championship, the USGA set regulations to control the distance a ball could travel. They were principally set around the concept of the ball's 'initial velocity'.

Initial Velocity: A ball did not conform to USGA standards if the velocity of the ball off the clubface was more than 255 feet per second (173 miles per hour).
NB: Initial velocity should not be confused with clubhead speed. The speed of the ball is always faster than the clubhead speed because of the 'trampoline effect'.

Similar to the discovery made over a hundred years earlier when it was realised 'nicks' in a smooth gutta percha ball could improve its flight, modern ball manufacturers discovered

that the dimple pattern had a significant effect on how far a ball flew in the air, its trajectory, and its spin. So by improving dimple patterns, a US ball company could slip around the USGA regulations and gain length without changing the initial velocity. Brilliant!

By 1971 the dimple war had begun. Equipment companies all around the world invested huge amounts of money into discovering how many dimples on a ball were best. They wanted to know what size, depth and dimple coverage gave the optimum flight. Meanwhile, most golfers were running trials with the wealth of new products and finding which ball best aided their game. Questions such as, 'Is a ball with a high trajectory or low trajectory more preferable?' were commonplace in top amateur and professional golf.

Technology was about to have a significant impact on the Old Course experience. The unique and gruelling examination that the Old Course had provided for hundreds of years, and that so many within the R&A had been trying to preserve, would be undone not just by slow decisions by the Ball and Implement Committee, but also by the clever minds of aerodynamic scientists and by stronger, fitter, seasoned professional golfers. Competitive players were looking for balls that suited their game and also certain courses. Questions emerged such as, 'What size ball with what spin rate and trajectory would be best for the windy conditions experienced on the Old Course?'

To show the prowess of the current crop of golfers, in 1971 golf analyst Jack Reddy published his 'Guideline to Golfing Success' in *International Golfer*. This was a series of check points that set the winners apart from the also-rans in the US Open. The research was based on two years of statistical analysis:

Driving: Drive a ball consistently between 250-270 yards and land in a fairway less than 35 yards wide four out of five times.

Long Irons: Hit a ball over 200 yards and on the average be able to come within 36 feet of the pin, or less than six per cent of the original distance.

Medium Irons: From a distance of 150-175 yards, land on the average within 26 feet of the target – or again within six per cent of the original distance.

Long Putts: From 75 feet away, putt to within 4 feet of the hole. On putts of less than 75 feet, come proportionately closer. A 40-foot putt should come within 2.4 feet on the average, one from 30 feet should be 1.8 feet away.

Short Putts: Under all conditions and on every variety of green, sink all putts up to 2.5 feet, half of all 6 footers and one out of every ten 20 footers.

Chip Shots: Chip nearly as well as you can putt; from 75 feet you should get within 5 feet, on the average.

Recovery Shots: Come within 10 feet of the hole when you are 75 feet out in deep grass and come within 12 feet from the same 75-foot distance when you are in a sand trap.

With most of the worlds top golfers also competing in the British Open, could the same level of skills be required to win the Claret Jug at St Andrews?

10 September 1972 – The 10th hole is named 'Bobby Jones'.

In 1973, concerned about the latest developments, the R&A decided the large ball that had been in use in the USA since 1932 would be compulsory for competitors in the 1974 Open Championship. But those intervening forty years had seen a great change in the ball, and figuratively speaking, in many ways the horse had already bolted. If the aim was to seriously reduce the distance a ball could be propelled, it may have been more appropriate for the USGA to also reduce the weight of the ball, as had been advocated since the 1920s. Another option was to introduce a tournament ball.

The USGA acknowledged the ongoing threat to golf courses (and indeed what some people thought was also a

OLD COURSE

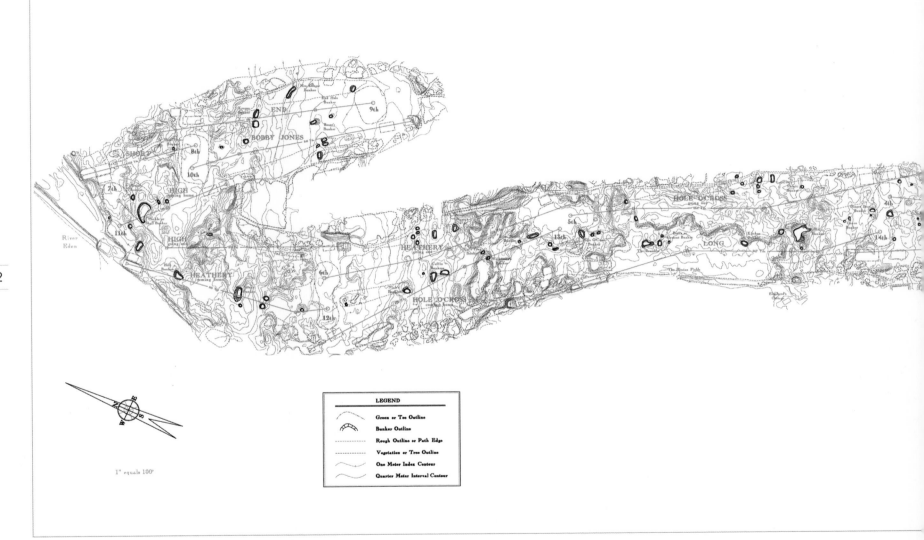

LEGEND

⌒ Green or Tee Outline

⌒ Bunker Outline

---- Rough Outline or Path Edge

---- Vegetation or Tree Outline

〜 One Meter Index Contour

〜 Quarter Meter Interval Contour

1" equals 100'

Above: This remarkable contour plan of the Old Course shows the undulations of the links. While difficult to fully appreciate at this scale, the numerous changes in elevation prove that, contrary to common perception, the Old Course is far from flat. Indeed, in some sections, the slopes could be described as steep. The plan was presented to the Royal and Ancient Golf Club by Jerry Pate Golf Design on 22 July, 1990. The plan reflects the length and setup of the course for the Open Championships held from 1978 to 1995 inclusive.

Plan courtesy of Jerry Pate Golf Design.

ST. ANDREWS

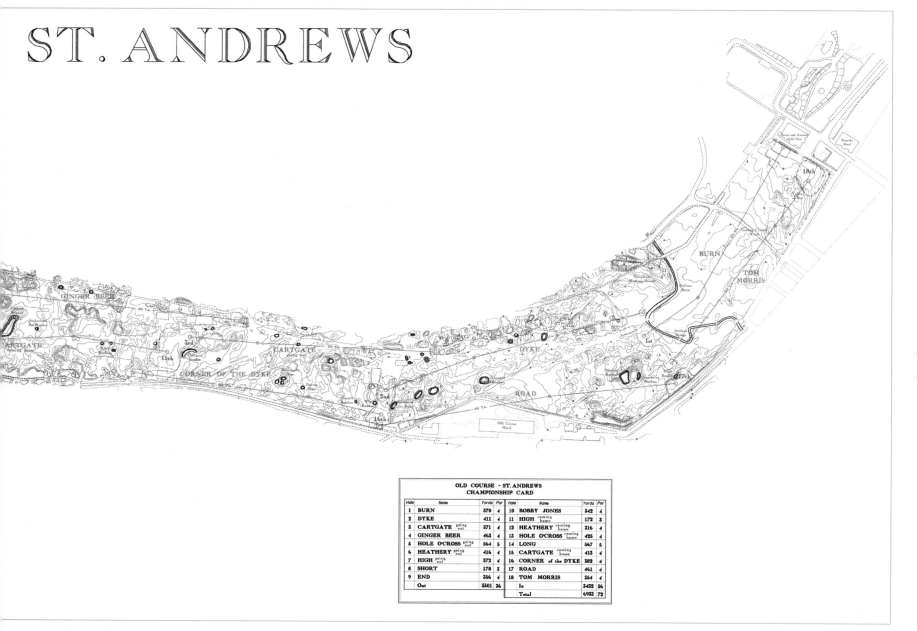

OLD COURSE - ST. ANDREWS
CHAMPIONSHIP CARD

Hole	Name	Yards	Par	Hole	Name	Yards	Par
1	BURN	370	4	10	BOBBY JONES	342	4
2	DYKE	411	4	11	HIGH coming home	172	3
3	CARTGATE going out	371	4	12	HEATHERY coming home	316	4
4	GINGER BEER	463	4	13	HOLE O'CROSS coming home	425	4
5	HOLE O'CROSS going out	564	5	14	LONG	567	5
6	HEATHERY going out	416	4	15	CARTGATE coming home	413	4
7	HIGH going out	372	4	16	CORNER of the DYKE	382	4
8	SHORT	178	3	17	ROAD	461	4
9	END	356	4	18	TOM MORRIS	354	4
	Out	3501	36		In	3432	36
					Total	6933	72

threat to the integrity of golf) from unbridled technology, and in 1976 imposed the 'Overall Distance Standard'. They mandated that no ball could travel over 280 yards, plus six per cent tolerance, or 296 yards in total, when hit by their USGA mechanical hitting machine. While this concept was good, and a crucial first step, the practical application on the golf course was less successful, as many top players had swing speeds greater than the 106 miles per hour the swing machine was set at. But the greatest challenge to this test was from two fronts: graphite shafts and various types of metal heads.

THE 1978 OPEN CHAMPIONSHIP

For the 1978 Open Championship, the Old Course was set up at 6933 yards. This was the fourth time in the history of the Open at St Andrews that the Old Course had been shortened from a previous length. This was perplexing considering the power of the new balls, but more astonishing in hindsight is the fact that the course remained at this length for the next four Opens. Additionally, no significant bunkers have been added to the Old Course for the best part of fifty years!

To shorten the course from 6951 yards to 6933, two changes were made. First, the ever-changing 3rd hole was returned to 371 yards, almost the exact yardage it was in 1964, and the 8th hole was made longer. This hole was extended to 178 yards, 5 yards longer than it had been in 1955, but 15 yards longer than in 1970.

These modest alterations saw a slight change in the difficulty of various holes, but not for the champion. Nicklaus took the championship with a score of 281, beating his score in 1970 by two shots. The average score of the other golfers making up the top ten was reduced by almost a full shot and the entire field improved by over half a shot.

Looking at the stroke average of the holes, shortening the 3rd made it easier and dropped it from the 11th hardest to the 15th hardest. The extra 15 yards at the 8th hole however, had no significant impact on the difficulty of the hole, except the hole's stroke average did drop below par, going from an average score of 3.07 to 2.99.

Far right: Jack Nicklaus tees off with his wooden-headed driver on the 2nd hole. Sixteen holes later he had seen off the New Zealander Simon Owen and won the 1978 Open Championship. In 2005 his face (and jersey) was etched into history on the Scottish £5 note.
Courtesy of Getty Photos

Right: The commemorative five-pound note was issued for the 2005 Open Championship at St Andrews to celebrate Nicklaus's last appearance at the Open and his great wins in 1970 and 1978. The note reproduced here has been autographed.

Hole	Birdies In 1970		Birdies In 1978	
4	15	(2)	21	(3)
12	86	(17)	65	(14)
17	5	(1)	7	(1)
18	87	(18)	56	(11=)

Note: Number in bracket denotes the rank. (1) is the fewest number of birdies.

On perfect greens, the holes most birdied in 1978 were the 5th hole with 149, then in a distant second, the 10th hole with 100. The 17th remained the most difficult after 453 rounds, with the second least birdied hole being the 13th. One interesting feature in the statistics is that while the par 5 5th hole was eaten alive by the field, the parallel

par 5 14th averaged above its par. From this, one might suspect that during the tournament the 5th hole played down wind, while the 14th played into it.

CARNAGE AT THE ROAD HOLE IN 1978
Tom Weiskopf = 6
Brian Barnes = 6. Putting for 3, putted into Road Hole bunker
Arnold Palmer = 7-7
Seve Ballesteros = 5-6-6-5
Tommy Nakajima = 9. After being on the green for 2, he, like Brian Barnes, putted into the bunker and took 5 shots to get out. If he had made the birdie he was trying for, he would have finished second. This remarkable disaster led to the Road Hole bunker gaining another name – 'the sands of Nakajima'.

Above: Back-to-back victories in St Andrews. Nicklaus clutches the Claret Jug again in 1978.
Courtesy of Getty Photos

Left: On the night before the 2005 Open began, two green staff mow the green that is shared between the 5th and 13th holes. Combined, they walked a distance of 3.5 miles to complete the task.
Iain Lowe

RANSOMES' LAWN MOWERS ARE THE BEST.

Patronised by HER MAJESTY THE QUEEN, H.R.H. THE PRINCE of WALES, H.R.H. PRINCESS VICTORIA of PRUSSIA, &c.

Only Gold Medal, International Horticultural Exhibition, 1892.

All Mowers sent on a Month's Trial. Carriage Paid.

TESTIMONIAL,
From the Hon. Sec., Prestwick Golf Club, Ayr, N.B., Sept. 8th, 1893.—"The Automaton Mower sent us gives great satisfaction and makes excellent work. I wish you to send a 22-inch machine, with extra side rollers for long grass, immediately.

RANSOMES' LAWN MOWERS produce a fine, even surface on the Putting Greens, and are in use on the CROMER, DEWSBURY, FELIXSTOWE, ISLAY, ISLE OF WIGHT LADIES', KILLARNEY, LEASOWE, LITTLESTONE, LOSSIEMOUTH, MID-SURREY, MORAY, MORECAMBE, PRESTWICK, ROYAL EPPING FOREST, RICHMOND, St. GEORGE'S, SEATON CAREW, SUTTON COLDFIELD, WOODFORD, WALLASSEY, WESTGATE-ON-SEA, WILDERNESSE, and other Links, giving the greatest satisfaction.

ILLUSTRATED CATALOGUES FREE BY POST.
RANSOMES, SIMS, & JEFFERIES, LIMITED, IPSWICH.

Left: Lawn mower advertisement from 1894.

Far left: The double greens on the Old Course are so large that sprinkler heads located on the perimeter do not provide enough coverage, so some sprinklers are located on the greens themselves, such as here on the 8th and 10th.
S. Macpherson

*See Chapter 8 for Old Course Green area and other calculations, listed under "Old Course Vital Statistics", p.173.

Far right: Every evening before a round of the Open Championship the sandy graves were carefully prepared. Here the vicious Strath bunker in front of the 11th green is addressed.
Iain Lowe

'One can feel so lonely at St Andrews missing a putt.' Anon.

The Old Course had become draped in a sacred cloak sometime during the Second World War. No new bunkers were to be cut in the course from then on. It is difficult to trace where this unwritten edict might have originated because it had not existed in 1905 or anytime before the mid 1920s, even though stern guardians such as Norman Boase had been at the helm. From this point on it was felt by many that cutting new bunkers on the Old Course amounted to sacrilege. From an architectural point of view, others felt that a few bunkers strategically placed further out than existing bunkers on certain fairways would replenish a special ingredient that was being neutralised by the power of the new ball. They encouraged long hitters to take less club off the tee and therefore return approach shots – the most difficult shots at St Andrews – to the value they had in previous generations.

But new bunkers were not to be. St Andrews had to rely even more on the unpredictable weather and its undulating fairways to prevent golfers at the height of their powers and armed with space age technology from destroying the course record and winning scores. What would the weather be like in 1984?

Before we get to that, little has been said about the improvement in the condition of the course during this period, but much had changed, and these changes had directly affected scoring. Most turf grass and maintenance improvements were due to improved techniques and equipment, but greater investment and more manpower also helped significantly. The greenkeeper, Walter Woods, was a traditionalist. In many ways he shared Old Tom Morris's belief that sand and time were the best solutions to most problems. He wanted roots of the turf to penetrate as deep as possible into the sandy fairways. He saw overuse of artificial fertilisers as counteractive to his goal. Rest and the use of natural products at certain times when the turf was under

stress was about the furthest Woods went. Old Tom once castigated a golfer who deplored the taboo of golf on a Sunday by saying, 'Weel, sir, the links want a rest on the Sabbath, even if you don't.'

One product Woods used several times before the 1984 Open on his 5.6 acres* of greens was called Seamac 600. It was made purely of plant hormones extracted from seaweed gathered from remote pollution-free oceans. Woods claimed that this product helped the vitality of the grass by encouraging a vigorous root system.

When Woods started in the 1970s much of the watering was still done by hand, particularly in the dry summer months. A brand new and almost revolutionary automatic sprinkler system had been installed in 1964, but due to under supply, over demand, and a rather inadequate system, hand-watering was still essential. Woods would often be at the course at five o'clock in the morning hand-watering the dry areas on the greens and undulations with a hose. The result, while not providing the coverage modern irrigation systems can provide, was a standard of care for the course that took its condition beyond any it had previously achieved.

While water to the course had improved by the mid 1970s, fairways were still not being cut during the summer. Due to the dryness of the summers, the gang mowers were not required. Only the lush hollows on the undulating fairways and around the greens needed to be cut – and when they were it was done by fly-mow.

For the 1978 Open, greens were being cut once a day at 3/16th of an inch (4.8mm). It wasn't until 1984 that this was lowered to 5/32nds of an inch (4mm), at which time greens were also being double cut. Cutting any lower than this resulted in scalping of the ridges in the greens. It is not known exactly how fast the greens were for the 1978 and 1984 Championships, but the greens were often described as 'fiery', and the wind could dictate the speed and line of a putt.

By the 2000 Open, with course machinery continually improving, the entire course was being cut by a fleet of ride-on mowers. The greens were being hand-cut with walk-behind mowers – a long and tiring exercise with greens such as the double 5th and 13th being a walk of 3.5 miles, but this method gave a better result. Greens could again have been cut to 4mm during the Open week, but the cut was never below 4.5mm. Such a low cut meant less grass blade resistance on the ball and an increase in the speed of the greens, but more importantly, the smoothness and overall condition was markedly better.

Even bunker maintenance has changed. Apart from their being regularly revetted and all equipped with their own rakes, the walls on the bunkers today are very steep – almost ninety degrees. Woods used to lay the face of a bunker back by stacking the turf sods half an inch offset to each other. The advantage of this was not purely for the golfers' benefit. It was found that in the summer when the sand is dry and the wind whips up, it was less likely that sand would be carved away from under the face and folded into the middle of the bunker – an event that could easily leave a ball in an unplayable lie under the face.

Woods would also fetch sand from the East Sands in St Andrews, and make the thoroughly trampled base of his bunkers in the shape of a saucer with this heavier sand. Come the Open Championship, bunkers would simply be topped up with 3 inches of fresh sand three to four weeks before the event.

It seems remarkable now, but up until the mid-1980s Walter Woods only had seven men working with him on the Old Course. They didn't have fairways to mow, but the hours of labour required to mow greens, water the course, tend bunkers etc, was only really eased when the Links Trust gave approval for five men to fill divots during the 1980s.

Back in place for the 1984 Open were the old railway sheds on the Road Hole. They had been taken down in 1967, but considerable extensions had been made to the Old Course Hotel. Some said the hotel had 'grown wings' since 1978, when Henry Longhurst likened the original block to a chest of drawers with all the drawers left open.

The 1984 Open Championship

When the 1984 Open rolled around in July, St Andrews was in a frenzy. Almost 200,000 spectators converged on the Old Course during the week and witnessed Seve Ballesteros tease and torment the Old Course like a matador would a bull.

Below left: Ian Baker-Finch's scorecard. Having led for three days, the young Baker-Finch had the Open in his grasp, but this final round ruined his chances. Watson, playing alongside Baker-Finch, and going for his hat trick and sixth Open, had his chances too, but the Road Hole proved to be his downfall. Eventually an excited Seve Ballesteros stepped in and birdied the 18th to win by two strokes with 276.
Card courtesy of the British Golf Museum

✓ 74 ✓   THE 113TH OPEN GOLF CHAMPIONSIP 1984   284 ✓

COMPETITOR ......Ian Baker-Finch...........................   Sunday 22nd July at ....2.30 p.m..............   Game No. ...32.....

Hole	1	2	3	4	5	6	7	8	9	Out		10	11	12	13	14	15	16	17	18	In	Total
Yards	370	411	371	463	564	416	372	178	356	3501		342	172	416	425	567	413	382	461	354	3432	6933
Par	4	4	4	4	5	4	4	3	4	36		4	3	4	4	5	4	4	4	4	36	72
Score	5	4	4	5	5	6	5	3	4	41		5	3	4	5	7	3	4	4	3	38	79

Signature of Marker ......Tom Watson..... ✓   Signature of Competitor ......Ian Baker-Finch...... ✓

The course was in good, firm condition and the weather during the week was also good. As a result, the Old Course lay down and surrendered herself in the heat. Ballesteros, at the height of his powers, took full advantage. He broke through the magical 70 barrier and averaged an incredible 69 shots per round. The Old Course played short, and during the mesmerising week, the 5th hole gave up over 200 birdies, and the course a total of 1246 birdies!

Birdie Count at the Open Championship per Year

Hole	1970	1978	1984
1	36	62	90
2	17	36	44
3	50	71	107
4	15	21	29
5	64	149	205
6	24	53	50
7	40	48	82
8	47	48	62
9	67	81	76
	360	569	745
10	55	100	121
11	23	40	28
12	86	65	85
13	29	17	35
14	73	56	46
15	37	49	50
16	38	39	45
17	5	7	11
18	87	56	80
	433	429	501
Total	793	998	1246

History remembers this Open as a landmark for equipment. This was the last time the champion used a wooden-headed driver. In 1990 Nick Faldo, with a new record-low winning score, used a metal-headed driver, and with it, ushered in an entire new era. Before that began in earnest however, the power of the class of 1984 was still evident, even with wooden clubs.

Where Craig Wood had hit his ball into the Swilcan Burn at the first hole on the roll in 1933, Fred Couples bounced his ball over the burn in his 1984 practice round (and then blamed his caddy for not telling him it was there!)

Innovations in the science of dimples improved again from the mid-1980s and into the 1990s. In *500 years of the Golf Ball*, John Hotchkiss wrote,

> *Instead of covering more of the ball's surface with large, shallow dimples, ball makers found it more effective to use smaller or various sized dimples which covered a greater percentage of the ball's surface. Not only did an increased number of dimples reduce drag, but it created a cushioning effect that made the ball softer when struck.*

Dimple counts varied considerably from 384 to 800, but in 1991 Titleist patented a ball with dimples that covered seventy-nine per cent of its surface area.

Many became increasingly concerned about how far the ball was travelling. Apart from comments about the power of the ball from leading players such as Sam Snead, Lee Trevino, and Jack Nicklaus, the following comments were made by authoritative organisations in 1994:

> *Our research indicates the ball travels 8 to 12 yards farther today than in 1960.*
> *– Chairman of the Implements and Ball Committee, USGA.*

> *The ball goes further and flies straighter, more accurately today. The lower flex point shafts and the improved flight path of the ball make it easier to be accurate.*
> *– Greens Committee Chairman, Augusta National.*

Still, the metal-headed driver was perhaps generating the biggest technology-aided distance. While the metal driver was

not a new invention, it had now improved to such an extent that in the mid- to late 1990s titanium, a lightweight yet durable material, could be used. The big break for titanium came when the golf industry learned how to cast titanium heads cost-effectively. It was known that the material had radically different characteristics, such as a higher strength than stainless steel, but it was a challenge for designers to optimise the thickness of the face to make it thin enough to increase the initial speed of the ball, but not so thin that the face broke at impact. The lightness of titanium also allowed clubheads made of this metal to increase in size.

> The metal driver was first patented in 1894 when Reginald Brougham invented the aluminium clubhead. When first produced it had a wood insert and was somewhat popular. Gary Adams and Taylor Made revitalised the metal-wood in the late 1970s.

Some advances in iron technology were also being made. No such club as a bi-metal iron had ever existed in the old days. As well, none of the very old irons employed a complete cavity surrounded 360 degrees by using raised metal.

THE 1990 OPEN CHAMPIONSHIP

No physical changes were made to the Old Course for the Open in 1990, and the effect of the new clubheads, balls, shafts and better conditioning of the players was clearly seen in the scoring. The 63 shot by Paul Broadhurst was the lowest score ever achieved in an Open Championship at St Andrews,

and only one off the course record of 62 set by Curtis Strange in the 1989 Alfred Dunhill Cup, but many others dipped into the mid-sixties.

Paul Broadhurst's card:

Hole	Length	Par	Score		Hole	Length	Par	Score	
1	370	4	3	-1	10	342	4	3	-8
2	411	4	4		11	172	3	3	
3	371	4	3	-2	12	316	4	4	
4	463	4	4		13	425	4	4	
5	564	5	4	-3	14	567	5	5	
6	416	4	3	-4	15	413	4	4	
7	372	4	3	-5	16	382	4	4	
8	178	3	2	-6	17	461	4	4	
9	356	4	3	-7	18	354	4	3	-9
			29 (12 putts!)					34=	63
								Total Length= 6933 yards	

Left: Paul Broadhurst's card. After the round he commented: *'It didn't feel right on the practice ground this morning. But when I got out here, it all came right.'*

However, while Faldo blasted Ballesteros's previous winning record by six shots, better proof of improved scoring and the diminishing resistance of the 6933-yard long Old Course is apparent when the scores of the entire field are examined. In 456 rounds, the Old Course gave up a record number of birdies, 1490 in all. This made an average of almost 3.3 birdies per person per round.

THE 119TH OPEN GOLF CHAMPIONSHIP 1990

✓71✓   270

COMPETITOR ...... Nick Faldo .... Sunday 22nd July at ......2.50pm........ Game No. ......36..... Playing Handicap ....

Hole	1	2	3	4	5	6	7	8	9	Out
Yards	370	411	371	463	564	416	372	178	356	3501
Par	4	4	4	4	5	4	4	3	4	36
Score	3	4	4	5	4	4	4	3	4	35

10	11	12	13	14	15	16	17	18	In	Total
342	172	316	425	567	413	382	461	354	3432	6933
4	3	4	4	5	4	4	4	4	36	72
4	3	4	4	5	3	4	5	4	36	71

Signature of Marker ...... Jn Baker Finch ✓ ......

Signature of Competitor ...... Nick Faldo ✓ ......

Left: Nick Faldo's scorecard on the final day in 1990. Having held off Greg Norman, the world number one player in the third round, Faldo had several shots in hand when he holed out for 71. It was his second Open win and followed his Masters victory earlier in the year.
Card courtesy of the British Golf Museum

Right: Chart comparing birdies from six Open Championships held at the Old Course.

Year	1970	1978	1984	1990	1995	2000
Birdies	793	998	1246	1490	1425	1452
Rounds	403	453	468	456	523	458
b.p.r*	1.97	2.20	2.66	3.27	2.72	3.17

* = Birdies per round

Course Length – Yards					
6951	6933	6933	6933	6933	7115

Far right: Plan of the 11th hole published in 'The Links' by Hunter and *Golf Monthly*, 1911. This plan shows the elevation of the green and the relative locations of the bunkers. Hill bunker is particularly notorious and is regarded by many as the most difficult bunker on the course from which to escape. The teeing ground arrangement has changed, particularly the elevation of the recently expanded main tee which is now level with the green surface. The Open tee is also over 20 yards further back than indicated on this plan.

When this chart is compared to the length of the Old Course during this time some correlations can be made:

1. Shortening the course in 1978 led to an expected increase in birdies.
2. Birdies increased from 1978 to 1990 as equipment and players improved but the course length remained unchanged.
3. Windy conditions in 1995 adversely impacted on scoring.
4. In calm conditions, tee extensions alone, such as those made in 2000, would not curb low scoring.

After the 1990 Open Faldo wrote of his victory, 'I am pleased that I played so well when I won on the Old Course in 1990. I missed only 3 greens and one of those, the 17th, was a deliberate miss… Although the fairways are big, you still need to go down the correct side… I was in one bunker all week – it was on the fourth on the last day.'

As regards the course itself, Faldo wrote:

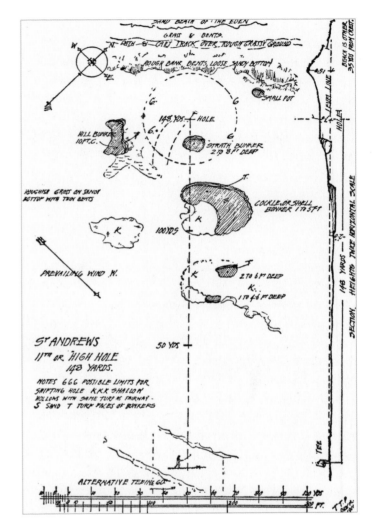

Right: A view from the tee of the 11th hole 1924-1925.
Golfing Diary

Far right: Waiting for golfers, Hill bunker defends the left side of the 11th green while the greens staff mow her pronounced slopes.
Iain Lowe

It is easy to be fractionally off line and then end up 30 yards from the hole. You only have to hit the ball slightly off centre, and it takes the wrong bump and goes a bit long. And putting from 30 yards can be hard work. Luckily I managed to be closer than that; in fact I don't think I was ever more than 30 feet from the hole all week.

St Andrews has some great holes. The 14th is one of the best par 5s in the world. The 11th, over that bunker, is wicked. You've only got 3 yards with which to work. The 17th is very tough. Whether you like it or not, it's a brute of a hole. Actually I think it's a good, but not great, hole. If you hit it straight down the middle of the fairway and they've put the pin behind the Road Hole Bunker, then you don't have a shot.

Over the years I decided to go left of that green. I think that's a far better percentage shot because then you are chipping back up the green and looking at a good chance of making a four. If you go to the right, you can either end up short and you won't make four from there, or you can go over the green and you won't make four from there. It is definitely a percentage shot to go left.

In December 1994, the American Society of Golf Course Architects released their 'Golf Equipment Impact Report' prepared by the chairman of their Golf Equipment Committee, Mr T.A. Marzolf. The report reflects on subjects such

Right: The traditional pin position (see Chapter 8, pp.177–179) for the Open Championship on this green is either back right – where there are two locations – or on a radius about 25 feet over Strath bunker in the front section of the green. Occasionally the pin may be located on the left side of the green during medal or casual play, but the left side of the green is not used during the Open because the slope of the green here is too steep (four to six per cent) when the greens are running at Open Championship speeds. With greens running at speeds of +/-10 feet on the stimpmeter, generally speaking, it has been found that a ball will not come to rest on areas of firm, tight bentgrass greens with a slope of greater than three per cent. However, the same slope may roll completely differently depending upon the mowing height and agronomic practices for each green (i.e. A green mown at 6.3mm with a three-per cent slope will be much slower than a green double cut at 4.6mm and rolled). However, during the 2005 Open when greens were double cut at a height of 4.5-5mm, the hole would not be cut outside these two areas.

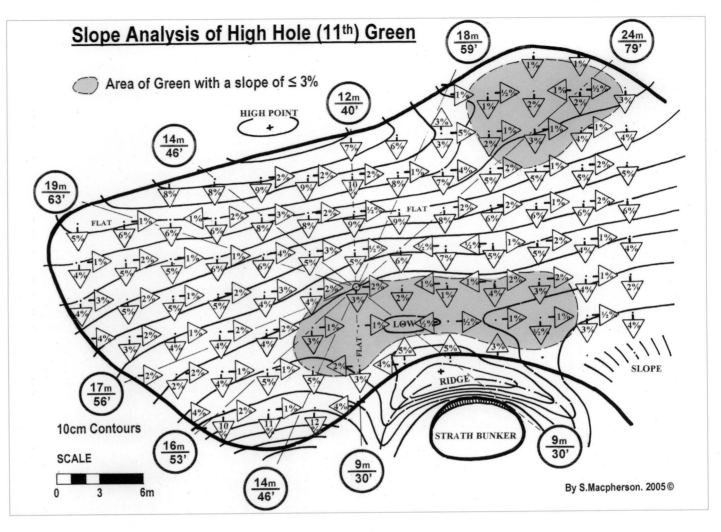

as 'How better club construction has allowed tour players to swing faster and get away with it', and 'How greens maintenance has changed golf architecture'.

Marzolf wrote about putting surface concerns,

Early 1900s greens averaged slopes of 5 percent to 8 percent (5 to 8 feet of fall in a 100 foot distance). This amount of pitch was considered fair play when cut by the greens' mowers of that time period... the steepness of the slope was a reaction by golf architects to achieve fun, challenging putting that matched the slower surface condition of the grass. In other words, a green is contoured to fit the intended level of maintenance.

At St Andrews, while the turf condition and the equipment used has improved, the contours in the greens have not been altered since Old Tom is said to have levelled the putting greens by the terracing up of their lower edges in the late 1800s. As a result, some areas of most greens are unsuitable for modern pin positions. Indeed, much of the famed 11th

GAME NO. 47	OFFICIAL SCORECARD	FOR R&A USE ONLY	DAY 4

COMPETITOR Tom Watson

SUNDAY 23RD JULY AT 1.45 pm.

124TH OPEN GOLF CHAMPIONSHIP 1995
THE OLD COURSE, ST. ANDREWS

THREE ROUND TOTAL 213
THIS ROUND 77
72 HOLE TOTAL 290
FINAL AGGREGATE 290

VERIFIED R&P.

ROUND 4

Hole	1	2	3	4	5	6	7	8	9	Out
Yards	370	411	371	463	564	416	372	178	356	3501
Par	4	4	4	4	5	4	4	3	4	36
Score	4	4	4	4	5	5	4	3	5	38

Signature of Marker

Hole	10	11	12	13	14	15	16	17	18	In	Total
Yards	342	172	316	425	567	413	382	461	354	3432	6933
Par	4	3	4	4	5	4	4	4	4	36	72
Score	5	4	4	5	4	4	5	5	3	39	77

Signature of Competitor Tom Watson

Left: Tom Watson's scorecard for his final round. Always a crowd favourite, Watson had returned to St Andrews and tried to win at the one venue he most wished to succeed at and which meant the most to him. Unfortunately, his good start was undone and ultimately he missed the playoff between Daly and Rocca by 8 shots. *Card courtesy of the British Golf Museum*

green is too steep for a flag location today. However these slopes increase the premium on hitting drives to certain sides of the fairways and approach shots to particular places on the greens if low scores are to be recorded.

Holes are cut in locations where the green has a slope of less than three to three and a half per cent. If the slope is any greater than this, the ball will not stop. Also, on most greens – essentially those not made of sand – green areas where pin positions are located must have a minimum slope of at least one per cent to ensure positive surface drainage should it rain.

Regarding the 11th hole at St Andrews and the speed of greens, Bernard Darwin wrote in 1936;

The green of the High hole coming in at St Andrews is sometimes admittedly too fast, but on the days when it is not, when the ball can just be made to stop and no more, is there any sensation equal to that of laying the putt dead from the brink of the Eden? The ball goes winding on its way down and across the slope; it seems now and then almost to stop, now and then fatally to gather speed; at last it nestles so close to the hole – and it must be very close on that green — that we are given the next one. That seems to me to be putting at its fullness, when up to the very last moment we are not

sure whether the ball will lie stone dead or, with a horrid little spurt when at its last gasp, run four feet past.

At 10+ on the stimpmeter (see p.128), during the Open Championship, the 11th green is running faster than Darwin preferred.

In the section, 'How better club construction has allowed tour players to swing faster and get away with it', Marzolf wrote:

Titanium, graphite, boron graphite, lightweight steel. These materials are now the norm for golf shafts used on the PGA tour. The great Bobby Jones played the game with hickory shafts. Flex points in shafts (high, low, medium and two-step) can now be custom fitted to match a player's height, arm strength and swing path to the ball. This high-tech advantage has allowed expert players a consistency that just wasn't there in early shafts. Because today's pros have a shaft that performs more consistently, they can swing harder and still be accurate.

Obviously, if you've got a club in your hand that has been built so specifically to match your particular swing, that's an advantage. Combine that shaft with a forgiving clubhead and perimeter weighting that

Above: John Daly lets rip with the driver on the 4th tee while on his way to winning the 1995 Open Championship. *Courtesy of Mattew Harris*

'His driving is unbelievable. I don't go that far on my holidays.' – Ian Baker-Finch on John Daly

reduces the penalty for off-centre hits, and now pros can really unleash their power.

These new metal woods and hi-tech shafts are a definite advantage to a professional golfer. Their predictable consistency has allowed swing changes that can produce more clubhead speed. In fact, several tour players have adapted their swings as a reaction to this new equipment (Davis Love and John Daly, for example).

Bobby Jones had a slight pause in the top of his swing, so that the hickory shaft could catch up to his hands. Davis Love III has an extremely late release of his hands that allows him to generate enormous clubhead speed. The equipment has changed, allowing tour players to swing fast...and get away with it.

While modern clubheads are more forgiving for the off-centre strike, in general players do not 'get away with it'. Rather, they benefit from modern equipment. The best players with the faster swing speeds select equipment that benefits their swing, that is, those with low torque and stiff shafts. Swings are no longer tailored to fit equipment, equipment is tailored to the swing, and the result is longer drives and lower scores.

Daly's play of the Road Hole was mesmerising. Nicklaus, sitting in the commentator's booth, could not believe it. Not only did Daly's play lack the cool strategic reserve that Nicklaus himself used to navigate around the Old Course, the white hot power of his play was in complete contrast to when Nicklaus won in 1970. Then, Nicklaus hit his driver, a 5-iron, into the green! For a further contrast, consider the difficulty of the hole a hundred years earlier. In *The Golfing Annual* of 1888, it noted that playing the hole was much harder. J.O.F. Morris described it, 'The (Road) Hole is a particularly difficult one, being not only long, but requiring careful work to keep clear of the hazards which the player has to encounter. There is a bunker about twenty yards to the left of the road (Cheape's), which runs alongside the "Corner of the Dyke," and into which, if trying to play the narrow course, you are very apt to get. However, there is plenty of room to the left of the bunker. It takes nearly three full drives to reach the hole, which is situated within a few yards of the turnpike road, and has a treacherous little bunker immediately in front of the putting green, with all the ground around it inclining to draw the ball. This consequently makes the green rather small.' Amazingly, through all these changes, and though it plays quite differently, both then and now, many regard this as one of the finest holes in golf.

THE 1995 OPEN CHAMPIONSHIP

If Nick Faldo's scoring demolition of the Old Course had not set off alarm bells in the Royal and Ancient Club's Green Committee, John Daly's distance performance in the 1995 Open certainly did. Though not as surgical as Faldo, and having to contend with windy and occasionally blustery conditions on the Saturday and Sunday, Daly showed how the Old Course could be reduced to a pitch-and-putt course. Using his driver on every hole except the par 3s – the 13th and the 15th, Daly's mammoth drives took bunkers like the Principal's Nose out of play, and allowed him to hit wedges into most holes, including the 17th. To Daly the Old Course had no par 5s and the 9th, 10th, 12th and 18th greens were all reachable, occasionally without using his specially-made, brand-new titanium 8-degree Wilson Invex driver!

One notable feature of the scoring in 1995 was that the winning score was forty shots less than in 1895. More amazing was the fact that the winning score in 2000 was also forty shots less than that recorded one hundred years earlier. Does this mean that, considering all the changes, the Old Course had become ten shots easier per round than a hundred years earlier?

Year	Winning Score	Year	Winning Score
1895	322	1900	309
1995	282	2000	269
Difference equals	40 shots	Difference equals	40 shots

At the end of this period, all golfers had the choice of more than a thousand golf balls that conformed to the specifications. This is a far cry from the 1930s when all balls were three-piece balata-covered balls with the same number of dimples. A player's skill was a greater factor in the final result then. Now, a less skillful player with better equipment may have the greater advantage. What would be the response to

Left: The Old Course on a warm summer's evening. In the foreground is the double green for the 2nd and 16th holes. Beyond that to the left is the old railway line and in the fairway the Principal's Nose and Cartgate bunkers can be seen.
S. Macpherson

these new challenges? Would the course be lengthened? Could par, in many ways considered the source of the evil, be abandoned? Would equipment rules be modified? With a new millennium looming, members of the Royal and Ancient Golf Club had many issues on which to ponder.

To see St. Andrews at its zenith you must watch an Open Championship when the big tents are erected away towards the sea and the crowds assemble in their thousands and the stage is set for the crucial test.
– Wethered & Simpson, *Design for Golf*, 1952

CHAPTER FIVE

MULTI-LAYERED BALLS and HOT FACED CLUBS

The Rebirth of the Old Course
– 2000–2005

It is an absolute fallacy to say that the Old Course has been 100 per cent the same for centuries, though probably in the last 50 years it has been less changed than at any time in its history. Bunkers have been put in, angles of holes changed. Look at the change by the 17th. The railway lines, the sheds, the road behind the 17th green have changed many times. People have memories of the past 20 years and think that it has always been so.

– Peter Dawson, Secretary of the R&A, speaking about the Old Course before the 2000 Open

After the 1995 Open, it was decided changes would be made to the Old Course in preparation for the Millennium Open. The championship test needed to be strengthened. To determine what changes needed to be made, a study was conducted and it was decided six holes would be lengthened: the 3rd, 7th, 10th, 14th, 15th and 16th.

Between these holes and a remeasurement of the course, an tremendous 182 yards were added to the length of the 1995 course (119 yards more than the 1955 course). This was the third biggest increase in length at any one time after the 200-yard gain between 1900 and 1905 and the 270 yards added between 1933 and 1939.

The biggest changes were made to the back nine. At the 10th hole, a new tee was constructed 37 yards back, where the whins (gorse) had been growing. The 14th, 15th and 16th holes gained an average of 32 yards each. The 14th also had a new tee built a little further back and on the edge of the Eden course, creating an even greater relationship between the hole and the out-of-bounds wall, while the 15th and 16th

were just pushed back. The philosophy with the 16th was to bring the Principal's Nose bunkers back into play.

If adding this yardage was an attempt to bring the course up to date and reconcile the improvements in equipment since 1955, was it also be sufficient to balance the significant improvements made between 1997 and 2000?

All discerning eyes were watching when the new championship tees were used for the first time in the 1997 Alfred Dunhill Cup. Those hoping for higher scores however were stunned when Jesper Parnevik and Justin Leonard set the new course record at 65. Confirming it wasn't just luck, the Paraguayan team equalled it twice in 1999. But these records were set under an unusual team format. So the question remained: in a high pressure stroke-play event like as the Open Championship, was the extra length enough to change the play strategy to make the holes harder? Only when the official hole statistics for the 2000 Open were were the answers revealed.

The years before the 2000 Open were an extremely active

Opposite page: Dreams at dusk. The sun sets on the 17th green and the Road Hole bunker.
S. Macpherson

time both on the Old Course and in the golf equipment development laboratories. First, the Old Course irrigation system was revolutionised. The first phase of the installation of the £2.5 million irrigation system was completed in the spring of 1999. The second phase of the single largest golf course irrigation system in Europe started in the winter of 2000. There are now four boreholes serving a 750,000-gallon reservoir and over 4000 sprinkler heads.

During the 2000 Open itself, the greenkeeping staff working on the course increased from fourteen full-time staff to fifty-six for the month of July. The greenkeepers were supported by a workshop staff of five. In the maintenance facility, a fleet of tractors supplied by New Holland and mowers by Textron, renewed on a rolling basis every five years, was now stored in two greenkeeping centres that had opened in the 1990s – the Eden and the Jubilee – and represented a capital investment of over £1.5m.

With all this labour and equipment, and under the direction of the R&A and Head Greenkeeper Eddie Adams, the Old Course was immaculately conditioned for the 2000 Open. Greens running at a stimp-reading of 10.5 feet were going to test the golfers, and possibly balance some of the effects of equipment on scoring.

Right: The stimpmeter measures the speed of a green relative to the surface conditions. Here, one ball is in the 'shute' and about to be released. The other ball has already stopped.
S. Macpherson

The stimpmeter was introduced in 1976 and its purpose is test the green's speed by releasing three golf balls down a chute from a set angle. The distance the ball travels in opposite directions is averaged and this is the stimpmeter reading. The measurement is in feet.

It is thought the average green in the 1920s and 1930s may have had a stimp-reading of about 3–4 feet. In recent times, greens have rolled as alarmingly fast as 13–14 feet in major golf tournaments, but depending on the slope of the green, above certain speeds greens can become unplayable.

The graphite shaft (invented in the 1970s by ex-USGA Technical Director Frank Thomas) was improved a great deal and provided the specific weight, flex, torque and strength characteristics desired. Additionally, metal club-heads were increasing, both physically and in popularity. Stronger and lighter materials such as titanium were being used so the cubic capacity could be increased without increasing the weight of the head. For example, the Great Big Bertha titanium driver was 250cc, but not the biggest at the time – the Yonex Super ADX was 300cc! The Invex driver Daly used to reduce the Old Course to a drive-and-chip course in 1995 was only 175cc. But things quickly became super-sized. Ping brought out the TiSI at 323cc, then TaylorMade released drivers in three sizes: 300, 320 and 360cc, and all were being used on tour. TaylorMade now has a steel driver which is 275cc – bigger than the 260cc Titleist Titanium 975D head that was used to great effect by Tiger Woods. The 975D was replaced by the 975J, which is twenty per cent larger at 312cc. Club heads have grown too: the Hippo Giant is 400cc, the Yonex V-Mass 400 is 410cc and Orlimar's biggest is 420cc. The only club head bigger still is the King Cobra bSS427 (named after a car from the 1960s), at 427cc, and with a barely legal COR (coefficient of restitution) or spring-like effect of 0.825.

During this time the new solid-core ball was also being perfected. For the Millennium Open, Nike released a new ball for the world's best golfer, 24-year-old American Tiger Woods. It was called the 'Tour Accuracy'. Experts at the Nike

ball division described the characteristics of the Tour Accuracy as the 'urethane cover solid construction golf ball that killed the wound ball. Long off the tee, better in the wind and spins. Around the green like balata.' Maybe some of this was promotional hype, but the competitive life of the wound ball became instantly threatened.

Devices such as the launch monitor had also come out to help professionals and top golfers get the most yardage out of their club-heads, shafts and balls. The launch monitor was designed to measure three factors; ball speed off the clubface, the spin rate of the ball, and the launch angle. It was not singularly responsible for players hitting the ball further, but became a catalyst, allowing players to be matched up with the best equipment for their game.

By 2000, the result of all of these advances was that driving distances had increased. The average drive on the PGA Tour in 1994 was 261.8 yards. In 1996 this increased to 266.4 yards, by 1998 it was 270.6 yards, and in 2000 it extended to 273.2 yards.

This creeping annual increase, and the almost 7 yards gained between 1997 and 2000, should have diluted the impact of the newly added length on the Old Course, but what effect did it

MOST RECENT OPEN CHAMPIONS BALLS				
Year	Ball	Construction	Number of Dimples	Cover
1978	MacGregor-Tourney	Two-piece wound ball	432	surlyn
1984	Titleist 384	Three-piece wound ball	384	balata
1990	Bridgestone, Rextar	Three-piece wound ball	396	balata
1995	Ultra Competition	Two-piece solid core ball	500	surlyn
2000	Nike Tour Accuracy	Three-piece solid core ball	392	urethane
2005	Nike Platinum TW	Four-piece polybutadine core	432	urethane

have on scoring during the Millennium Open? Yardage added to a course does not affect all golfers proportionally. For the longer hitters, it was conceivable that some added length would have almost no impact at all on the way they played and scored. It may have assisted their championship chances by removing a percentage of the shorter-hitting challengers. However, the same distance could make the course exponentially more

Below: This table indicates the number of bunkers in specific zones from the tee during the 1995 and 2000 Open Championships.

OLD COURSE BUNKERS BROUGHT INTO PLAY BY NEW TEES IN 1995 AND 2000

	200-230 yds		231-250 yds		251-270 yds		271-290 yds		291-310 yds		311+ yds	
Hole	1995	2000	1995	2000	1995	2000	1995	2000	1995	2000	1995	2000
3	1	1	0	1	1	0	0	1	1	0	0	1 (333)
7	0	0	0	0	0	0	2	0	0	2	0	0
10	0	0	0	0	1	0	0	0	1	1	0	1(336)
14	2	1	1	2	0	1	0	0	0	0	0	0
15	1	1	0	0	0	1	0	0	0	0	1 (311)	1 (353)
16	PN	0	0	0	1	PN	0	0	0	1	0	0
	5	3	1	3	3	3	2	1	2	4	1	3
	PN = Principal's Nose											
											1995	2000
			Total Bunkers In play								14	17
			Bunkers In play between 250 yds and 290 yds								5	4

perilous for the short hitter as landing areas decreased in size, more bunkers were brought into play, and longer iron shots are required to reach the greens, particularly if these extended holes played into the wind. This situation was especially true at the 4th hole where into the wind shorter hitters found it difficult to get over the rough dunes in the middle of the fairway, and so either had to play down the narrow fairway right and risk getting caught in the hill, or way left to the 15th fairway – a shot which left a very difficult approach to the green. (See page 90.)

Driving Distance: Measured Drives are the average number of yards per measured drive. These drives are measured on two holes per round. Care is taken to select two holes that face in opposite directions to counteract the effects of wind. Drives are measured to the point they come to rest regardless of whether they are in the fairway or not.

CHART CONCLUSION

The added length brought more bunkers into play, but also made the course less hazardous in the critical distance between 251 and 290 yards – the distance where most drives land or finish.

THE 2000 OPEN CHAMPIONSHIP

When the first day of the eagerly anticipated 2000 Open Championship arrived, one man stood at the top of the golfing world. Tiger Woods was at the peak of his powers. His prodigious length, accuracy and ability would have been nearly impossible for any course to have withstood, especially in the near-perfect weather conditions of that year. And so it proved. Woods' performance and scoring was exceptional. With an average driving distance of 297.4 yards in 2000, Woods' eight-stroke victory showed his dominance in golf and in his game, as he walked away not only the champion golfer of the year, but also the youngest winner of the Grand Slam. His best round was 66, but his average was an incredible 67.25. The winning total was the lowest ever, beating Faldo's victory in 1990 by one shot.

It has been well reported that during the course of the

four rounds Woods avoided all 112 bunkers on the Old Course. This was a magnificent achievement. Steve Williams, Tiger's caddy wrote of them,

Our approach that week was to play short of them or play over them, and that is exactly what he did. Tiger's iron play was brilliant this week thus never bringing any of the greenside traps into play. Regardless there was still an element of luck involved as it is very easy to hit the ball in a trap on holes 10 and 12 when you are trying to knock the ball on the green.

But it is interesting to theorise about how many bunkers may have been in play for Tiger Woods during that week of calm, sunny weather – possibly only between three and eight.

Hole	Bunkers in play	Hole	Bunkers in play
			BUNKERS MOST IN-PLAY FOR WOODS AT 2000 OPEN
1	0	10	Bunker short and right of green
2	0	11	Strath
3	0	12	Last bunker closest to green (Woods played over green each day)
4	Bunker greenside, left	13	Last Coffin
5	0	14	0
6	0	15	0
7	Shell	16	0
8	0	17	Road Hole bunker
9	End Hole	18	0
Front Nine- 3		Back Nine- 5	TOTAL= 8

A look at the of number of birdies the Old Course had yielded during the previous six Open Championships indicates a correlation between improving technology, golfer ability, and scoring relative to course length. The course was 6951 yards

in 1970, then 6933 yards until 2000, but when it became 7115 yards long, the birdie count remained over 1400. In 1995 it was slightly down due to the weather, but from 1978–1990 when the course length was unchanged, a definite increase occurred.

BIRDIE COUNT AT THE OPEN CHAMPIONSHIP PER YEAR

Hole	1970	1978	1984	1990	1995	2000
1	36	62	90	134	75	73
2	17	36	44	66	47	65
3	50	71	107	108	115	99
4	15	21	29	34	22	53
5	64	149	205	189	152	203
6	24	53	50	68	41	99
7	40	48	82	92	68	97
8	47	48	62	49	30	37
9	67	81	76	102	102	92
	360	569	745	842	652	818
10	55	100	121	138	66	118
11	23	40	28	54	31	55
12	86	65	85	83	132	143
13	29	17	35	23	41	43
14	73	56	46	109	201	115
15	37	49	50	59	60	45
16	38	39	45	69	40	27
17	5	7	11	15	13	13
18	87	56	80	98	189	75
	433	429	501	648	773	634
Total	793	998	1246	1490	1425	1452
Unusually high number						
Unusually low number						

The back nine holes in 1995 recorded a remarkable increase in birdies. This may have been due to the prevailing wind direction that week.

The way the wind changes, it's a different course every time. I think 17 is a great hard hole, but 18 is one of the best holes I've ever seen. You just can't do anything wrong on 18; you've got to birdie it every time. Only you can't. – Pete Dye

After the Open, statistics were released documenting the difficulty of the holes. In a chart comparing the two championships, one can see the effect the added distance had on the stroke average of the lengthened holes. (See p.129.)

The windier conditions during the 1995 Open had some effect on these figures, but it is interesting to note that in general, on a firm, undulating links like the Old Course, distance alone does not increase the difficulty of a hole.

Since the 2000 Open, the industry has continued to improve the equipment available to golfers, most notably with the introduction of the large solid-core, multi-component constructed, urethane elastomer-covered Titleist Pro V1 ball. When unveiled at the PGA Tour in 2000 and released to the market in December 2000, this became the most successful golf ball introduction in the game's history – and the start of the latest revolution in golf ball technology. Unaware of the impact this ball would have, but wise to the threat of new equipment, the governing authorities took some significant strides to limit the power of the club. To reaffirm their position on equipment and the rules, the R&A and the

Above: In the final hours of the last practice day, Open competitors tried to unlock the secrets to success at the short 18th hole. One preferred target off the last tee is the clock on the R&A clubhouse. If the flag is on the right side of the green, this leaves a shot up the slope of the green and the Valley of Sin can be avoided.
Iain Lowe

132

Right: Ernie Els' final round scorecard in 2000. Taking runner-up honours for the third successive major competition, he said afterwards, 'I suppose you could say I'm going for the "second-place Slam!" I'm playing a different tournament from Tiger. Even if I had played as well as I could I don't think I would have got to 20 under to beat him.'

Ernie Els										
Game No. 33										
Sunday 23 July at 2.00 pm										

OFFICIAL SCORECARD
129TH OPEN GOLF CHAMPIONSHIP 2000
OLD COURSE, ST ANDREWS

FOR R&A USE ONLY DAY 4
THREE ROUND FINAL AGGREGATE
TOTAL 208
THIS ROUND 69   277
72 HOLE TOTAL 277

VERIFIED *the.*

ROUND 4

Hole	1	2	3	4	5	6	7	8	9	Out
Yards	376	413	397	464	568	412	388	175	352	3545
Par	4	4	4	4	5	4	4	3	4	36
Score	3	4	3	3	4	4	4	3	4	32

Signature of Marker ......

10	11	12	13	14	15	16	17	18	In	Total
379	174	314	430	581	456	424	455	357	3570	7115
4	3	4	4	5	4	4	4	4	36	72
4	4	4	4	5	4	4	4	4		69

Signature of Competitor 37

USGA in May 2002 issued a joint statement of principals. In it, they stated their continued desire to closely monitor the effects of advancing equipment on the playing of the game:

The R&A and the USGA are also aware that this subject has attracted wide-ranging comment and a number of conflicting views. History has proved that it is impossible to foresee the developments in golf equipment that advancing technology will deliver. It is of the greatest importance to golf's continuing appeal that such advances are judged against a clear and broadly accepted series of principals.

...The purpose of the Rules is to protect golf's best

traditions, to prevent an over-reliance on technological advances rather than skill, and to ensure that skill is the dominant element of success throughout the game.

Could it be said that by not restricting the power of equipment earlier, the R&A and USGA have prevented, and continue to prevent future generations of golfers from enjoying the test classic courses that have given us the game's best players in the past?

The R&A and the USGA continue to believe that the retention of a single set of rules for all players of the game, irrespective of ability, is one of golf's greatest

EFFECT OF ADDED DISTANCE ON STROKE AVERAGE

Hole	Par	1995 Length	Stroke Average	2000 Length	Stroke Average	yardage increase	stroke difference
3	4	371	3.88	397	3.88	25	no change
7	4	372	4.07	388	3.90	16	easier
10	4	342	4.03	379	3.85	37	easier
14	5	567	4.69	581	4.97	14	harder
15	4	413	4.04	456	4.20	43	harder
16	4	382	4.22	424	4.17	42	easier

strengths. The R&A and the USGA regard the prospect of having permanent separate rules for elite competition as undesirable and have no current plans to create separate equipment rules for highly skilled players.

This can be taken to mean that no 'tournament ball' will be introduced.

Golf balls used by the vast majority of highly skilled players today have largely reached the performance limits for initial velocity and overall distance which have been part of the Rules since 1976. The governing bodies believe that golf balls, when hit by highly skilled golfers, should not of themselves fly significantly further than they do today. In the current circumstances, the R&A and the USGA are not advocating that the Rules relating to golf ball specifications be changed other than to modernize test methods.

The R&A and the USGA believe, however, that any further significant increases in hitting distances at the highest level are undesirable. Whether these increases in distance emanate from advancing equipment technology, greater athleticism of players, improved player coaching, golf course conditioning or a combination of these or other factors, they will have the impact of seriously reducing the challenge of the game. The consequential lengthening or toughening of courses would be costly or impossible and would have a negative effect on increasingly important environmental issues. Pace of play would be slowed and playing costs would increase.

The R&A and the USGA will consider all of these factors contributing to distance on a regular basis. Should such a situation of meaningful increases arise, The R&A and the USGA would feel it immediately necessary to seek ways of protecting the game.

Head size: 460cc +10cc measurement tolerance.
Club length limits: 48"
The R&A developed a new testing machine, the Pendulum Tester, which was designed to test the flexibility or spring-like effect of the club-head for driving clubs. The test was brought into effect on 1 January 2004. Though initially limited to clubs with loft of fifteen degrees or less, it is likely that it will extend to clubs with a greater loft if it has certain features which are consistent with a driver, for example, head size, face dimensions and club length. It is possible that the R&A in the future may also develop a Driver Head list which will work pretty much in the same way as the existing list of Conforming Golf Balls does, i.e., there will be a condition of competition (for elite players) stating something like the following:

> Driving Clubs: Any driving club the player carries must be composed of a shaft and a head that is named on the current Conforming Driver Head List issued by the R&A.
> Penalty for Breach of Condition: Disqualification.

Speaking about the new test, David Rickman, Rules Secretary of the R&A said:

> *The introduction of the Pendulum Test is the culmination of a lengthy period of work carried out by both the R&A and the United States Golf Association. The new test is relatively simple and non-destructive and the device is portable. We believe that in developing this new test we have satisfied not only our requirements, but also those of manufacturers and other interested parties such as the Professional Tours.*

The R&A and the USGA then announced a final rule on

the spring-like effect, which was to be approved after 15 July 2002. This rule established a limit by measuring the coefficient of restitution (COR) of a driving club.

The major provisions of the rule were:

1) For most competitions and all recreational play, there will continue to be no spring-like effect test or COR limit until 1 January 2008;

2) From 1 January 2003 until 31 December 2007, the Committee in charge of a competition restricted to highly skilled players may decide to introduce a Condition of Competition limiting COR to 0.830. The R&A will introduce this Condition of Competition at the Open Championship in 2003 and beyond and will recommend its introduction for all events on the major professional tours;

3) From 1 January 2008, the rules of golf will be changed to include a conformance test with a COR limit of 0.830 (or the equivalent).

In the R&A's area of rules jurisdiction, from 1 January 2004 until 31 December 2007, the new test is only relevant in elite level competitions (where an appropriate Condition of Competition has been introduced). For most competitions and all recreational play, there will continue to be no spring-like effect test or conformance limit until 1 January 2008.

As an indication of the advances technology has had on players, Tom Watson could hit a ball further into a 10 mph wind in 2003 than he could in the 1970s:

	Wound Ball & Persimmon Driver	Precept Ball & Modern Driver (<0.830 COR)
Distance (Carry)	245 yds	264 yds

This is a 20-yard gain, and this despite the fact his swing speed has slowed.

Director of Marketing for TaylorMade, Tom Olocsky,

said COR accounts for only 8–10 yards: 'It's really a matter of managing launch conditions… figuring out the best ball, and the best launch angle that will create the least amount of spin. Guys are figuring this out and when they do, the ball takes off.'

In essence, the less the ball spins as it comes off the club face and the higher it gets launched into the air, the further it will fly. Average players don't have the same advantages as pros because they don't swing at the same speed, or hit the ball as consistently and squarely in the centre of the clubface. Club and ball technology experts who follow the tour believe launch conditions – the combination of low spin balls and launch angles – result in an approximately 15- to 20-yard increase in average driving distance on the PGA Tour.

Where spin is concerned, the 1.62 size ball generally spins more than the 1.68 ball because it has a lower moment of inertia. The smaller ball, however, tends to go further because it has a lower drag force (the drag force increases proportional to the frontal area of a sphere, so the difference between the 1.68 and the 1.62 works out to about a seven and a half per cent increase in drag for the bigger ball). The wound balls tended to launch lower with more spin, but the cover influenced this relationship, and there are now blends of surlyn and urethanes that can produce more spin than balata.

The difference in distance, performance and spin, between a two- and three-piece ball for a player with a swing speed below 85 miles per hour is minimal. As reported in *Golf Digest* in September 2003, the largest difference between ball types came in half-wedge shots where the modern three- and four-piece balls generated significantly more spin than any other type of ball. This extra spin and control is in part why professional golfers expect to hit wedge shots to within 10 feet of the flag.

A recent study conducted by Douglas Winfield looked to determine why PGA Tour players hit the ball farther now than in 1980. His results were:

	1980: Distance = 256.9 yds	2003: Distance = 286.3 yds
Swing Speed	110 mph	115 mph
Ball Velocity	158 mph	167 mph
Launch Angle	7.5 degrees	10 degrees
Spin	3600 rpm	2750 rpm

Simply, a ball hit harder, with less spin (resistance) and at an optimum trajectory, will travel further. Research has indicated that to gain maximum distance for a ball hit with an initial velocity of 160 mph, the optimum launch angle is around twenty degrees with a spin rate of about 1000 rpm. Fortuitously or sadly, depending on one's viewpoint, it has also been discovered that these are almost impossible conditions to attain.

THE RELATIONSHIP BETWEEN LAUNCH ANGLE, BACKSPIN AND DISTANCE
Courtesy D. Winfield. 2004

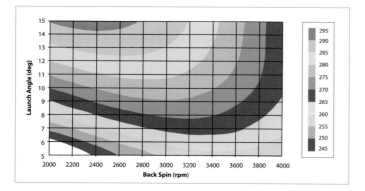

Improvements in driver technology are partly responsible for the increase in the average driving distance on the PGA Tour from a rate of 0.3 yards per year from 1968 to 1995, to a rate of 2.3 yards per year till 2000. The jump in 1997 corresponds to a time when many players embraced the new titanium club technology. For example, John Daly averaged 288.8 yards off the tee in 1996, but 302.0 yards in 1997.

Four club-related factors have contributed to this increase:
1. Steel to graphite shafts: graphite shafts are up to 70 grams lighter than steel shafts resulting in faster swing speeds, longer clubs and heavier clubheads.
2. Longer clubs: Driver lengths have increased by one to three inches, resulting in faster swing speeds.
3. Wood-to-steel-to-titanium clubheads: The spring-like effect increases ball speed resulting in an approximate increase of between 10–15 yards in driving distance on the tour.
4. The ability to find the best combination of head, shaft and loft for any one player. Prior to the new technology, wooden clubs were unique and each had special character. Players were reluctant, once they found a driver they liked, to change the shaft or adjust the head – perhaps by any method other than adding lead tape. A top player might have used one favourite club for years and treasured it like a child. Now players can take ten titanium heads of varying lofts, sizes and weights and the same amount of shafts out to the range and experiment until the best club with the most appropriate flight for a player, continent, course or even wind condition is found.

As added proof of the continuing momentum of technology, the following is a comparison of ball distance improvement since 1600.

Date	Type of Ball	Length of Drives	Spin Rate
1600–1845	Feathery	120–160 yds	
1845–1903	Gutta percha	175–200 yds	
1903–1950	Haskell three-piece wound	200–240+ yds	4000–8000 rpm
1950–2000	High-tech two-, three- and four-piece	240–285 yds	3000–5000 rpm
2000–2005	Multi layer, urethane-covered, solid core	280 yds+	2700–3000 rpm
2004	Titleist Pro V1	290 yds+	2700 rpm

Right: The Titleist Pro V1 (*left*) is a two-piece ball. The Nike One (*right*) has a four-piece construction but both are solid-core balls.

	Swing Speed (mph)	Ball Speed off Club face (mph)	Distance carry (yards)
T. Woods	135	190	300*
PGA Average	125–126	177	260–280*
* Depending on the wind speed and direction.			

* Measured on a standardisation machine at an increased swing speed of 120 mph with a modern type ball and non-branded titanium head. Individual drives may hit the ball farther because of increased swing speed and other factors.

Far right: The average distance players on the Tour can drive the ball has been increasing. The advent of spring-faced golf club technology and modern balls such as the Titleist Pro V1 have contributed directly to the most recent increases in the driving distance. Interestingly, it is the longer hitters who have gained the most yardage comparatively over the last five years, with a current difference between the two averages of over 20 yards.

On 27 May 2004, the R&A and the USGA imposed limits on the ball. These limits included:

- Minimum diameter: 1.68 inches.
- Maximum speed: 250 feet per second plus two per cent tolerance
- Maximum distance (overall distance standard): 317 yards plus three per cent tolerance*

From 2000 to 2004, the average increase in driving distance on the US PGA Tour accelerated to a rate of 3.3 yards per year. However, this average hides the fact that in both the 2000–2001 and 2002–2003 seasons, the average driving distance shot up by over 6 yards. The cause for the huge increase in 2000 was mostly the mass change by tour players from the soft, wound balata balls to the new harder, low-spin golf balls. The increase in 2002 was more a result of the governing authorities' (the USGA and the R&A) quest to limit the spring-like effect, and announcing a 0.85 test limit. As soon as this happened, almost every club on the market hit 0.84–0.85 and all of the pros used clubs at that limit. As a result, more professionals were hitting the ball significantly past the 300-yard mark off the tee, and sometimes on the fly. At the end of the 2003 PGA season, the driving statistics had nine players averaging over 300 yards, with Hank Kuehne topping that category averaging 321 yards. Previously, the only player to average over 300 yards on the PGA Tour was John Daly.

In 2003 Tiger Woods was using a Titleist 975D Driver with a COR of 0.795, and a 43.5-inch-long Dynamic Gold X-100 shaft tipped to length. He achieved:

At the end of the 2004 PGA season, the average driving distance decreased slightly from the previous year to 287.2 yards but Hank Kuehne remained at the top of the list of the longest drivers, averaging 314.4 yards. However, while his average may have dropped 7 yards, six more players averaged over 300 yards, taking the total to fifteen. The longest was recorded by Davis Love III who struck a huge 476-yard drive.

In 2005, twenty-six players averaged over 300 yards off the tee with Scott Hend the longest at 318.9 yards and Tiger Woods second with 316.1 yards. The average drive on the PGA Tour increased to 288.8 yards, with the average of the top ten being 309.8 yards.

2006 saw the number of players driving the ball over 300 yards on average fall to twenty, but the average driving distance for the top 196 players on the PGA Tour increased to 289.52 yards.

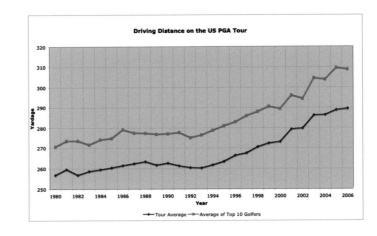

Club and ball technology are not the only factors influencing the achievement of greater driving distances. Player ability and course conditions are also contributing factors. More players are better taught, better conditioned and with more quality golfing opportunities, and this has resulted in a stronger group of elite golfers. It is difficult to quantify exactly how improvement in a player's diet, fitness, or the use of sports psychologists, swing analysts, and personal managers translates into a performance improvement on the course. Though it may be reasonably assumed that different types of assistance helps players to different degrees, debate continues as to whether such assistance aids the elite players or 'Journeymen Pros' more, or whether any benefit improves a player's average performance more than their best game during weeks of peak performance. Only individual players could answer this. But of the different types of support available to players, technical guidance is the most popular, although elite players often treat the physical and mental with equal importance. Obviously such support has a cost, and the players hope that the advice received results in a better on-course performance – if for no other reason than to offset the often high consultancy costs.

As for the courses, fairways and greens are mowed much lower and more consistently than they were in the past. This can affect driving distance by +/- 20 yards per tour event. Also, golf course greenkeepers, armed with the latest equipment, more information and better maintenance programmes, improve the quality of a course year round.

At the 2004 American Society of Golf Course Architects Conference, it was proposed that the following factors had contributed to the increase in driving distance:

Balls = 40%

Clubs = 30%

Players = 15%

Course Conditions = 15%

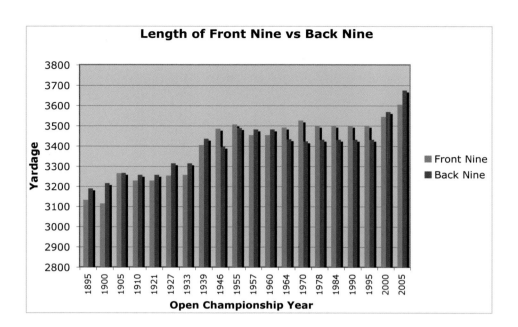

Length of Front Nine vs Back Nine

Yardage / Open Championship Year

■ Front Nine
■ Back Nine

There are constant improvements in the clubs, balls, course equipment and player conditioning. As a result driving distances will only continue to increase on the tour.

The regulations governing ball and club development put in place since 2000 are a crucial and substantial step, even if, as some argue, they are a little slow in coming. A critical acknowledgement in the joint principles issued by the R&A and the USGA is the importance of protecting both the integrity of the golf course and the cost that is passed on to golfers through green fees and memberships. But in the case of the Old Course, would the course set-up for the 2000 Open be long enough to maintain the challenge of the game for the 2005 Open?

The R&A and Links Trust did not believe so, and they were proved right at the 2004 Dunhill Links Championship, when Northern Irish golfer Graeme McDowell shot a new course record of 10 under par. On a calm, warm day in October, off the 2000 Open Championship tees, McDowell's card was:

Above: The difference between the lengths of the front and back nines on the Old Course has altered frequently over the past hundred years depending upon the nature of the course extensions. The back nine was traditionally longer, but in 1946 the extensions to the front nine made it 89 yards longer. This relationship was reversed in 1957, but in 1964 the creation of new tees on the front nine again made it longer than the return holes. Only the changes in 2000 reversed the trend.

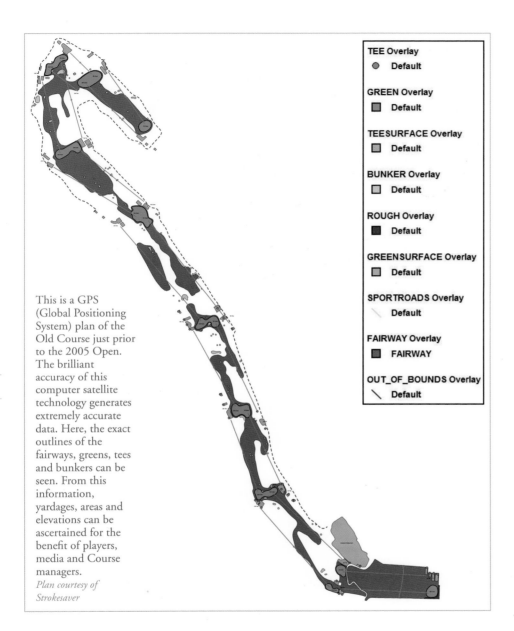

TEE Overlay
● Default

GREEN Overlay
■ Default

TEESURFACE Overlay
■ Default

BUNKER Overlay
■ Default

ROUGH Overlay
■ Default

GREENSURFACE Overlay
■ Default

SPORTROADS Overlay
╱ Default

FAIRWAY Overlay
■ FAIRWAY

OUT_OF_BOUNDS Overlay
╲ Default

This is a GPS (Global Positioning System) plan of the Old Course just prior to the 2005 Open. The brilliant accuracy of this computer satellite technology generates extremely accurate data. Here, the exact outlines of the fairways, greens, tees and bunkers can be seen. From this information, yardages, areas and elevations can be ascertained for the benefit of players, media and Course managers.
Plan courtesy of Strokesaver

Hole	Length	Par	Score		Hole	Length	Par	Score	
1	376	4	4		10	379	4	4	
2	413	4	4		11	174	3	2	-6
3	397	4	3	-1	12	314	4	3	-7
4	464	4	4		13	430	4	3	-8
5	568	5	4	-2	14	581	5	4	-9
6	412	4	3	-3	15	456	4	4	
7	388	4	3	-4	16	424	4	4	
8	175	3	3		17	455	4	3	-10
9	352	4	3	-5	18	357	4	4	
Total Length = 7115 yards									

Prior to this incredible performance, in the winter of 2003/2004 six new tees were added to the Old Course. While the second course extension in as many championships was not surprising, the location of the new tees was. For the first time, the new tees had been placed outside the recognised boundaries of the Old Course. One tee is now located on the Ladies Putting Course, one is on the New Course and two are on ground recognised as belonging to the Eden Course.

In October 2003, Peter Dawson, Secretary of the R&A, commented about the changes saying,

> *We're not trying to change the character of the course – we just want to re-instate the old decisions players had to make… Yet because of the history of the place and the fact so many people who are average golfers come here from all over the world to play the course, moving hazards is not the option it would be at many other places. You simply can't move a bunker here or there on the Old Course. All that leaves is to move tees. We shifted six tees at the 2000 Open and these latest changes are on a par with what happened last time. This time the course will be 160 yards longer – a rise of just two per cent.*

So what are the changes? The 2nd hole has had a new tee added 40 yards back into the Ladies Putting Course or Himalayas. The aim was to bring Cheape's bunker back into play and, as Dawson said, 'to encourage a second shot with a feathered longer iron rather than a spinning pitching wedge.' The hole now plays at 453 yards. (See the plan on p.140.)

The new tee at the 4th hole is 16 yards further back. The aim of the extension is to bring the central humps back into play and make the players choose between a left-hand line or right-hand line (see the plan on p.90).

A new tee was also added to the left and below the current championship tee on the 9th hole. While this tee was not used in the 2005 Open, its slight change in orientation and elevation would make the fairway blind, but more significantly it would make players hit a right-to-left shot to avoid the End Hole and Boase bunkers.

The new tee on the 12th hole sits on top of the landform behind the 11th green that has been more often used as a spectator viewing area. It is hoped that the added 34 yards will bring the hidden bunkers back into play on this hole and discourage many longer hitters attempting to hit over the green and chip back.

The aim of the new 13th tee is to bring the Coffins bunkers back into play. If the wind is in the player's face, it should do

so, as it is now 285 yards to carry these bunkers. Extending the tee back 35 yards has made the hole 465 yards.

The changes at the 14th hole were perhaps the most significant because by moving the tee back 37 yards, the Beardies bunkers may again be brought back into play, as well as the out-of-bounds wall when the wind blows. Consequently, the fearsome Hell Bunker will again challenge the second shot. At 618 yards, this hole is now the longest on any Open Championship course. 'Even with just a wee bit of breeze in your face this one is going to be a real cracker', Dawson grinned. 'We had no problem with players getting up in two at the 5th or 14th. Latterly, they've been getting up at both. Nothing wrong with that, but the drive at the 14th had become hazard-free. So we're

Far left: The second tee now sits alongside the Swilcan Burn. The new target line is the TV camera at the top of the crane in the distance. Most players hit their driver, some hit 3-woods to avoid Cheape's bunker.
Iain Lowe

Above left: Though Cheape's bunker still poses a threat, it is not as difficult as it was in the past when it was deeper and not raked. Indeed, unless an elite player is buried or under the lip of the bunker, most can reach the putting surface from this hazard. Regardless of this however, players still try to avoid it.
Iain Lowe

Below left: The view from the grandstand behind the 11th green shows the new 12th tee for the 2005 Open, its angle, the Eden estuary and the hollow between the 11th green and the new tee. The white path down the right running between the Old Course and the New Course is not out-of-bounds. Many caddies advise players to lay up close to it to get a good angle into the many pin positions on this unusual plateau green.
Iain Lowe

Play-Lines on 2nd Hole from Championship Tees

Prevailing Wind Direction

Old Course Hotel

Out-Of-Bounds

N

SW

Wind Disrupted
by Hotel

Cheape's Bunker

New Line

Old Line

165y

125y

2nd

3rd Tee

Scale

0   50   100y

300y

1st Green

Ladies Putting
Course

Swilcan Burn

40y   413y   2000 Open Tee

453y   2005 Open Tee

KEY

– – – Preferred play-line during 2000 Open

——— Preferred play-line during 2005 Open

© S.Macpherson. 2005

Length of Old Course for Open Championship

current medal tees (which were Open tees in years gone by) and making them play with a ball of similar design and character to that used when those tees were in championship use. On the Old Course, the benefits of using a less powerful ball are that a greater number of hazards are returned to play, a reduction in maintenance costs, greater spectator movement around the course, and a greater ability to watch tee shots land. And proportionally, with the less powerful ball, as MacKenzie said in 1934, those who swing faster will still hit the ball further than those who swing slower.

It seems that even if golf equipment and the assembly of the tees, greens and bunkers remain unchanged, the character of the game and the natural environment golf is played in will cause the course to change anyway. The impact the grazing of sheep alone had on the turf and gorse convinces one of the changing character of the Old Course. To preserve the playing

character of the course, authorities would have to resist the advances (and benefits) of maintenance equipment over the past century, but even were this possible, it would not have stopped the natural laws of disorder, erosion, growth and consquently the natural evolution of the course.

Bill Campbell is the only man to have served both as president of the USGA and captain of the R&A. He shared with members of the American Society of Golf Course Architects at the group's Donald Ross Dinner in 2003 his personal views that 'recent, ongoing increases in driving yardage seem to be exponential and are indefensible and not in the game's best interests.' His concerns centred on the dramatic changes that took place in a very short and recent period. He said,

The size of the problem is manifestly in the distances that the long-hitters are driving the modern ball. I don't mean just Tour-average statistics, but rather stats for the longer Tour Hitters when using drivers. It is apparent that most par-5 holes are now easily reachable in two shots by most Tour pro and top amateurs, and even by some college and school team players; and that longish par 4s have become drive-and-pitch opportunities for many, and lesser par-4s are drivable by some...How can this be good for the game? Must top-rated courses extend to 8000 or more yards? And then, what next?

The respected Campbell then called for action:

Since the status quo is actually a moving target, something should be done to fix it ASAP. I am impatient by nature, and now by age, that the game be preserved as we have known it, based on one's all-around skills, that classic courses not be rendered obsolete, and that golf course architects not have to design longer and longer tests or else trick courses up

BUNKERS BROUGHT INTO PLAY BY NEW TEES IN 1995, 2000 AND 2005

Yardage	Yards Added		Hole	200-230 yds			231-250 yds			251-270 yds			271-290 yds			291-310 yds			311+ yds		
78-'95	2000	2005		78-'95	2000	05	78-'95	2000	05	78-'95	2000	05	78-'95	2000	05	78-'95	2000	05	78-'95	2000	2005
370			1	0	0	0	0	0	0	0	0	0	0	0	0	0	0	0	0	0	0
411		40	2	1	1	0	0	0	1	1	1	0	0	0	0	0	0	1	0	0	0
371	26		3	1	1	1	0	1	1	1	0	0	0	1	1	1	0	0	0	1(333)	1(333)
463		16	4	0	0	0	1	1	1	0	0	0	1	1	0	0	0	1	1(311)	1(311)	1(327)
564			5	0	0	0	0	0	0	3	3	3	1	1	1	1	1	1	0	0	0
416			6	0	0	0	2	2	2	0	0	0	5	5	5	0	0	0	1(317)	1(317)	1(317)
372	16		7	0	0	0	0	0	0	0	0	0	2	0	0	0	2	2	0	0	0
178			8																		
356			9	0	0	0	0	0	0	1	1	0	0	0	0	1	1	1	0	0	0
342	37		10	0	0	0	0	0	0	1	0	0	0	0	0	1	1	1	0	1(336)	1(336)
172			11																		
316		34	12	2	2	2	0	0	1	0	0	1	1	1	0	0	0		0	0	0
425		35	13	2	2	0	0	0	0	1	1	2	0	0	1	0	0	0	0	0	0
567	14	37	1 4	2	1	0	1	2	1	0	1	1	0	0	2	0	0	0	0	0	0
413	43		15	1	1	1	0	0	0	0	1	1	0	0	0	0	0	0	1 (311)	1 (353)	1(353)
382	42		16	P.N	0	0	0	0	0	1	P.N.	P.N.	0	0	0	0	1	1	0	0	0
461			17	0	0	0	0	0	0	0	0	0	0	0	0	0	0	0	0	0	0
354			18	0	0	0	0	0	0	0	0	0	0	0	0	0	0	0	0	0	0
6933	7115	7279	Total	10	8	4	4	6	7	9	9	9	10	9	10	4	6	9	3	5	5

	Holes extended for 2000 Open		PN= Principal's Nose
	Holes extended for 2005 Open		Par 3

Above: This chart shows that the extension of certain holes has generally brought more bunkers into play. The now critical area of 271–290 yards provides interesting data. While very few could hit the ball more than 290 yards on the full in 1978, and indeed the average drive was almost 270 yards, this area has not seen an increase in the number of bunkers during the past twenty-seven years. What has happened is that bunkers in this area have gone from being generally just beyond the length of an average drive to being in range, and in the latest two Open Championships, these bunkers have been carried by the longer hitters. So now the next zone becomes of interest, if the aim is to take the driver out of the hands of the long hitters. In this regard, the authorities have been able, by moving back the teeing grounds, to bring more bunkers into play. From 1978 to 1995, four bunkers were 291–310 yards from the tee. The tee extensions for the 2000 Open Championship brought two more bunkers into play, and the most recent new tees have brought three more into play on the 2nd, 4th and 12th holes.

*to "protect their integrity" – a well-worn euphemism
for preserving the difficulty of their par.*

An excellent amateur golfer in his own right, Campbell's solution was simple – a shorter ball, 'especially since otherwise the yardage dilemma would recur time and time again.' This would be easier for those setting up courses for championships having to resort to his pet peeve of 'making greens unduly hard and fast – too slick for their slopes as originally designed – compounded by making tighter hole locations.'

The administrators at Augusta National, free of the red tape that bound the hands of the USGA and the R&A, were considering that solution: 'If technology brings about change in the next several years like we've seen in the past several years, then we may have to consider equipment specifications for the Masters,' said Augusta Chairman Hootie Johnson in 2002. Ernie Els had another idea though, and said in 2003: 'I am not totally against technology but they do have to put a governor on the ball... perhaps even the administrators should just consider bringing back wooden headed clubs.'

Jack Nicklaus is passionate about the subject of golf balls, and in an interview at the 2004 Masters said,

Amateurs can't make a ball respond. Things that are designed today are designed for the good player to hit. Because spin rates on the golf ball are so low, the golf ball won't stay in the air when mis-hit [as most amateurs do], *so they have not only lost the 30 yards they have gained* [due to equipment improvement] *they lose 20-30 extra yards going the other way. How can you improve doing that? You can't! The good player hits it in the rear end every time and gets the good result – the extra 50 yards. No wonder they tear apart the golf course. But the average golfer can't play it because he can't learn how to play. How can you learn how to play when you hit one ball 220 and the next ball 170 with a 3-iron?*

In an interview after he won the team event at the 2004 Dunhill Links Championship on the Old Course, professional golfer Fred Couples agreed with Campbell's solution. 'What they should do is make us all use another ball – that would solve a lot of things.' Regarding the changes to the course for the 2005 Open, and if the ball is not limited, Couples commented, 'If they lengthen a couple more holes, I think the Old Course would be really awesome.' He suggested, 'Perhaps No.3. Maybe the tee could be pulled right back there. Also if the two par 3s measured 200 or more yards, it would make the course another half a shot harder.' Before concluding, he delicately added, 'However, when you start to do things like that you start screwing around with things that have been around for so many years and that's probably not the right thing to do.'

On many courses, the distance the ball can be hit has not been reflected in scoring because courses are set up harder (fairways narrowed, rough thickened, bunkers added, water hazards enlarged and flags tucked ruthlessly behind bunkers).

This has not happened at the Old Course. Acknowledging agronomic improvements, the course continues to be set up in a reasonably traditional way and as a result, scores more greatly reflect the improvement of the ball, the club, and player. The effect of new tees introduced for the 2005 Open was reflected in the 2005 Open Championship summary statistics. (See p.150.)

The increasing steepness and now vertical faces of the Old Course bunkers have made the process of extracting oneself from their sandy depths more precarious. As a result, some golfers may give the 'greedy wee enemies' as Darwin described them, a wider berth. But it is interesting to hypothesise which category of player – the long hitter, middle-weight or feather-weight – will be more inconvenienced by bunkers with the new tees. It seems the aim is to affect the long hitter, but unless the Old Course constructs a Scottish version of 'Hell's Half Acre' so that all the fairways end at 300 yards from the tee on every par 4 and 5, the longer hitter will still have an advantage off the tee.

A Shorter Ball

Leading up to the 2005 Open there was considerable pressure was to consider the development of a shorter ball. The USGA senior technical director Dick Rugge made it a priority to open up lines of communication with equipment manufacturers, including in the April of that year asking thirty-five of them to submit two prototype golf balls – one that could travel 15 yards shorter, and the other 25 yards shorter than the current USGA limit. This is roughly a five to eight per cent reduction of the distances. Most companies took part in the test to find shorter standards. Rugge said, 'We expect that testing balls made to conform to the reduced limits will enable an appropriate evaluation of how a reduced-distance golf ball would affect playing of the game,' adding that the prototypes would be tested both on-course and with a robot.

Chairman of Augusta National Golf Club Hootie Johnson, who had been outspoken about the effect new balls were

144

Right: Mowing the 18th fairway (crossing Granny Clark's Wynd). Two Triplex mowers operate in an offset formation.
S. Macpherson

having, commented on the USGA directive saying, 'We think this is a favourable step by golf's ruling bodies in regard to the golf ball.' However, the R&A and USGA continue at this time to believe that no rule changes are needed under current conditions. Rugge said, 'The research project has no goal except to be prepared. [If] in the future we need to make some changes, we will have that research already done.'

Length could continue to be an issue, and if the USGA and R&A proceed at a speed too slow for Augusta National, Hootie Johnson has said, 'We are concerned, as are others, about the golf ball. I know the USGA and R&A are working hard on this issue. We are willing only to wait a finite time to see what can be done.' Augusta National has little land left to extend its course, so a shorter ball may be its best option. It is the only option if classic courses such as Prestwick Golf Club in Scotland or Merion Country Club in Pennsylvania are to ever host another major. At present they are simply too short.

This research by the USGA and R&A is significant because it is a move away from the Joint Statement of Principles published almost three years earlier to the month, which stated they saw no need to rein in the ball. Titleist, Callaway Golf and Nike Golf, three of the most high-profile ball manufacturers, either have reservations about the USGA request or are remaining silent.

'There are a lot of noises affecting them to make decisions there's no need to make,' said Wally Uihlein, chairman and chief executive of Acushnet Co., which makes the Titleist ball, and is the industry leader with forty per cent of the world market. 'They're talking about a distance rollback without any evidence the game is on the edge of ruination. We've already jumped to the conclusion that something has to be done before we know anything is wrong.'

While distance statistics for the 2005 PGA season indicated that the large increases in recent years have stabilised, and therefore any need to limit the ball have receded, history suggests equipment advances have just slowed momentarily. It will only be a matter of time before another clever mind invents a ball or club with a new combination of materials that works to propel the ball even further. This is why the authorities need to keep researching the matter, and possibly impose limits.

Tiger Woods fears that if limits are needed and the USGA and the R&A are too slow, Augusta National Golf Club will impose their own ball on Masters competitors. He believes the standardised ball may not reach the expectation of top players in areas such as spin, trajectory and launch angles. 'I don't think that a standard ball for everyone would be the right way to go,' he said. 'It's too personal.'

He is right, it is personal, especially with large sponsorship deals at stake. However, the facts remain: the person who creates the cleanest strike with the greatest swing speed hits it further, the lowest score wins, and many classic courses can't get any longer. If classic courses are to remain tournament venues and playing costs are to stabilise, something will need to change. For the sake of the average player, whose greatest benefit from the new equipment is greater fun, the best solution may be to develop a competition or PGA Tour ball. After all, it's the average player who would be punished the most if all balls are rolled back. However, the USGA and the R&A do not intend to make two sets of rules. They say, 'We believe good golf is played under one set of rules.'

Far left: An increasingly tired looking Road Hole bunker in 1998. But this bunker would not be renovated until the run up to the 2000 Open Championship.
S.Macpherson

While they may not intend to make two sets of rules, it is clear that professionals and amateurs are playing two very different games. And reports from the National Golf Foundation in the USA are saying that, contrary to the USGA's belief that golf is getting easier, many golfers over the age of forty are quitting because of golf's difficulty. This is not necessarily due to clubs and balls, but a comment on the way golf courses are being set up to try and counter the advances in equipment. Back tees, narrow fairways, fast greens, lots of water, and deep bunkers make the going tough for an average player, as well as expensive because of the number of lost balls. While not all of these factors have been introduced to the Old Course, elsewhere it is rife, and the outcome may be the worst scenario for all sectors of the golf community – fewer players.

Above left: Out with the old, in with the new. Taken in January 2003, this photo shows the new bunker revetted and the soil surrounding the Road Hole bunker prepared for new turf to be laid. However, it was completely remodelled prior to being turfed, in favour of a wider, shallower version.
S. Macpherson.

PREPARING THE OLD COURSE.

The Old Course is always prepared when it is due to host an Open Championship, but the level of this preparation has escalated with each Open. The increasing costs of treatment reflects this trend. In the last hundred years the course has gone from costing approximately £700 to maintain in 1904, to over £420,000 in 2004 – of which around £400,000 is staff wages. This 2004 figure is 600 times more than the expenditure incurred a hundred years ago.

APPROXIMATE COSTS FOR MAINTAINING THE OLD COURSE IN 2004

- Seed £2700
- Chemicals £200
- Fertiliser £2400
- Topdressing £6000
- Incidentals £4000
- Shell and road materials £3500
- Staff payroll £400,000
- Machinery costs too variable to cost.

Above left: The new Road Hole bunker ready for the 2005 Open Championship. Ready to gobble up any off-line shots, and a few that get an unlucky bounce!
Iain Lowe

Right: Paired with Tiger Woods in the final group on the Saturday, Colin Montgomerie had a chance to make up some shots on Woods, but few putts fell, except a 30-foot bender on the last hole. His round of 70 was one better than Woods 71, but not the round Montgomerie had been hoping for. The total of 207 left him tied for third at -9, three shots behind Woods with one round to go.

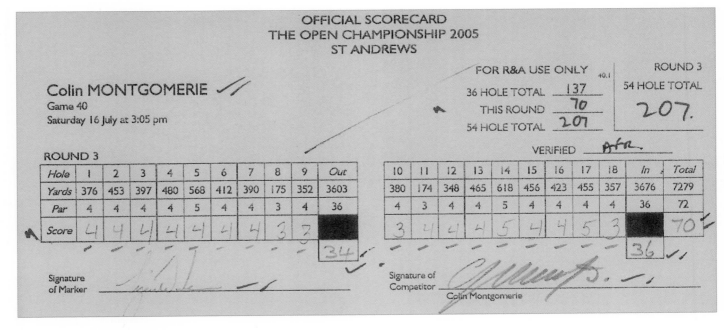

OFFICIAL SCORECARD
THE OPEN CHAMPIONSHIP 2005
ST ANDREWS

Colin MONTGOMERIE ✓✓
Game 40
Saturday 16 July at 3:05 pm

FOR R&A USE ONLY 40.1

36 HOLE TOTAL 137
THIS ROUND 70
54 HOLE TOTAL 207

ROUND 3
54 HOLE TOTAL
207.

VERIFIED AfR.

ROUND 3

Hole	1	2	3	4	5	6	7	8	9	Out	10	11	12	13	14	15	16	17	18	In	Total
Yards	376	453	397	480	568	412	390	175	352	3603	380	174	348	465	618	456	423	455	357	3676	7279
Par	4	4	4	4	5	4	4	3	4	36	4	3	4	4	5	4	4	4	4	36	72
Score	4	4	4	4	4	4	4	3	3		3	4	4	4	5	4	4	5	3		70
										34										36	

Signature of Marker _____

Signature of Competitor _____
Colin Montgomerie

As regards the physical treatment of the course, basic principles underpin the management programme adopted by the current Head Greenkeeper Euan Grant and Links Superintendent Gordon Moir. Pesticide and fertiliser application is kept to a minimum, with only 20-25 kg/ha of nitrogen being applied to the greens on an annual basis. Irrigation is only used to keep turf alive while deep aeration is carried out regularly to alleviate compaction. This is done using Verti-drain during the winter and HydroJect (water injection) through the spring and summer. Mowing heights are kept to approximately 5mm with surface refinement operations including light top-dressing, rolling, and occasional verti-cutting. These combined procedures are aimed to enhance the health of the turf, keep it growing upwards and to promote smooth putting surfaces. Perhaps the most significant change in the maintenance operation since Old Tom controlled the links is the quality of machinery used to implement the various operations, and the frequency with which the operations are conducted.

THE 2005 OPEN CHAMPIONSHIP

A tremendous amount of work went into the preparations of the Old Course for the 134th Open Championship. With Tiger Woods eager to defend his win of five years earlier and Nicklaus making his final Open appearance, the world was watching the 'Home of Golf' with eyes more transfixed than usual. To have the course in top condition, work began well over a year before with the revetting of over ninety bunkers and the construction of new tees. Two months before the Open, the landing areas for the Open competitors were roped off, and rough left to grow. A month before the Open the course was closed to play entirely. In the final countdown, the greens were increasingly intensively groomed with double cutting and periodic treatment of the roller (Graden turf irons) when required. In the last days before the Open, the greens were running at 9.5 on the stimpmeter, and with little rain and warm days in the low- to mid-20s heating the links and adding fire to the fairways, the greens were sure to reach the 10.5 feet the R&A were aiming for by the Thursday of the first round.

Looking back at the course in the days before the staging of the 27th Open held at St Andrews, the course really was in excellent shape. The heat had burnt off the grass on the peaks of the fairway undulations, yet the hollows held some colour. Only the growing up of the rough grasses around some fairways was controversial. It had turned fairways traditionally regarded as double fairways into single fairways – most notably the 6th, 14th and 17th. The protestors thought the rough removed some important play options.

One patch of rough destined to cause havoc was that down the right side of the Road Hole. While the rough on the left of the fairway was deep, the 'cabbage' on the right was viciously so. Those who strayed into it in an attempt to get the best line into the green would almost certainly be kept from reaching the putting surface. In the statistical summary at the tournament's end, this proved to be true. The hole had maintained its stern reputation. Only 45.9% of golfers hit the fairway, and even fewer, 43.9%, hit the green in regulation, making the Road Hole the hardest during the 2005 Open.

The 14th hole, which had become the longest hole in championship history at 618 yards after its 37-yard extension, did not prove as difficult as the authorities had hoped. Indeed, only three holes played easier. With the average drive being 326.9 yards, and Woods averaging 342.75 yards, many competitors could reach the green in two shots – often with irons – and this resulted in 168 birdies. Much to the chagrin of the R&A, the Beardie bunkers were relatively easily skirted and Hell bunker did not come into play at all. Even with the Elysian Fields encircled by rough, the hole had once again played below its par – the last time it hadn't was 1984.

In the shaping of the fairway lines, the fairway mowers had been directed to glide in and out between the bunkers. This method can produce some very attractive fairway lines, but it can also leave some bunkers surrounded by rough grass if smaller, more mobile, mowers are not utilised to clean-up around bunker edges. The fairway set-up of the course for this Open saw such bunkers as the cluster on the right side of the

6th hole in the rough, and others with several feet or yards of semi-rough in front of them. This was the case for the bunkers known as the Seven Sisters on the 5th hole – shots that would have traditionally rolled into it were held up on the front lip by a yard of semi-rough.

In the search to find the champion golfer that year, rough grass was a legitimate and viable test, and it did prove to be a threat to those who missed the uniquely wide fairways. But the challenge is to cultivate this rough in places and densities that are in keeping with the strategy of the course. When Daly won in 1995, he took on many of the bunkers off the tee. He had the power and nerve to do so, and the Championship Committee had set up the course to allow for it. In 2005 the course set-up guidelines changed, and perhaps the new set-up removed some of the risk/reward strategy that has characterised the Old Course. On the 4th hole for example, when the tee was set right back, some

Left: Tiger Woods holding the Claret Jug after he won the 2005 Open Championship.
Courtesy of Ian Joy Photography

BIRDIE COUNT AT ST ANDREWS OPEN CHAMPIONSHIP PER YEAR

Hole	1970	1978	1984	1990	1995	2000	2005
1	36	62	90	134	75	73	87
2	17	36	44	66	47	65	46
3	50	71	107	108	115	99	103
4	15	21	29	34	22	53	27
5	64	149	205	189	152	203	211
6	24	53	50	68	41	99	56
7	40	48	82	92	68	97	85
8	47	48	62	49	30	37	39
9	67	81	76	102	102	92	212
	360	569	745	842	652	818	866
10	55	100	121	138	66	118	78
11	23	40	28	54	31	55	34
12	86	65	85	83	132	143	105
13	29	17	35	23	41	43	19
14	73	56	46	109	201	115	168
15	37	49	50	59	60	45	48
16	38	39	45	69	40	27	34
17	5	7	11	15	13	13	19
18	87	56	80	98	189	75	220
	433	429	501	648	773	634	725
total	793	998	1246	1490	1425	1452	1591

Unusually high numbers
Unusually low numbers

Year	1970	1978	1984	1990	1995	2000	2005
Birdies	793	998	1246	1490	1425	1452	1591
Rounds	403	453	468	456	523	458	472
B.p.R	1.97	2.20	2.66	3.27	2.72	3.17	3.37
YARDAGE	6951	6933	6933	6933	6933	7115	7279

Above: Average birdies per round at successive Open Championships.

and on the final round, moved the tees up approximately 10–15 yards.

Additionally, on the 16th hole, almost all players laid up short of the Principal's Nose because the rough grass over it and the Deacon Sime bunkers had been left to grow. There was very little encouragement to take on the bunkers. Of course, this didn't stop Daly, who in his last round in 2005 used his driver... but the ball went into the rough. Of course, for his boldness, he was left only a little wedge to the green, but even he couldn't get the spin to stop it on the green. Assessing these strategic areas is a fine art but the balance must be to test a golfer's power occasionally, test accuracy mostly, and test their skill always. With that in mind, had some areas been left as fairway, more competitors may have taken on the bunkers and instead of watching a procession of mid-irons, spectators might have been treated to a greater variety of shots as each player tried to play the course in a method that maximised their individual strengths.

THE CHAMPION AND POST-CHAMPIONSHIP ANALYSIS

Hail the champion! All credit must go to the victor. Using the new Nike One Platinum ball described as 'a four-piece ball that allows the experienced player to apply variable loads on the ball and still get superior action on every shot', Tiger Woods played excellent golf all week to become back-to-back champion at St Andrews. With twenty-one birdies and rounds of 66, 67, 71, 70, he rarely gave any other player so much as a whiff of victory. He drove three of the par 4s in the first round, had eight birdies, and even the three bunkers he found couldn't stop him leading the Open. Woods birdied the 5th hole every day and birdied the 9th and 12th holes three out of four days. Only the 13th, 16th and 17th holes provided any resistance to his scoring by leaving him one over, two over, and one over after four rounds respectively. Woods only found one more bunker after round one, and it was on the 10th hole in the final round when he was trying to drive the green. But, while he struck the ball well, on the

players could not carry the 285 yards required. While this is not apocalyptic in its own right, what caused the stir were the unappealing and agonisingly few lay-up options for the short hitter. Even the viewing corridor to the green was blocked by a stand of gorse. Into the wind some players had to play left to the 15th fairway. Authorities realised the issue

HOLE	PAR	EAGLES						
		1970	1978	1984	1990	1995	2000	2005
5	5	4	4	12	13	2	18	15
7	4	1	1	1	0		0	1
9	4	1	0		1	2	0	9
10	4	2	1	3	1		1	0
12	4	3		1	2	5	4	2
14	5	1		0	2	14	6	3
18	4	2		1	1	1	0	9
TOTALS		14	6	18	20	24	29	39
OTHERS		0	0	2	3	1	0	0
TOTAL		14	6	20	23	25	29	39

Left: Eagles scored in the last seven Opens held at the Old Course.

149

MULTI-LAYERED BALLS AND HOT FACED CLUBS

famous greens he also putted very well, ultimately averaging 1.67 putts per green and leading the tournament statistics. The combination of power and accuracy resulted in a very deserving champion.

One day I'll be able to tell my kids
and my grandchildren about what happened
to me at the Old Course. Without a doubt,
I like it best of all the Open venues.
It's my favourite course in the world.
– Tiger Woods

In 1970 *Golf Monthly* wrote about the sharp improvement in scoring in that year's championship compared with the 1964 event, saying, 'This year no fewer than 14 eagles were scored during the championship; in 1964 the total was eight.' Ever since then the eagle count has continued to soar. In the 2005 Open Championship a new record of 39 was set, with the 9th and 18th holes giving up far more than ever before.

What effect did the new tees have on how the course played? Woods described how he played the holes with the new tees. He said from the 2nd tee he played a 3-wood to the right and short of Cheape's bunker. On the 4th hole he hit the ball high to carry the hill and on the 12th, he hit using the driver and 'fit' the ball left or right of the last bunker, because at 309 yards off the tee it was too far for him to carry it. The 14th hole got a lashing from his new 45-inch graphite-shafted driver. For the rest of the field the effect of the new tees was greater. The angle of the new 2nd tee did bring Cheape's bunker more into play, so many hit short to avoid it. This however left a long shot into the elevated green – a difficult shot to get the ball close, particularly as the front of the green slopes away for the play line. If this hole was harder, it was the 4th tee that caused the most consternation. Those without the power to hit it higher like Woods just tried to hit it harder. Some shorter hitters relied on a good bounce to get them over the rough and on to the fairway, even those who aimed left. Those who failed to make it struggled to reach the distant green. Lastly, the new 13th tee had a significant effect on scoring. The change to it brought the Coffin bunkers into play and forced players to play left or right – many with a metal wood. The danger level was high, and under the pressure, many either found

the bunker or hit the drive to a position from where it was difficult to get near the flag.

Calculating the actual impact of the new tees is easier. In comparing the statistical difficulty of the holes in 2000 to those in 2005, it reveals that the new tees caused most holes to play slightly harder, except the highly publicised change to the 14th hole, which ultimately played easier.

The extension of teeing grounds is often thought to favour the longer hitters. To examine this theory, a look at how the players who finished in the top ten in driving distance played these new lengthened holes provides some interesting data.

lower, but the field have not made the same impact. How has this balance been maintained? Perhaps partly due to the weather, partly to more bogies because of greater amounts of rough grass, and partly due to the increasingly steep faces of the bunkers. But the heart of the answer may lie with the greens. Putting is the final frontier where the battle against sub-par scoring by tournament authorities can be waged. If the accessibility to the flags is reduced, almost regardless of the increased driving distances, hitting the ball close to the hole will be difficult. Additionally, if the slopes around the flag location are particularly fast or undulating, putting difficulty is also increased.

Right: This table compares the stroke averages of the modified holes between 2000 and 2005. Results indicate the added length did not make all the holes play harder for the Open competitors.

150

Far right: This table shows the effect the new tees at the Old Course in 2005 had on the scoring of the players who ranked in the top 10 in driving distance.

Hole	Par	2000 Length	Stroke Average	2005 Length	Stroke Average	yardage increase	stroke diff.
2	4	413	4.09	453	4.24	40	harder
4	4	464	4.1	480	4.27	16	harder
12	4	314	3.89	348	3.99	34	harder
13	4	430	4.21	465	4.39	35	harder
14	5	581	4.97	618	4.86	37	easier

This group of players, who finished between 1st and 60th on the leader board and averaged over 332 yards off the tee, had an advantage on the holes made longer. However, this didn't happen on the one hole where the fairway runs out at their average driving distance. On the 13th, where the run-out was 300 yards, if a player went left over the Coffins, or about 330 yards right of the bunkers, their distance advantage was negated by the in-range rough, dunes and bunkers. As a result the field overall averaged a lower score on this hole. This suggests those with skill but less power, not only can compete, but also beat players where the strategy of the holes requires control and accuracy.

With the improvements in player fitness, training and skills, and with new hi-tech equipment resulting in more birdies and eagles being recorded than ever before, and the highest average of birdies per round regardless of course length, it is interesting to note that in the modern era (i.e., since 1970) the average score per round is still above par. Yes, the top ten finishers are scoring

	Stroke Average		
Hole	Field	Top 10 in Driving Distance	Difficulty
2	4.24	4.05	easier
4	4.27	4.15	easier
12	3.99	3.83	easier
13	4.39	4.50	harder
14	4.86	4.83	easier

A look at the flag positions used in the 2000 and 2005 Open Championship (Chapter 8, 'Traditional Pin Positions' pp.187–189) compared to where traditional flags were located by the R&A for medal competitions in 1937, indicates that flag positions have, in general, moved closer to bunkers, slopes or the edges of the green. This is more apparent on some holes than others. For example, the flag locations on the 2nd hole are fairly close to traditional locations, as they are on the 3rd, 7th, 11th and 17th. However, on holes like the 1st, the preferred flag position is

much closer to the Swilcan Burn. On the 5th hole too the flag is positioned much closer to the front on the green to make access harder. The 8th hole the pin has been located just over the bunker or right at the back of the green – again reducing the room for error for players attacking the flag. On the 11th hole, when the green speeds are averaging 10.6 feet on the stimpmeter, as they were during the 2005 Open (the 1st was the fastest at 11 feet, the 18th the slowest at 9 feet 10 inches), flag locations are limited by the slope of the green. But the Championship Committee is not averse to locating a flag where players are not expecting it. This happened on the 7th hole in the first round of the 2005 Open when the flag was set back right on an area usually associated with the winter flags. In the third round in the 2005 Open, another unusual position was utilised, but this time on the 17th hole. It was just in front of the Road Hole bunker and just up the slope, the philosophy being that this would bring the bunker more into play. As it turned out, players generally played short of the green and attempted to get up and down for a par 4. The final hole is interesting also. The spread of flag locations during the 2005 Open shows a conscious use of the Valley of Sin to protect the flag. A flag set at the back of the green would almost certainly yield far more birdies and eagles than one just over the Valley of Sin.

The Old Course has traditionally produced great champions, and this was certainly true in 2005. However, after the 2005 Open some commentators suggested the R&A Committee responsible for setting up the Old Course had conspired against its traditions of double fairways and wide play options, and in bringing in the rough, changed the character of the course. If true, this hurtful accusation implies that in the eyes of the R&A the Old Course does not have enough natural defences to protect itself against the modern player armed with the latest equipment. But if growing thick rough down the side – and occasionally in the middle of each fairway – is a strategic effort to stem low scoring, is it not also reducing

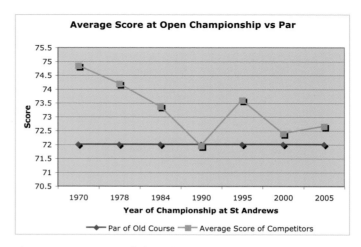

Left: Only once since 1970 has the average score of Open Championship competitors fallen below the Old Course par. That was in 1990 when par was 72 and the average score was 71.95.

the greatest virtue of the Old Course, which is the various lines and options a player can take in getting from the tee to the green? Would it not be better to keep the course comparatively free of rough, and just let the Open competitors play the traditional set-up regardless of the possible low scoring effects? As golf architect Tom Doak wrote, 'The Old Course at its best is as fast as a snooker table and where its undulations take the place of other balls on the table'. The presence of rough grass only slows the speed of the table and counteracts the effect of the undulations.

The Royal and Ancient Golf Club has always been averse to changing the character of the Old Course, but if the set-up of a course changes, the character of the course will also change. Equally, if equipment changes, the playing experience changes. If neither of these events happen, the Old Course is still slowly physically changing anyway – if only for the simple reason that it is built on sand.

For the 2010 Open Championship at St Andrews, it will be intriguing to see what technology the players will bring with them, how the course will be set up, and indeed what sex the competitors will be. With the R&A now extending the Open Championship invite to female golfers, could other decisions that are widely perceived now as being radical be on the horizon? Could we see a shorter-travelling tournament ball introduced? Will the concept of 'defending par' be

Above: After heading to the most northern part of the course (the 7th green), golfers turn south. On a clear day, the long views back to the distant hills, coastal cliffs and the town of St Andrews itself can be captivating. As seen here from the 9th tee, even the R&A Clubhouse can be made out just right of the flag on the 9th green. When playing this hole, the biggest challenge can be negotiating a way past the two fairway bunkers. Generally, play is to the left, but when the flag is tucked behind 'Boase' and 'End Hole' bunkers, as it is here, golfers may play left or right of the bunkers. On calm days, or when the hole is playing down wind, many longer hitters attempt to drive the green. As a result this hole is statistically one of the easier ones on the course during the Open Championship.

S. Macpherson

abandoned? Will more bunkers be cut on the Old Course? While it may take a tsunami to change the current tide of opinion on the state of golf and the Old Course, the passage to the next Open Championship at St Andrews is likely to be unsettled. Time always brings historical, social, cultural and technological pressures to the door of the Royal and Ancient Golf Club. While the days are long past when the men of the R&A could dictate freely to the golfing world the specifications of the ball and clubs, they still maintain control over the rules for the Open Championship and the set-up of the Old Course. And so it can be said that the competition and the evolution of the course is still in their hands. Only time will tell if the direction they take – that plotted with their strong historical compass – while sailing on the forceful and unsettled seas of technology, will ensure the future vitality of the Open Championship, St Andrews and golf around the world. May providence be with them at the helm.

Above: The big clock on the R&A clubhouse.
S. Macpherson

I know no other course on which, if you do not lay your shot down in the right place, an apparent insignificant bunker in your path can make it so utterly impossible to remain anywhere near the hole. As a necessary corollary there is great scope for thought and for taking alternative routes. The course always keeps you thinking, and you must think afresh with every change of mind. Nowhere in the world is golf so little cut-and-dried. Because you make a bad shot, it does not follow that you will be immediately punished; very likely you will not; but it is still more likely – it is almost certain – that your next shot will be made exceedingly difficult. You will be able to reach the green, but unless you are very skilful indeed, you will not be able to stay there. There will be a bunker to avoid and you may avoid it, but it will be cunningly reinforced by a slope that will take your ball exactly where you did not want it to go. It is a course of constant risks and constant opportunities of recovering, of infinitely varied and, to the stranger, unorthodox shots, of a certain amount of good luck and bad luck, of great differences in result due to very small differences in direction. It is occasionally the most exasperating course in the world; it is always the least dull.

– Bernard Darwin, *Lonsdale Library: The Game of Golf*, 1931

CHAPTER SIX

SERENDIPITY'S SCORECARD
Conclusions

*If there be added to its golfing charms the charms of all its surroundings – the grand history of St. Andrews
and its sacred memories, its delightful air, the song of its numberless larks, which nestle among the whins,
the scream of the seabirds flying overhead, the blue sea dotted with a few fishing boats, the noise of its waves
in the bay of Eden as seen from the high hole when the tide is full, the venerable towers and the broken
outline of the ancient city, and in the distance the Forfarshire coast, with the range of the Sidlaws, and,
further off, the Grampian Hills, it may be truly said that, probably, no portion of ground of the same size
on the whole surface of the globe has afforded so much innocent enjoyment to so many people of all ages
from two to eighty-nine, and during so many generations.*

– James Balfour, 1887

It has been just over a century since, as Simpson and Wethered wrote in their book *The Architectural Side of Golf*, '…[G]olf architecture was spoken of for the first time and recognised as belonging to the art of the game'. The year 2005 also marked one hundred years since the first radical changes were made to the Old Course for an Open Championship in response to new technology. The original natural, ragged-edged, open, sandy pits that were eroded by the many feet and niblicks of the early golfers have long since been formalised. Now the Old Course is wider and longer than ever before and many of its features are known around the world. But questions remain, such as, is the modern game in good health, and what is in the future?

It seems important to state that golf on the Old Course was very difficult up until the 1900s. The course was narrow, the turf was relatively unkempt, and off-line shots were punished mercilessly. The initial widening of the links and improvement in the turf was a very positive development, and though it changed the character of the course, it was a change that should be looked back upon with much affection because it led to the celebrated layout that is played today. The stimulus for this change was technology, and mostly the development of a newer, better, and more affordable golf ball. The gutta percha ball in 1845 gave life to golf by lowering the cost of participation and broadening the pleasure of playing. With the new rubber ball, golf became cheaper, more fun and more popular.

Advances in equipment in the early 1900s continued to encourage more players to golf. The introduction of the superior rubber-cored ball in 1903 gave another massive injection to golf's popularity. But with this new ball came a new type of concern. The authorities saw the greater distance and control the new ball gave, and felt, perhaps for the first time, that the test the Old Course offered was not sufficiently stern. Buoyed by the relaxing of the rules surrounding the placement of teeing grounds, the R&A added 200 yards and thirteen bunkers to the links for the 1905 Open Championship. It was the start in earnest of the duel between equipment, course set-up and scoring.

155

Opposite page: Hell
Bunker in 2006.
S. Macpherson

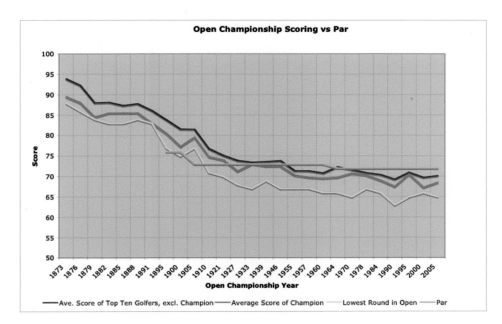

Open Championship Scoring vs Par

Open Championship Year

— Ave. Score of Top Ten Golfers, excl. Champion —— Average Score of Champion —— Lowest Round in Open —— Par

Above: All scoring in the Open Championship at St Andrews has continued to fall. Despite a drop in the value of par, the score of the Open champion has been consistently below par since 1946.

Since then, while much has changed, the battle has not. On the equipment side, hickory shafts have gone, titanium and graphite have been introduced, dimple patterns have been near perfected, golf ball regulations have been set, plus-fours are out, and distance laser finders are with us. On the Old Course, a further 700 yards has been added, all bunkers have become revetted and the greens now roll at over 10 feet on the stimpmeter during the Open Championship. The overall result is that scoring during the Open Championship has continued to fall.

As a governing body of golf, the Royal and Ancient Golf Club is responsible for formulating the rules and standards of the sport, but like many clubs and course owners, it must also respond to inventions and advancements by the commercial sector of the industry. However, over time the relationship between the R&A and the industry has changed. In the earliest of times, the golf industry was small and mostly local. At the same time the men of the R&A were very influential, as captains of industry, members of the judiciary or politically engaged, etc. Within this relationship, golfing innovations deemed contrary to the betterment of the game

were easily legislated against, and physical changes to the course, such as the cutting of new bunkers easily completed. Time has almost reversed this relationship. The golf industry is now a very strong, global and wealthy sector, while the members of the golfing authorities themselves are comparatively less influential. As a result, when it comes to legislating against a club or a ball, or instigating changes to the Old Course, it is a significantly more difficult prospect, regardless of the deemed importance.

One thing that has not changed however is how the R&A's regulations resonate around the golfing world, and how the golfing world in turn responds to them. Decisions passed down at the 'Home of Golf' have global implications. One of the areas where the influence of the R&A has been particularly felt has been in the controversial topic of ball technology. Most members of the R&A probably play with the new club and ball technology with similar enthusiasm to the rest of the world. The R&A Championship Committee must consider the effect new and better equipment has on their flagship event.

Increasing the length of the links has been seen as the greatest weapon in slowing the rate of scoring. But the length by which the links has grown has been at a slower rate than that the more skilful players can propel an aeronautically engineered ball with the latest high-tech clubs. The effect that added length has had on scoring has been minimal. In fact, scoring has continued to fall despite the increases in the yardage of the Old Course.

The length the Old Course would need to extend to in some way redress the balance between the challenge the Old Course offered in 1905, when the average drive was around 200 yards and now, is quite bewildering. Using approximate average driving distances from the early periods and accurate measurements from the US PGA Tour since 1980, we can estimate that the Old Course would need to be almost 9000 yards long today. Perhaps more startling is the realisation that the difference between the current yardage of the Old Course and that required to keep pace with the newest advances in equipment is growing!

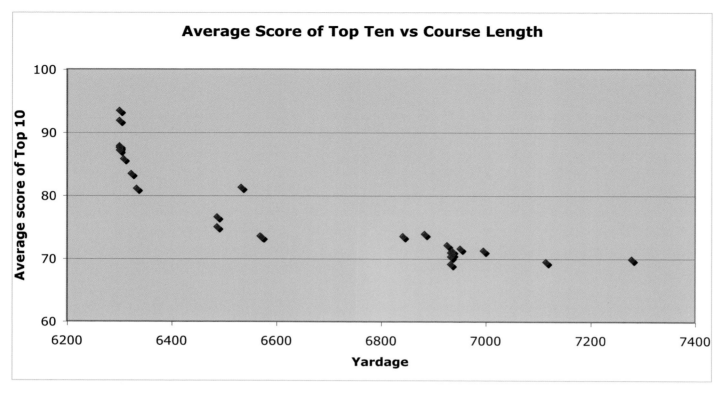

Average Score of Top Ten vs Course Length

Y-axis: Average score of Top 10 (60, 70, 80, 90, 100)
X-axis: Yardage (6200, 6400, 6600, 6800, 7000, 7200, 7400)

Left: Over time, an increase in the yardage of the Old Course has not prevented a decrease in scoring. Indeed, scoring has continued to fall despite an increase in the yardage.

No change can be looked at in isolation. While the course has been lengthened in response to advances in the equipment available to players, players themselves have improved. The modern player is bigger, stronger, better trained, has better fitness and access to physiological and dietary advice, and is generally more professional in this era of power golf. The quality of maintenance equipment available to the greenkeepers has also improved. Sheep and rabbits were replaced by the horse-drawn mower, then the power mower, and now all manner of high-tech, finely-adjustable mowers and satellite equipment is on hand to the greenkeeping staff. In the run-up to the hosting of a modern Open Championship, watching the green staff making the final preparations is like watching a highly choreographed ballet. Synchronised machinery flows up and down the fairways in perfect rhythm, while on the greens hand-mowers cleanly cut the turf grass to low heights for the sake of smooth, speedy

putting surfaces. Overall, the benefit has been a greater ability to prepare the entire course to a higher standard, for better players year round.

The evolution of equipment has been well documented. Equipment manufacturers, players and the governing bodies

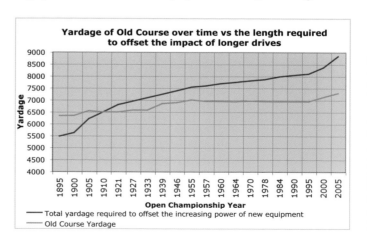

Yardage of Old Course over time vs the length required to offset the impact of longer drives

Y-axis: Yardage (4000–9000)
X-axis: Open Championship Year (1895, 1900, 1905, 1910, 1921, 1927, 1933, 1939, 1946, 1955, 1957, 1960, 1964, 1970, 1978, 1984, 1990, 1995, 2000, 2005)

— Total yardage required to offset the increasing power of new equipment
— Old Course Yardage

Below left: The Old Course was considered a long and difficult course. Since the advent of the gutty, improved golf clubs and balls have contributed to the significant change in this situation. Since the 1950s the gap between the length of the Old Course and the length required to offset the power golfers can propel their ball has been ever widening. Chart based on calculations by Max Behr in 1937 (p.79).

will all agree that hitting the ball is an easier activity today than in bygone days. The fruit of this progress has led to the greater enjoyment of golf by a wider group. Indeed, it has allowed golfers to play longer than they may have at any other time in history, and encouraged more people to play. Some nay-sayers argue that new equipment has de-skilled the game, and players can achieve better results today with less skill than it took to achieve the same scores in years gone past, while extremists claim new technology has become a purchasable substitute for skill. This rationale is hard to support. The ball still needs to be struck cleanly and squarely, and regardless of the size of the sweet-spot on the club head, the club will not swing itself. If certain shots and skills have been retired with the old brassy and niblick, some new shots

have been developed with the lob wedge and 'rescue' club. Shot-making skills have perhaps been transformed, but the skill to swing a club powerfully, repetitively, on-line and at a target has not been lost.

Among all the changes at St Andrews, some have been compelled to ask, 'When was the Old Course the best test of golf?' The answer depends somewhat on how you measure 'best'. If par is the yard-stick, then possibly between the late 1920s or early 1940s. During this period, with wooden clubs, hickory shafts and small wound balls, the average score of the champion was below par, but the average score of the remaining top ten golfers was slightly above par. It was not until the 1955 Open that the average of the top ten finishers and the champion was below par.

Right: The red line representing the increase in the course length, as featured in Chapter Five, has been laid over the improving scores of Open Championship participants. It was apparent these two lines would bisect each other, and while it would be misleading to quantify the area between the lines (due to scaling variations of the two vertical axes) or hypothesise about the relationship of the these two lines in the future, it is indicated that where the lines bisect each other (in the late 1920s and late 1930s) that the length of the course was in tune with club and ball technology and player ability to deliver winning scores about par.

Since then the power of the ball, the power of club technology, better conditioned courses, and better conditioned players have combined to achieve scores below the par rating of the course. It is impossible for the authorities to mandate on the condition of the players (though slightly entertaining to imagine), and unimaginable for the Old Course controllers to return to the days when the course was being mown by a horse-drawn mower, but it is possible, if change is deemed important, for the authorities to limit the power of the ball or club.

Some claim the modern course is providing the best test of golf because of the power players exhibit to get to the green, which contrasts with the fine skills required on the smoother, faster putting surfaces. Others say the modern greens are 'tricked-up' to excessive speeds and the fetish for length is leading to the desiccation of golf's gentle fun. It seems as equipment and the Old Course have changed, the Old Course has offered not one test better than another, merely different tests. Perhaps the examination has swung from the long game towards the short game, but both are still examined.

If the aim is to find a balance where scoring and the length of championship courses are in harmony with par, several conclusions can be reached:

1. Modern equipment is too powerful for the current length of the championship courses.
2. Courses need to be strengthened (lengthened, and more hazards introduced), or
3. If they cannot be extended, either the characteristics of the ball and club need to be altered to make them less powerful – perhaps via the introduction of a tournament ball.

If, however, it is par itself that is the fly in the ointment, its removal as a standard for which a score is rated should be considered. Old and antiquated, and once already changed, birdie could be adopted instead of par as the ideal score per hole, as it is for most good players today anyway. Alternatively, the whole hypothetical system could be abandoned, holes given only a length, and the players left to just shoot their best score. After all, ultimately it is the lowest score that wins, not the player's score relative to par.

While it is clear that advances in equipment have remained the main instigator of physical changes to the Old Course, there is little discussion as to why. Why must the tees be moved back? What is the problem with the top modern players playing the Old Course off the same tees that were good enough for say the 1955 Open Championship? The answer is usually that scoring will be too low and that because the ball travels so far, the players will not be playing the true character of the course. However, if the players shoot lower because they are better, and better equipped, well done them. And what is the true character of the course anyway? The version of it in the1880s? The 1920s? The 1960s? It has always changed.

A possible solution often raised is to regulate a less aerodynamic ball. The popular argument against this it that the current ball, combined with the new and larger metal woods gives golfers greater enjoyment, and removing that pleasure will turn golfers off. There is no doubt that new equipment is making golf easier, but a shorter-travelling ball may only be for competitive golfers – those who present the greatest threat to the viability of the courses. However, to the authorities this act would create one set of rules for some golfers, and another set for the rest, and as such is against a guiding principle of the game. Others don't see it that way. Casual golfers could choose to play the competitive ball if they want to experience the challenge the top golfers have, and the top golfers will still experience the challenge the Old Course has offered a succession of Open Competitors from the same set of tees. As a result, the character of the course will not be changed and par may remain the unit of standardisation for a round of golf, and both sets of players get a relative challenge.

So far this solution has not been chosen. Instead, the ball

Right and far right: In the almost one hundred years between the times these two photos were taken, so much has changed in golf, the Old Course and the Open Championship. In a quick comparison one notes the change to the bunker's form and face, and the improved maintenance techniques. Another physical change includes the gorse that now exists between the 13th and 6th fairways. How will the course look in another hundred years?
Left photo courtesy of Book of the Links *by Sutton.*
Right photo S. Macpherson

has remained reasonably unbridled and the Old Course lengthened – a decision that has had other wide-ranging consequences. Apart from most other courses needing to follow suit and extend their lengths, and new courses needing to be designed, built and maintained to longer specifications, the primary concern is safety. If the ball is travelling further, yes, holes will play shorter, and par will be more easily defeated, but the ball is also more likely to trespass onto neighbouring fairways and more distressingly, into property outside the boundary of the golf course. The solution is for existing courses to buy the land surrounding them and new courses to be built on larger parcels of land. But sadly for most existing courses, buying surrounding land is impossible, and for new courses, buying more land may make the cost of building a golf course prohibitive, or push the cost of playing golf further from the reach of the average person. Should this happen, and the classic courses become outdated, and the cost of golf rise disproportionately, we may begin to see the demise of the great game of golf.

Back at St Andrews, if the ball remains unbridled and conceivably goes further in the future, the Old Course can make other physical changes to redress the balance between the links and the improvement in the skill of golfers. Bunkers could be re-cut in line with modern driving distances, and re-cut around greens in places that will improve the strategic merit of the course. While this may be controversial to modern minds, there is a great deal of evidence proving that

many bunkers have come and gone from the Old Course in its history. The authorities could justify any new bunkers to the increasingly watchful and protective public as being reversible, in line with historical precedents, and will improve the challenge that the Old Course offers.

Since 1870 and the completion of the 1st and 18th greens, no major construction that materially changes the right-hand course that is used for the Open Championship has been approved. If, due to some amazing and unforeseen innovations, the golf ball can be hit a great deal further in the future – by a bionic shaft, for instance – would the authorities consider the renovation of holes such as the 9th. A new green complex further back has long been touted. Or more radically, they could hold competitions at St. Andrews on a composite course formed from the Old and the New courses. This could be done without destroying the separate lives or identities of either course and may result in a better 'viewing course' for spectators. No major upheaval would be required.

Of course, such larger physical changes to the Old Course are inconceivable nowadays. However, strong decisions may need to be made again if the changing – and many say deteriorating – relationship between power, skill and the shot values on the Old Course are to be strengthened. The fear is that any further erosion of these shot values may lead to the ultimate – the loss of the fun, enjoyment and challenge of the Old Course for those players who visit it, especially the longer-hitting and elite players.

The venerable and wise within the Royal and Ancient Golf Club understand that each generation has a responsibility to the next. They know that it is their responsibility as governors of the game to balance the modern challenges of a popular, multi-billion dollar worldwide sport with the traditions of the past, and the requirements for the game's future success. With that understanding, they sit in an unenviable position, watching some traditions mix with new technology like oil and water. The character of the Old Course is being changed with time and by playing and maintenance equipment, and the best that is being done to scare off low scoring is lengthening the links. But by locating tees outside established course boundaries, what message is being sent about the impact of the modern playing equipment, and what precedent is being set for golf courses around the world?

We are in a modern golfing watershed where the tees on many courses – some being classics – can no longer be extended, and this predicament is likely to continue in the foreseeable future. If nothing changes, two scenarios are likely. First, if tournaments continue to be played at those constricted courses, scores during elite competitions will fall at a faster rate. Or second, the authorities will formulate a set of firm equipment guidelines to regulate against inventions that act to propel the ball, especially that of the competitive golfer, any further. The cost of legislation for a shorter club and ball may be high, but the cost of changing the world's golf courses, and possibly losing future generations of golfers, is much higher.

How far have we come in the evolution of the Old Course? A long way indeed. From balls and bunkers to greens and grasses and length and lattitude. But the nature of evolution is that it is never complete. It never stops. The character of the Old Course is somewhat like a river; while it appears to be taking its traditional course, it is always changing. And whilst we have enjoyed it at many different times, freezing it in time is impossible. Even if the modern layout was frozen for future generations, like a frozen river, below the surface changes are still taking place – and in the case of the Old Course this is especially true, because it is built on sand. The Old Course is an amazing tribute to golf with its greatest strength being its adaptability. Designed by serendipity and massaged by man, the Old Course has resisted and embraced change simultaneously. It has been at the forefront of golf's evolution, yet preserved the pleasures and idiosyncrasies of golf's traditional adventure and mystery. Long may she live.

If I had ever been sat down and told I was to play there and nowhere else for the rest of my life, I should have chosen the Old Course at St Andrews.

– Bobby Jones

CHAPTER SEVEN

THE YEARS AHEAD

*Golf can claim without exception to be the most flexible game in the world…There are no lines or circles
to denote areas of play; nothing in fact, but a starting point and a final goal. The widest liberty of action
is allowed between these points with facility for every kind of manoeuvre.*
– Tom Simpson and H.N. Wethered, 1929

The modern player is playing on a course specifically modified to suit the modern game. The cross-country adventure that golf began as is a remnant of the past. Just as the gutty ball reduced the difficulty of the Old Course by an estimated six shots, new technology has continued to help golfers reduce the distance and control difficulty of the modern game. Like the gutty, which also reduced the expense of playing golf and inspired an influx of new pilgrims, each significant new invention has usually had an effect on the popularity of golf. It is difficult to argue against any invention that makes golf more popular, but what equipment will the future players be using, what configuration will the Old Course be in, and what will scoring be like?

THE BALL

At his press conference after missing the cut at the 2005 Open Championship, Jack Nicklaus was asked if he would rather play off the old tees with a shorter ball, such as that being proposed by the USGA, or the 2005 Open tees with the current ball. Adamant in his answer, he said he would have preferred to play the shorter ball.

And in fact, it is easy to conceive of the introduction of a shorter ball or a tournament ball. It would be a simple adaptation that would provide another product line for manufacturers, preserve the challenge of classic courses, slow the cost of maintaining modern golf courses, harness scoring closer to the par of a course (if that is important), while embracing and enhancing the best characteristics of the sport. The new ball would most likely be more affected by the wind, generate less spin, and probably be lighter, or have a specific dimple configuration. Such an introduction will affect not just tournament players, but aspiring tournament players. Those wanting to play competitively will begin to practice with the new ball in preparation for tournament play. Those aspiring to win championships will need to play all their golf with such a ball prior to turning professional because switching between two types of ball – say a ball that isn't affected by the wind, and one which is – would be very difficult.

Opposite page: The white flag flutters on the lower plateau of the second green.
S Macpherson

Should a tournament ball be introduced, the key to its success and acceptance would have to be its availability to all. It should be sold in shops alongside the regular ball. That way those wanting to experience the increased challenge of the tournament ball are able to do so. Conceivably it could be a bit like selecting which run to take on the ski slopes, or if playing off the same tees, doing the same run as your friends but doing it with only one ski. The shorter ball could also act like a handicap. For instance, a player on a low handicap could use a short ball while taking on a higher-handicap who is using a long ball.

The desire to experience the challenge of varying balls is well documented. At St Andrews, golfers can hire hickory clubs and gutty balls if they want a taste of the old game. But a shorter ball could produce marketing opportunities and a new challenge for modern golfers, for example, 'Compare your score to the Open Champions – play the same tees with the same tournament ball!'

Tiger is carrying the ball consistently 300+ yards since he went to the 460 Ignite. Amazing and intimidating!

– Kel Devlin, Nike Golf, 2005

SHAFTS

Shafts have long been described as the 'engine' of the golf club, and never was that more apparent than when the top golfers realised that golf was a simpler game when a steel shaft provided the link between the hands and the club head. Steel shafts were a great leap forward in price, quality and uniformity for players all around the world sixty years ago – especially for golfers in those countries without hickory. But since the graphite shaft was invented around 1970, it has improved beyond recognition and can now, in some cases, cost more than the club head!

The manufacturing technique of graphite shafts has become an extremely fine science with weight, kick-points, torque, etc., all being precisely honed. The manufacturing process now uses a higher quality of graphite, and as a result, produces greater uniformity between shafts and a greater range of shafts.

Range has become increasingly important. Older players,

woman golfers and casual players have all benefited from graphite shafts, but in the past the players with faster swings have not. That has now changed. With players getting stronger, the industry has developed extremely strong and longer shafts that have lower torque. This allows players with fast swing speeds, such as Tiger Woods – who notably switched to a graphite-shafted driver at the 2005 Open Championship – to maintain their technique and swing speed and get the club head back squarely to the ball at impact.

Greater distance and control for golfers in the future will be when the improving shafts are matched to their specific requirements. However, it is not inconceivable that in the future a new material may be discovered that works to propel a ball straighter and further than ever before. With this in mind, should the governing bodies who have worked to limit the ball and COR (co-efficient of restitution) of the club head set the parameters for the shaft? Failure to do so may lead to another rear-guard action.

CLUB HEAD SIZE

It's hard to know where the search for the ideal club head size will end. The USGA developed a proposal to limit the size to 385cc, but the manufactures rejected it. The USGA raised the limit to 470cc, but that failed also – particularly at Integra where they made the 'SoooLong', which is 600cc. It remains to be seen if this size will sell, but if it does not, perhaps that is when the ultimate limit will be imposed on club-makers.

CLUBS

The way forward can sometimes be better seen by looking back. If returning shot-making skills and reducing the impact of pure power is important to golf, authorities may look to increase the minimum loft of clubs and redefine a set of clubs.

If the lowest loft of any club in the bag (except the putter) was fifteen degrees, players would need to fashion low shots into the wind. Drives would also fly higher, and the average score could possibly increase. Alternatively, shot-making may

return more if a set of clubs during competition was reduced from fourteen to say, a maximum of nine. Players would effectively have a half-set of irons and the distance gap between shots could be 25 yards. This would require players to hit more controlled half-shots to suit those in-between distances.

Grooves might again become a focal point in the future. With professionals regularly able to keep grooves clean and machine the edges sharp, accuracy off the tee appears to be less important than distance. In 2005 the top three players on the PGA Tour – Tiger Woods, Vijay Singh and Phil Mickelson – finished 188th, 147th and 161st respectively in the driving accuracy statistics. While not currently illegal, the resharpened grooves could become deeper and wider and as a result top players could generate greater amounts of spin and control of the ball – even out of the rough. Simply put, many professionals would prefer a wedge from the light rough than an 8-iron from the fairway. So if courses cannot get any longer, reducing the control players can get from the clubface may cause a return to driving accuracy rather than distance for some elite players.

DISTANCE

Should the ball be limited in the distance it can fly though the air? How much more distance can equipment manufacturers get out of the ball and club at the current specifications? Who is benefiting the most from new equipment? It is right to look at the effects of ball, shaft and club head technology separately, but the fact is that the distance a ball travels is a result of their combined effect.

While many golfers believe they are getting some benefit from the new technology, it is really only the best golfers with the fastest swing speeds who are benefiting. At faster swing speeds the ball and clubface are compressed and the ball gains considerably more distance. The result of this is those players who possess the fastest swings do not need to use their longest hitting clubs to negotiate their way around some golf courses.

Tiger Woods said he was hitting his driver 400 yards at the 2006 Open Championship at Hoylake in the practice rounds but it gave him so little control on the hard and fast fairways that he choose to use a 2-iron for the majority of his tee shots during the Open itself -– just like he did at St Andrews in 2005. If technological advances allow the ball to be propelled still further in the future and it becomes commonplace that the driver and 3-wood are no longer required by players to negotiate the courses, then it may be agreed that equipment advances have removed an important test from the game and reduced the range of skills golfers require.

If the vast majority of golfers are not getting any significant distance benefits from new equipment, what would be their reaction if they were to learn now how much extra yardage the equipment manufacturers believe they can get out of the current club and ball specifications for players with faster swing speeds? We have seen tremendous advances in the last ten years and there is nothing to suggest that we could not see similar advances in the next ten years. If it were announced that we could expect to see the top players hitting a version of the current ball another 30 yards further, would this cause regular golfers to become unsettled about the distance a ball can be hit?

Once all the distance has been wrung out of the current specifications, it is possible to imagine a shorter travelling 'competition' ball being introduced. It could bring the strategic merits of many classic courses back into play, prevent some collateral damage to houses alongside golf courses, and importantly, give equipment manufacturers another source of revenue. One difficulty however, may be for the authorities to find a new ball specification that none of the ball manufacturers already have a patent on.

Meantime, it is hard to imagine casual players not purchasing new equipment in response to the greater distance a ball can be hit. Most golfers feel they must buy the latest technology just to maintain a 'level playing field' with their playing partners. Simply, the temptation of 'more yards' is

too great for many, even if the players don't have the swing speeds to get the advertised benefits.

Lastly, it can be guaranteed that if the clever and well-funded designers and engineers at the club- and ball-making companies do have 'more gas in the tank' with the current equipment technology, and it's almost certain they do, it will not be all released at once. It can easily be predicted that any advances would be released in small amounts – say in five-yard increments every two years. This drip-feeding of distance allows the equipment companies to sell a new model of driver every two years to maximise their profits and recapture the costs of intensive research and development. It also makes the effect of a longer travelling ball less apparent, and presents golf courses with time to adjust.

Scoring

There is little doubt the winning scores set in the future will be better than that set in 2000. If weather conditions are against low scoring in the next Open, maybe it will be in the Open after that, but like the relentless march of time itself, all scoring records at St Andrews will eventually surrender to new technology and to the fearless golfers who best harness their strength, ability, courage and luck.

How low the scoring will eventually get in the future is anyone's guess. Rough calculations show that averaging four rounds of about 78.5, and making a total of about 314–315, in the last ten years before the gutty ball was ousted in 1902, would have carried a player to victory. In the ten years after the Haskell ball was introduced, an average of 302–303 would have been needed. So the rubber-cored ball was worth about twelve shots. If we jump to the period 1946–51, you would have had to shoot four rounds of 71 and score about 285–286 to get close to the Claret Jug. So at this point, as Mortimer and Pignon discovered in 1952, the 'rubber-cored ball is worth about 29 strokes to you over the man who is using a gutty before 1902'. Since then scoring has improved further. With the modern ball you would need to average about 68 to have

a chance to win with a total of about 270-272. That is as much as forty-five shots lower – more than eleven shots better per round. With stronger, fitter golfers playing with further enhanced equipment and another new type of ball, it is easy to imagine the winning score continuing to decrease in the future. Only a massive jump in the technology of the equipment available for use and the set-up of the Old Course would alter this prediction.

There could be a greater move back to match-play in the future. From the first days when golf began, up until the more recent times, perhaps to the middle of the 20th century, a match was decided by holes and not strokes. Some lamented the growing preference for stroke play: 'This mode of scoring does not seem to partake of the real spirit of golf… If in those days a hole was lost, it was no great matter: there were plenty more to play. There was ample opportunity to give and take, and keep up the fun and frolic of the game to the end.' While the Open has always been a stroke play event, greater numbers of casual golfers may be encouraged to play the Old Course under match-play rules. For visitors to the Old Course, this can be a particularly enjoyable experience on the unorthodox links.

Par

The standard of rating holes has changed from bogey to par in the past, and it would be an interesting discussion if the USGA and R&A ever felt it was time birdie became the new standard score rating for a hole. However unlikely this scenario is, it would solve some issues and ensure holes satisfy the original definition of par, where it was the ideal score of a scratch player on any hole. Especially now, when scratch golfers consider the ideal score on a hole to be birdie.

In terms of what the length of a hole should be to fit within the category of being a par 3, 4, or 5, it is hard to know. Length is not the only factor influencing the par of a hole. But if a competition ball is introduced, the yardage at which a par 4 becomes a par 5 would not need to change. If however,

the ball continues to travel further, we could expect a par 4 to become even longer. How much? Well if an average drive becomes 300 yards, and an approach iron can be hit 250 yards, then who would be surprised if future par 4's measured over 500 yards. Would a par 5 then need to be 650 or 700 yards off the back tees?

COURSE MAINTENANCE

The equipment available to greenkeepers is constantly improving. So is the knowledge of modern greenkeepers. Detailed scientific data and analysis of such things as nutrient levels, organic matter, soil structure, pH and conductivity are all part of modern agronomy studies. Long gone are the days of every turf trouble being cured just by throwing down 'mere sand'. The types of machinery, equipment, and soil amendments will continue to improve but it will be the knowledge of the greenkeepers that will become the most important. With or without limited budgets, good decisions will need to made about what equipment to use and when. For instance, when are the best times to carry out certain operations? How should the greenkeeper balance the traditions of maintaining an old links, but using new techniques – fertilizing, top-dressing and watering, for example? For that matter, what old techniques still work and are needed to maintain the traditional appearance of the Old Course – i.e., revetting bunkers? The professionals responsible for making these decisions will find themselves being better remunerated, but it is also likely they will be on a stricter performance contract. Those who excel can expect a longer tenure than those who don't.

THE OLD COURSE

Perhaps the greatest failing of the Old Course is in its role as a spectator venue. Modern grandstands have done a lot to improve matters during the Open Championship, but where they are are not in place, following the golf can be very difficult. Fifty years ago, just after the 1955 Open, people

were 'rope-shepherded in their thousands along the sidelines, standing 12 and 15 deep, and sometimes 150 yards from the player'. It was suggested by Douglas Brownie in the *St Andrews Citizen*,

> *Why – as a constructive suggestion – could they not design a really modern championship course out of the Old and New Courses? I discussed this last week with several people interested in golf course architecture, and they all agreed that it could be done without – and this is the point – destroying the separate lives and identities of either the Old or the New. The idea is that the special course be laid out within the general framework of the two courses, each hole of the special course being one of the 'ordinary' holes of either the Old or the New.*

A composite course would never be accepted at St Andrews, though a stranger to the course might be sold on the merits of the idea. And the R&A must be praised for increasing the number of stands available to spectators, and making what is quite a difficult place to watch golf quite enjoyable.

Working to balance the set-up of the Open Championship course for both power and skill could become increasingly important in the power-golf era. Having noted the effect fairway run-out areas had on scoring, it would appear from the 2005 Open results that having more run-out areas may reduce the impact pure length has on scoring. On holes where a fairway turns sharply, ends, or is blocked by a hazard at the landing area, and the power of a long hitter is negated off the tee, accurate golfers can compete with and beat those longer hitters.

BUNKERS

For the professionals, how many bunkers should be in play to constitute a good test? On a course such as the Old Course, which has so much latitude and generally small bunkers, a minimum of ten or fifteen must be in play for most top-flight

golfers. Though taking some tees back for the 2005 Open Championship brought more bunkers into play, the solution in the future may be simply the solution the R&A used a century ago – cut more bunkers.

As for style, the relatively new fascination with vertical faces adds an element of danger and luck to the Old Course bunkers, but it could also be argued that such a style counteracts the skill of recovery. As part of the course's evolution, it is easy to imagine the faces in time becoming less sheer, and return to a more traditional, tapered style.

All the sandy waste areas that once existed on the Old Course have long since been grassed over or formulated into bunkers. The large hollow in front of the 5th green was once a sandy area. Restoring it to such a state may return a degree of difficulty to the hole that modern equipment has removed. Players may be more likely to play short of the spectacle bunkers than risk being in an unraked sandy wasteland. It is more likely, however, that the Royal and Ancient Club and the Links Trust will cut new bunkers on the Old Course – and be justified in doing so. Several in strategic locations will add more interest and strategy to the Old Course adventure for modern golfers.

Another consideration for the future may be returning to a situation whereby bunkers are unraked. While many small, rural or municipal courses around the world do not have rakes in bunkers, and perhaps the majority of casual golfers are more familiar playing from imperfect lies than not, most professionals shake at the thought of encountering a ball in a footprint. Just because more money is riding on the outcome of golf events now should not mean the abandonment of a once strong-held tradition – namely the unpredictability of a lie in a hazard – especially when the maintaining of that tradition is being used to justify maintaining other aspects of golf. If a half-measure is more palatable to the governing authorities than removing all rakes, then perhaps the wide-toothed rake once proposed by Peter Thomson should be reconsidered. It would create furrows where a ball could be sitting up on a sandy ridge or could equally be sitting down in a rut. Either way, making bunkers more unpredictable hazards again may be beneficial to golf clubs and the spirit of the game.

GREENS

In 1891 Dr J.G. McPherson, a keen golfer and student of the game, wrote of the greens, '…there was a variety of surface which brought out the greater skill; now all are nicely turfed over and artificially dressed like billiard tables. Then, at the Heather Hole one had to dodge about and watch the lie of the green… Now, a dead straight putt suffices. The Sandy Hole puzzled the uninitiated with its heavy putting surface; now it is a stroke easier.' The Old Course received no attention in these earliest days and the only greenkeepers were the rabbits. It is therefore one of the greatest transformations in golf that courses now double cut and roll greens with the aim of establishing uniformly smooth and fast greens of the same colour. There has been a slight drift away from having greens green, focusing more on having them healthy, but the fascination for speed and smoothness has increased.

In the past, greens were never uniform. Each had a separate size, shape, slope, colour and speed. The predominant reason for practice rounds prior to the Open Championship was to learn each green's 'personality'. The challenge of putting was to remember which green was faster or slower, and which side to approach the flag from to get the smoothest line to the hole. Uniformity in green speed has shifted some of the focus of practice rounds to other areas, but it is conceivable that to re-create the art of putting, the speed of greens could in the future be made to vary. Such a scheme may seem contrary to the concept of progress, but it has happened in other places – roading being one example. In the past, roads were rough and pot-holed. Better construction techniques, equipment and materials over time resulted in better roads that were sealed and smooth. As a result of better roads, speeds on them increased. Now, in an attempt to slow down cars, road authorities are effectively reversing progress and

deliberately making perfectly good roads bumpy by the addition of speed controls such as humps.

Good greens already have humps, slopes and undulations, but more of these could be used if some greens were slowed down. For example, on the famous High Hole (the 11th) on the Old Course, the left side of the green can no longer be used in the Open Championship because at four to six per cent, the slope is too steep when the greens are running at 10+ feet on the stimpmeter. Slowing this green down would allow greater variation in the flag placements.

Costs

The cost of playing golf in the future will rise. This is guaranteed. But decisions made by the golfing authorities may be accelerating the costs of playing golf beyond the general cost of living increases we have each year.

By permitting equipment that allows the golf ball to be hit such prodigious distances, golf courses need to be built on larger plots of land. This is because a golf ball that is going further, has the potential to go further off-line also. So for safety and legal reasons, longer courses need to provide greater separation between the golf holes and their property boundary.

The group first to bear these costs, and the group generally most vocal in opposition to increasing costs, has been the golf course owners and operators. There is an obvious reason why other industry groups do not object as much. It is simply because many benefit financially from the ball being hit further. In no particular order, equipment manufacturers stay reasonably quiet because they want to sell more clubs and balls. Golf course architects generally keep a hush because a longer ball presents more opportunities to lengthen and renovate existing courses, and teaching professionals have found that the new clubs perform better when being hit at higher launch angles etc., so make money by teaching new swings to eager or desperate golfers. Additionally, maintenance supply companies sell more mowers, fertilizer, and seed to courses that have a larger acreage. Ultimately, however, all these costs are transmitted to only one group — the golfers– via increased green fees and membership dues. Only time will tell if golfers, as the largest and most powerful group, ever feel sufficiently aggrieved to mobilise themselves against the long ball and longer courses.

As the situation is today, it is the tiny minority of long-hitting players (i.e., golf professionals) who are making golf more expensive and less accessible to the majority. On a global scale, more expensive golf could reduce the growth of the game in established golfing nations and it may slow or stop golf being taken up in new countries. If so, this would be a tragedy and a shameful legacy. It is in the game's greatest interest for the cost of playing golf to be affordable to future generations of golfers.

The Years Ahead

In the years ahead, all sectors of the golf industry will experience further change. For the club-makers this will mean new innovations, for the Old Course they may take the shape of new tees or bunkers, and for the Open Championship, the biggest change may be the participation of women. It is impossible to predict how a host of factors will impact on the golf industry, but the authorities will respond to these changes, which in turn will set off a new string of innovations. This is the endless cycle of evolution.

The original charm of golf, its simplicity and naturalness, cannot be too strongly emphasized; and this was in a great measure lost when the demand for fresh courses grew, since it became necessary to imitate what in the first instance had come into being spontaneously.
– Tom Simpson and H.N. Wethered, 1929

CHAPTER EIGHT

FACTS, FIGURES and FINDINGS
Charts and Tables, Bibliography, Acknowledgements, Index

The first few rounds a golfer plays on the Old Course are not likely to alter his first estimate that the course is vastly overrated. He will be puzzled to understand the rhapsodies that have been composed about the perfect strategic position of its trapping, the subtle undulation of its huge double greens, the endless tumbling of its fairways, which seldom give him a chance to play a shot from a level stance. Then, as he plays on, it begins to soak through his pores that whenever he plays a fine shot, he is rewarded; whenever he doesn't play the right shot, he is penalised, in proportion; and whenever he thinks out his round hole by hole he scores well. This is the essence of strategic architecture: to encourage initiative, reward a well-played, daring stroke more than a cautious stroke, and yet to insist that there must be planning and honest self appraisal behind the daring.

– Robert Trent Jones, *The Complete Golfer*, 1954

Left: In tallying up the changes, this old post-card of the Links at St Andrews shows nicely how much and yet how little some things have changed. The lack of infrastructure then, e.g., the Old Course Hotel, Links Clubhouse, Golf Practice Centre, Clubhouse on the Ladies Putting Course etc., is a most obvious change that is representational of the growth of golf, and the popularity that the game at St Andrews now enjoys.

Opposite page: When the Old Course is played in reverse (the left hand course) this is the view from the 18th tee. The hole plays from the regular 1st tee to the regular, and famous, 18th green.
S. Macpherson

Above: On the eve of the 2005 Open Championship, all wait in eager anticipation for the Open to begin. St Andrews is humming with excitment. Out on the course, the R&A have employed security guards to protect each hole. They may keep the galleries off, but they can do little to protect the par of the course from the world's best golfers armed with modern technology! That will be up to the forces of Nature.
Iain Lowe

Old Course Vital Statistics

An ideal or classical golf course demands variety, personality, and, above all, the charm of romance.
– C.B. Macdonald, 1928

Global Positioning Systems, or GPS, have become an excellent new tool for the golf course design, construction and maintenance industry.

The following table is a series of measurements taken from the course and off the GPS model of the Old Course.

Hole	No. of Tees	No. of Bunkers Pots	No. of Bunkers others	AREA of Bunkers sq m	AREA of Back Tee sq m	AREA of Main Tee sq m	AREA of Fairway sq m	AREA of Green sq m	AREA of 1st cut Rough sq m	AREA of Rough, Heather, Gorse sq m	Total Area sq m
1	1	0	0	0	0	980	12,180	1043	2400	650	
2	2	7	3	225	60	625	9720	1820	7100	5200	
3	4	7	1	216	55	694	8220	2412	3100	4400	
4	2	9	2	444	90	836	10,320	2328	2650	5650	
5	3	12	1	202	72	692	11,020	3516	2500	13,600	
6	3	7	2	97	54	530	8870	2808	3900	7900	
7	2	3	1	342	222	440	10,660	2023	2100	6450	
8	2	1	0	18	142	784	0	3350	650	6700	
9	3	5	1	147	215	707	6500	1377	2950	7150	
Front 9	**22**	**51**	**11**	**1691**	**910**	**6288**	**77,490**	**20,677**	**27,350**	**57,700**	**192,106**
10	3	6	0	63	52	545	8050	Double with 8	2100	6100	
11	2	3	0	85	575	595	1160	Double with 7	750	3250	
12	2	5	1	161	153	256	8700	Double with 6	3100	7200	
13	3	5	0	174	94	490	8080	Double with 5	6400	9150	
14	3	13	2	605	78	649	14,510	Double with 4	11,200	12,250	
15	3	5	0	59	73	745	8430	Double with 3	6100	9200	
16	3	6	1	80	57	642	9330	Double with 2	4200	4150	
17	2	1	2	121	150	338	8050	660	4750	8850	
18	3	0	0	0	225	290	17,180	1446	850	600	
Back 9	**24**	**44**	**6**	**1348**	**1457**	**4550**	**83,490**	**2,106**	**39,450**	**60,750**	**193,151**
Total	**46**	**95**	**17**	**3039**	**2367**	**10,838**	**160,980**	**22,783**	**66,800**	**118,450**	**385,257**
Total Bunkers			**112**								

Area of...	Sq m
Cartgate Bunker	138
Cottage Bunker	256
Shell Bunker	299
Hell Bunker	387
Road Hole Bunker	9
Cheape's Bunker	54
Principal's Nose	10+13+15
Spectacles	21+19

Practice Putting Green (PPG)
Old PPG   495 Sq m
New PPG   460 Sq m

NB – Cheape's bunker only counted on hole 2
NB – Back tee on 8th is Up Top & not used in Open.
Number of bunkers that come into play both ways = 7

Total Area of Course =   38.5 Hectares

A common delusion is that fairways should be flat. There are few things more monotonous than playing every shot from a dead flat fairway. The unobservant player never seems to realise that one of the chief charms of the best links is the undulating fairways, where one hardly ever has a level stance or level lie. It is this that makes for variety, and variety is everything in golf.
— Dr MacKenzie, 1920

The variety of the holes at St Andrews have inspired many of the hole's names, such as 'Burn', 'Heathery' and 'High'. However, hole names have changed through the years. In 1821 Martin listed the names of the holes then. The 1st hole played from the Hole o'Hill to the Bridge Hole – the current 17th and was called 'Bridge'. Martin erroneously names the 2nd hole on his 1821 Plan as the 'Cunnen Hole' when in fact the *4th* was the Cunnen Hole. The ballfield or 'ba'field' that the 2nd hole was named after is thought to have existed south of the 17th fairway.

In Chalmer's Plan, printed in 1836, it is unknown who 'Leslie' was. Additionally, it is unclear what 'Rhi' means on the 7th hole. Some suspect however that it is an inaccurate translation of the Scottish word *ree* or *reegh*, meaning a sheep-pen, or small square area open towards the sea or water that receives small vessels.

	Martin's Plan	1821	Chalmer's Plan	1836
	Hole Names		Hole Names	
1	Bridge Hole	361	Bridge Hole or Hole of Leslie	355
2	Cunnen Hole	436	Hole of Bafield	440
3	Cartgate Hole	328	Hole of Cartgate	325
4	Ballfield Hole	378	Hole of Cunnin Links or Ginger Beer Hole	376
5	Hole o'Crofs	503	Hole o'cross	467
6	Muir Hole	379	Hole of Shell or Heather Hole	417
7	Eden Hole	350	Hole of Rhi or High Hole	348
8	Hole o'Turn	152	Hole of Turn or Short Hole	147
9	End Hole	302	Hole of Return or Last Hole	291
OUT		3189		3166
10				
11				
12				
13				
14				
15				
16				
17				
18	Hole o'Hill		Hole o'Hill	
IN		3189		3166
TOTAL		6378		6332

THE MODERN NAMES OF THE HOLES AND THEIR ORIGINS.

1. **Burn**: This hole has had numerous names including 'Hole of Leslie' and 'Bridge Hole.' It was called the Bridge Hole because the first drive was made towards the stone bridge. However at some time, the Bridge was exchanged in favour of the Swilcan Burn – also spelt Swilkin or Swilken in the old days – which has always flowed across the links, but its first reference in a book comes in 1863. The hole has no bunkers now, but up until about 1842 Halket's Bunker existed mid-way between the 1st and 18th fairways, and just west of Granny Clark's Wynd – about where a good drive can land.

2. **Dyke**: The Dyke is the old wall that forms the boundary between the Old Course Hotel and the 17th fairway. Cheape's bunker – originally called Cheap's Dyke Bunker on Chalmer's 1836 Plan – is named after Sir James Cheape, who saved the Links from the rabbit farmers in 1821. His descendant, another James, sold the links to the R&A in 1892, which sold it to the Town in 1893. It is unclear when this name replaced those before it but the Dyke must have been present in 1836 for it to be referred to in the original bunker name as stated above. The name began to appear constantly from about the turn of the 20th century.

3. **Cartgate (out)**: So named because it is close to the cart track that crossed the fairway and led to the beach. These tracks can still been seen on the fairways, especially on

aerial photographs. Cartgate Bunker exists just short of the green.

4. **Ginger Beer**: Old Daw Anderson used to set up his refreshment stall on this hole in the 1850s, but usually sold more potent drinks than the name suggests. The feature bunkers on this hole are named Sutherland's, Students' and Ginger Beer.

5. **Hole o'Cross**: Referred to more locally as 'Hole a'Cross', this hole may have gained its name because of the gully in front of the green that golfers had to cross to get to the green. The Spectacle Bunkers and the Seven Sisters are more identified now than they ever were in days gone by. It is not known when the Seven Sisters became known as such, but there is no reference to that name before 1968.

6. **Heathery (out)**: This name is almost certainly a reference to the green that was covered largely in heather. It is believed to have begun in the 1830s, and one of its first printed references comes in 1836 on Chalmer's Plan of the Links.

7. **High (out)**: This green is the highest on the course, and this is most likely to be the inspiration for the name. Cockle or Shelly Bunker is the feature bunker on this hole and is so named because of the sea-shells (often cockles) that could often be seen on the floor of the bunker.

8. **Short**: The name of this hole is explained by its length. However, prior to this name, it was often called the 'Hole o' Turn', which is perhaps a reference to the fact that this hole turned play in a difference direction – from northwards to eastwards.

9. **End**: The name of this hole is as self-explanatory as the hole before it. It is the final hole on the front nine, and the last hole before players turn back for the clubhouse. The Kruger Bunkers were built during the Boer War (1899–1902) when the British were fighting in the Transvaal, and named after Transvaal's president, Paul Kruger.

10. **Bobby Jones**: This hole was the last hole named. It was named on 10 September 1972 after Bobby Jones, a man who loved St Andrews and was loved by St Andrews. Jones had died in 1971 and this was seen as an ultimate commemorative gesture.

11. **High (In)**: As part of the shared green with the 7th, this hole shares the name, defining its elevation. 'In' further defines it as the hole played on the way back in. The Strath Bunker which guards this green is in reference to the Strath brothers, especially Davie, a friend and golfing partner of Young Tom Morris, who had particular difficulties with this hazard.

12. **Heathery (In)**: Like the 6th, this hole gets its name from the fact it was once covered in heather. The broad fairway and smooth green gives no hint of its former difficulty. Only the five hidden bunkers and tier green provide the strategic test. The curious hidden nature of the fairway bunkers can only be explained by the fact that when the hole is played backwards as it often was, all the bunkers can be seen. Stroke Bunker, the largest of the five, was the most feared. Its name reflects its difficulty – once in it, a player almost certainly lost a stroke.

13. **Hole o'Cross (In)**: This hole shares a green and name with the 5th. Again, it is unclear whether this hole was named 'Hole o'Cross' or 'Hole a'Cross'. Either way it was a troublesome hole, and remains so today with bunkers such as Nicks, The Coffins, Cap's Trap and Lion's Mouth all difficult bunkers to extricate oneself from. Walkinshaw was a particularly difficult bunker for one local golfer whose enthusiasm exceeded his proficiency. Indeed, he ended up in it so often, it now bears his name.

14. **Long**: This is the longest hole on the course and its name reflects this feature. This hole also has the largest bunker, Hell Bunker, which is approximately 140 to 110 yards short of the green, and 27 yards wide. This lurking enemy is particularly troublesome to carry for most

golfers, especially in adverse weather conditions. It has wrecked many good rounds, and also said to have been the spot where lives have ended. Other bunkers of note on this hole are the Beardies, Kitchen and the Graves.

15. **Cartgate (In)₅**: Named for the same reason as the 3rd, this hole has a notable bunker named Sutherland. Its notoriety comes from the determination of the man whose name has become forever linked to the sandy enemy. Mr A.G. Sutherland believed the bunker had keen strategic merit and was aghast when, in 1869, it was filled in. He wrote many letters to the R&A and pleaded his case with vigour, but to no avail. In fact it was only after a late-night dinner when two men, who for many years ran unidentified but were cousins, roused a local gardener from his sleep and bribed him with gold to come and re-cut the bunker. This was done under the cover of darkness, and a simple note with Sutherland's name on it left in the newly formed bunker.

Cottage Bunker on the 15th refers to the old Pilmour Cottage, which is now Pilmour House and part of the Eden Clubhouse – headquarters of the St Andrews Links Trust.

16. **Corner of the Dyke**: The name of this hole refers to the corner of the wall which is behind the green. No dyke is ever known to have run parallel to this hole before or since the railway line existed. The most prominent bunkers are Principal's Nose and Deacon Sime. Principal's Nose is thought to have been named after a principal of St Mary's College in the early 19th century, Mr Haldane, a man who was endowed with a prominent, bulbous nose. It could be true. The Reverend Principal Haldane did have a connection with the course: he both baptised and married Old Tom Morris!

17. **Road**: This hole is simply named after the road which runs behind the green. Its fame is matched by its degree of difficulty as it continues to bring down many top professional golfers. The bunker lurking in front of the green is instrumental in the difficulty of this hole. In an attempt to avoid it, golfers rarely hit good shots into the green. Tommy Nakajima was a victim of the bunker in 1978 when after being on the green for 2, he putted into the bunker and took 5 shots to get out! Six years later, Tom Watson was on the road to victory, but it quickly became the road to ruin when he hit over the green in 1984. The Road Hole has taken many victims. When reporters asked Ballesteros about his bogey on 17, he responded, 'What bogie? For Seve it is a par five.' This often remains the safest way to play the famous hole.

18. **Tom Morris**: Named after Old Tom on the 29th of September 1908, he considered the green on this hole his finest work.

Postscript

A most mysterious anomaly was the Hole of Craig, which is difficult to locate exactly, although it must have been named after the Rock called Doo (or Dhu) Craig in St Andrews Bay.

Traditional Pin Positions

The best way to whet the appetite and improve the game of any golfer is to offer an incentive and provide a reward for high class play, and by high class play is meant simply the best of which each individual is capable. Placing a premium on accuracy with due consideration for length should be the aim of all men who design golf courses, for accuracy in the play signifies skill and skill is generally the master of brute force... the object should be to provide holes of proper length to accommodate the more important clubs after the drive has been made. It naturally follows if this play is carried out that holes of character and variety can be had.

— William Flynn, 1927

After playing a medal round on the Old Course in 1937, Sir Guy Campbell wrote a letter to the Royal and Ancient Golf Club querying the position of some hole locations and requesting the details of 'Traditional positions of the Medal Holes on the Old Course'. Answering the request, the R&A soon laid out the traditional positions in writing. The descriptions were given by the cross bearings of natural objects, and 'the intersection of these lines gives the centre of some 2 yards diameter within which the medal hole is placed'. Directions were supplemented by measurements from fixed objects on or near the green (hydrants, edges of bunkers etc.).

Today some of these fixed objects, most notably the bridge that crossed the railway track, the power lines along the railway track and the hydrants, are long gone. However, the locations of the traditional pin positions can be identified. It is now of interest if any of the positions that were favoured by the authorities in the Haskell and late hickory/early steel shaft period, are still favoured today. If not, have the favoured positions of the flags been tucked closer to bunkers, or nearer the edge of the greens – as has been the trend worldwide – in order to increase the difficulty and precision of the test?

From the diagrams that follow, it is apparent that the positions of some modern hole locations have moved away from the traditional ones. Certain pin positions have migrated away from the centre of greens and towards the edges, slopes or bunkers. Combined with green speeds of between 10 and 11 on the stimpmeter this returns a premium to the control and approach accuracy of golfers, and on a longer hole, often the position of the tee also.

Holes where there has been a significant movement of the pin position towards a slope or hazard include the first green. Here the Swilcan Burn has been brought more into play, and it is almost impossible for golfers to stop their ball short of the pin when it is forward. On the 5th hole also, the cup is often located at the front of the green and while this makes the hole shorter, the slope at the front makes getting an approach shot more difficult. On the 8th hole, the authorities have taken to putting the flag both just over the bunker at the front and near the tricky slopes at the back. On the back nine the 15th and 18th holes are examples of where a slope has been used to limit the sides from which the flag can be approached. On the 15th hole, when the flag is set at the front right position, players must play left of the pin and slightly long to get the best putt back uphill to the hole. Lastly, on the 18th, the Valley of Sin has been used as a defence, and again golfers favour playing over the flag and putting back towards it.

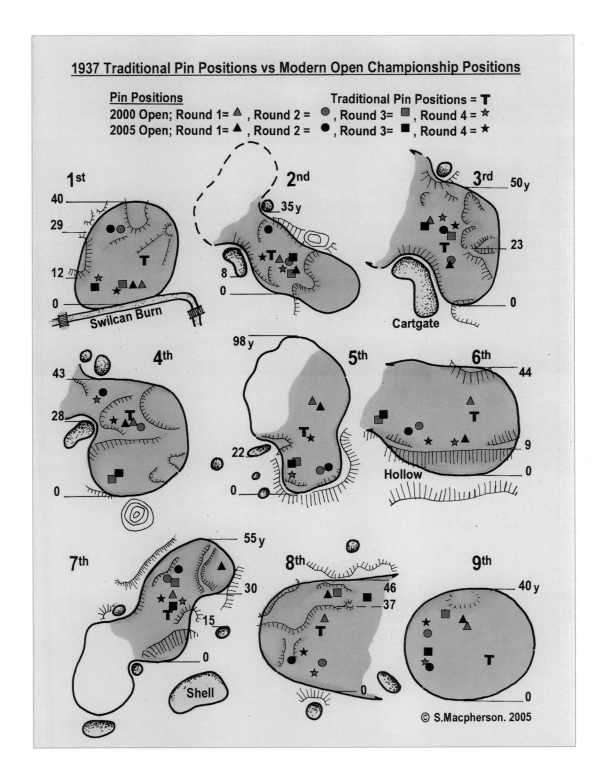

St Andrews: The Evolution of the Old Course · The Impact of Time, Tradition and Technology

178

© S.Macpherson. 2005

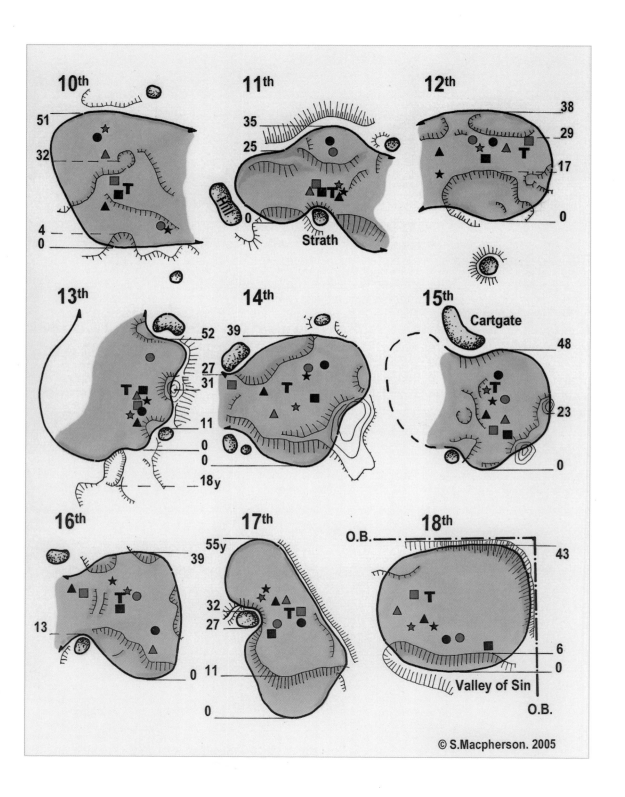

© S.Macpherson. 2005

Does St. Andrews stand where it did? As the most enchanting, exciting, interesting place in which to play golf, and especially top play for any length of time, it certainly does. Perhaps as the strictest and fiercest test of the game of golf as played by the modern champions with the modern ball it has lost some ground. It needs a wind and a fast turf nowadays to worry the champions and make them scratch their heads enough. The ball is hit so far that it can no longer be said that 'the majority of the holes are so disposed that they may be reached with two, or maybe three real good drives.' Though for that matter there are very few courses of which it can be said, and those few seem to many people a weariness of the flesh.

– Bernard Darwin, *Lonsdale Library: The Game of Golf,* 1931

180

The originals of the aerial photographs on the following nine pages are courtesy of Strokesaver.

The Old Course has undergone significant changes since the first ball was struck on the sandy Links. While nature has had her hand in the changes, the hand of man has shaped most recent events.

The aerials of the 2005 course are accurate photos of the holes on the Old Course as they stood then. Modern computer technology has allowed the adaptation of these images. It has been the goal of the author to try and recreate – as accurately as possible with the information at hand – visual representations of the holes as they may have stood over a hundred years earlier in 1900. Some tolerance may, however, have to be given to these images in regard to the size or area of hazards, tees and greens. The representations are only approximations.

For comparison purposes, the two sets of images have been aligned side by side. Captions have been added to assist in highlighting the most significant changes. Further documentation and explanation can be found in the main text, or on pages 191–195 in the Description of Hole Changes: 1842–2005 and pages 196–199 in the list of Hole Changes Chronologically: 1866–2005.

Holes 1 & 18
1900 Open Championship

Hole 1 = 365 yds
Hole 18 = 361 yds

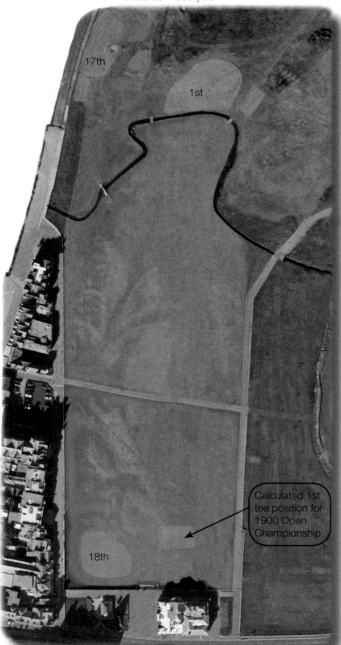

17th

1st

Calculated 1st tee position for 1900 Open Championship

18th

Holes 1 & 18
2005 Open Championship

Hole 1 = 376 yds
Hole 18 = 357 yds

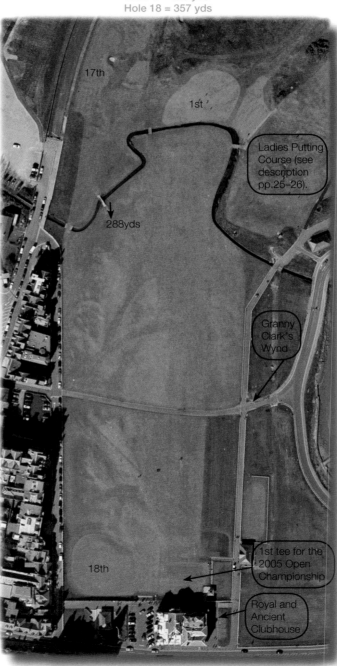

17th

1st

288yds

Ladies Putting Course (see description pp.25–26).

Granny Clark's Wynd

18th

1st tee for the 2005 Open Championship

Royal and Ancient Clubhouse

Recent changes to the Old Course

Of all the holes, these two have perhaps experienced the least change. This said, the notable changes that have occurred between 1900 and 2005 are the several new teeing grounds built on the first hole, starting with the current back tee put in place in late 1904, and the widening of the Swilcan Burn by 2 to 3 feet in 1933.

On the 18th hole, the green was constructed by Old Tom Morris in 1866 and it has changed little between 1900 and today. Perhaps the only notable changes are the right side of the hole becoming out-of-bounds in 1911 and Granny Clark's Wynd being realigned and later tarsealed in 1923.

Recent changes to the Old Course

Many changes have occurred on the 2nd hole. Firstly the tees have moved back. The first new tee built after 1900 was in 1904 when it moved towards the burn. The next tee backed onto the burn and most recently – for the 2005 Open Championship – the tee has moved back onto the 'Himalayas'. The total increase in yardage has been over 50 yards. Secondly, new bunkers have been cut. The bunkers on the right side of the fairway are thought to have been cut just before the 1905 Open, and three of the four bunkers just right of the green were added by 1924. The fourth bunker was added later. Thirdly, the green has been extended to the right. This occurred between 1924–1932.

By comparison, little change has occurred on the famous Road Hole. The road behind the green has been tarsealed and the width of the grass fringe behind the green reduced, but other than that, perhaps only the regular reshaping for repair of the bunkers has caused any obvious change.

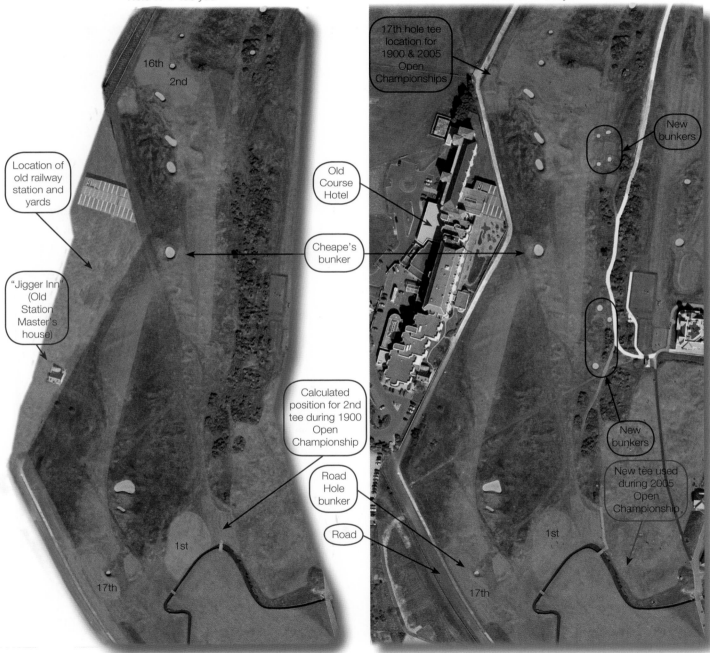

HOLES 2 & 17
1900 OPEN CHAMPIONSHIP

Hole 2 = 402 yds
Hole 17 = 456 yds

16th
2nd

Location of old railway station and yards

"Jigger Inn" (Old Station Master's house)

Cheape's bunker

Calculated position for 2nd tee during 1900 Open Championship

Road Hole bunker

Road

1st

17th

HOLES 2 & 17
2005 OPEN CHAMPIONSHIP

Hole 2 = 453 yds
Hole 17 = 455 yds

17th hole tee location for 1900 & 2005 Open Championships

New bunkers

Old Course Hotel

New bunkers

New tee used during 2005 Open Championship

1st

17th

Holes 3 & 16
1900 Open Championship

Hole 3 = 341 yds
Hole 16 = 338 yds

Holes 3 & 16
2005 Open Championship

Hole 3 = 397 yds
Hole 16 = 423 yds

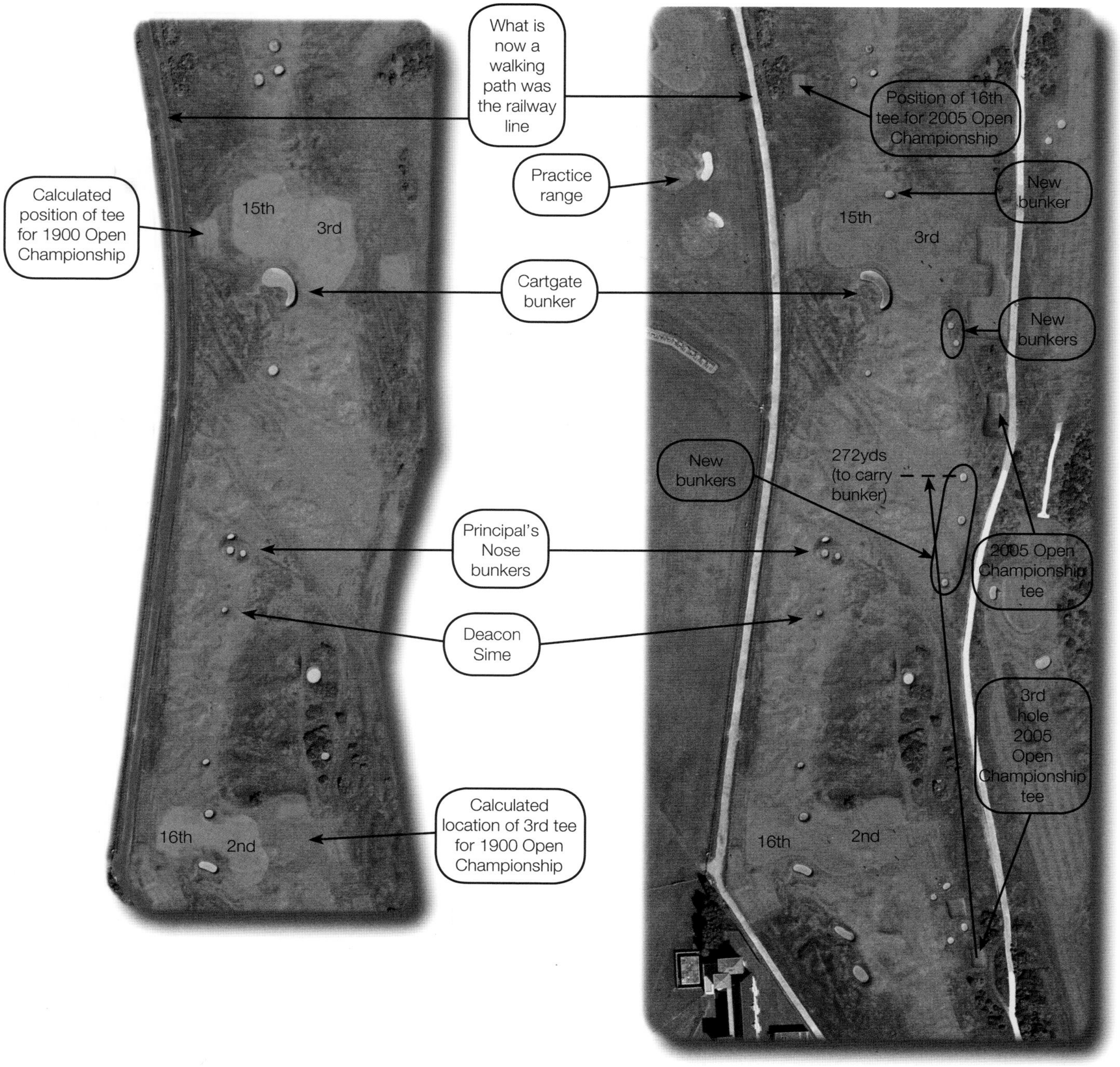

What is now a walking path was the railway line

Position of 16th tee for 2005 Open Championship

Calculated position of tee for 1900 Open Championship

Practice range

New bunker

15th

3rd

15th

3rd

Cartgate bunker

New bunkers

New bunkers

272yds (to carry bunker)

2005 Open Championship tee

Principal's Nose bunkers

Deacon Sime

3rd hole 2005 Open Championship tee

16th

2nd

16th

2nd

Calculated location of 3rd tee for 1900 Open Championship

The tee on the 3rd hole has moved back several times, adding about 56 yards to the hole. Additionally, up to five new bunkers have been cut, probably between 1905 and 1908, at various intervals along the right side of the hole to provide golfing hazards where the gorse once grew.

The 16th hole has had at least three new back tees between 1900 and 2005. The first was built about 1924, the second in 1936 and the latest in 1997. These have added no less than 85 yards to the length of the hole. The railway line down the right of this hole became out-of-bounds in 1911.

Recent changes to the Old Course

At least two new bunkers were cut on the right side of the fourth fairway in 1905. One more bunker was cut next to Students' Bunker between 1920 and 1924. Since then only two new tees have been built. The first in 1963 added 46 yards, and then an extension in 2003/2004 that provided a further 16 yards.

On the 15th hole, apart from the five tees that were built between 1904 and 1997 and added 91 yards to the length of the hole, the most interesting changes are to the bunkers. In 1905 a new bunker was cut in the left front of the green, and then in 1949 Hull bunker – that was located adjacent to Cottage Bunker – was filled in. This is the last bunker know to have been filled in or cut on the Old Course.

HOLES 4 & 15
1900 OPEN CHAMPIONSHIP

Hole 4 = 385 yds
Hole 15 = 365 yds

HOLES 4 & 15
2005 OPEN CHAMPIONSHIP

Hole 4 = 480 yds
Hole 15 = 456 yds

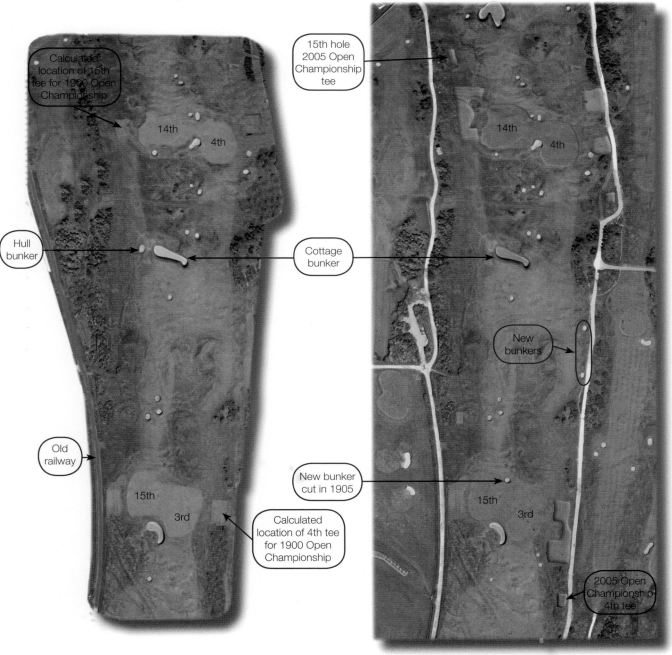

Calculated location of 15th tee for 1900 Open Championship

14th

4th

Hull bunker

Cottage bunker

Old railway

15th

3rd

Calculated location of 4th tee for 1900 Open Championship

15th hole 2005 Open Championship tee

14th

4th

New bunkers

New bunker cut in 1905

15th

3rd

2005 Open Championship 4th tee

HOLES 5 & 14
1900 OPEN CHAMPIONSHIP

Hole 5 = 533 yds
Hole 14 = 516 yds

Calculated location of 14th tee for 1900 Open Championship

13th

5th

Calculated location of tee for 1900 Open Championship

14th

4th

HOLES 5 & 14
2005 OPEN CHAMPIONSHIP

Hole 5 = 568 yds
Hole 14 = 618 yds

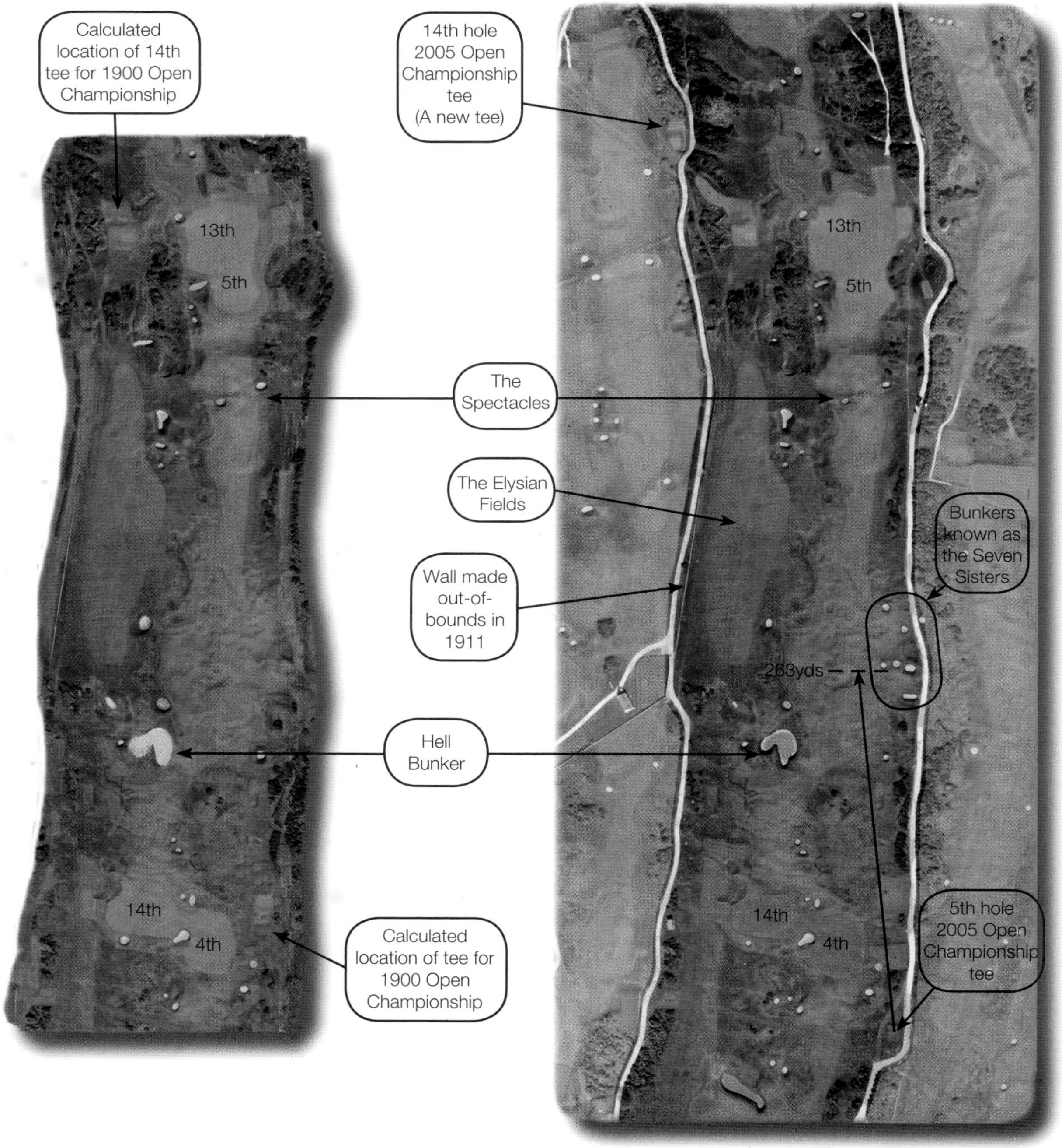

14th hole 2005 Open Championship tee (A new tee)

13th

5th

The Spectacles

The Elysian Fields

Bunkers known as the Seven Sisters

Wall made out-of-bounds in 1911

263yds

Hell Bunker

5th hole 2005 Open Championship tee

14th

4th

The biggest change to the 5th hole has perhaps been down the right side of the fairway. Where once there were whins, now there is a nest of bunkers known as the Seven Sisters. These were cut between 1905 and 1908 in an attempt to narrow the fairway. The last new tee, built about 1936, added 46 yards to the hole. This tee has since been remodelled with the path around it altered, but no significant change has occurred to the hole's length.

The 14th hole stretched the most in length during this period. For the 2005 Open Championship it was measured at 618 yards – over 100 yards longer than it was for the Open in 1900. It has taken five new teeing grounds to achieve this increase over the years, but the tees have not just gone back, they have also moved to the right. This has somewhat altered the strategy off the tee, with the angle of play now being away from the wall.

The bunkers on the 14th hole have changed shape slightly, with some gaining size, and others losing. Interestingly, documents suggest that sometime between 1897 and 1905, the small bunker to the West (right) of Hell was cut. No reason for this change has been found.

Recent changes to the Old Course

The 6th hole has had several new bunkers and tee extensions. As for the bunkers, past the first two bunkers, a cluster of four bunkers was cut on the right side of the fairway. This most likely occurred over a four-year period between 1905 and 1908. Later, between 1920 and 1924 the long bunker about 240 yards from the current Open Championship tee was cut. As regards the teeing grounds, through the years three new back tees have been built and added 67 yards to the length of the hole.

In contrast to most holes, the 13th hole has lost more bunkers than it has gained. Between 1924 and 1932, two bunkers just forward and left of the front tees were filled in. The hole has now gained length, with tees constructed for the 2005 Open Championship being built on the adjacent Eden course.

Holes 6 & 13
1900 Open Championship

Hole 6 = 345 yds
Hole 13 = 403 yds

Holes 6 & 13
2005 Open Championship

Hole 6 = 412 yds
Hole 13 = 465 yds

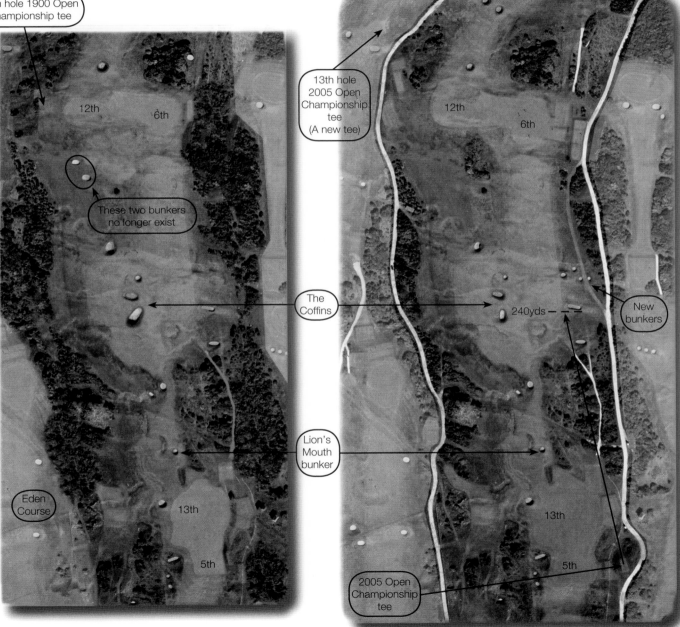

13th hole 1900 Open Championship tee

These two bunkers no longer exist

The Coffins

Lion's Mouth bunker

Eden Course

12th

6th

13th

5th

13th hole 2005 Open Championship tee (A new tee)

12th

6th

240yds

New bunkers

13th

5th

2005 Open Championship tee

Holes 7 & 12
1900 Open Championship

Hole 7 = 333 yds
Hole 12 = 318 yds

Eden Estuary

Calculated location of 12th tee for 1900 Open Championship

7th

11th

6th

12th

Calculated location of 7th tee for 1900 Open Championship

Holes 7 & 12
2005 Open Championship

Hole 7 = 390 yds
Hole 12 = 348 yds

Construction of the sea wall added greater distance between the green and the Eden Estuary

12th tee for 2005 Open Championship

7th

11th

Hill bunker

297yds from tee to Shelly bunker

Crushed shell paths circumnavigate entire course

6th

12th

7th hole 2005 Open Championship tee

Hill bunker

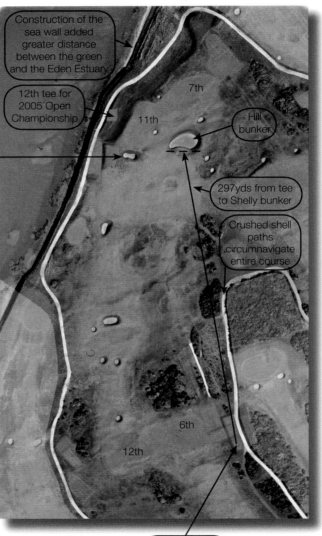

Little physical change has occurred to the 7th hole. One bunker in front of the tees was filled in about 1920, while the remaining bunkers are just better maintained. The hole appears to have gained some length, but with few documented changes to the teeing grounds, the gain in yardage may be due in part to extensions in the teeing ground, but also in new methods of measuring the hole and its slight dog-leg.

The 12th hole has had a reasonably quiet period. The most radical changes have been to the back tee which has come (for the 1955 Open) and gone (for the 1964 Open) and was reconstructed in a slightly different form for the 2005 Open Championship.

Recent changes to the Old Course

The short par 3 8th hole has had its green relaid in late 1904 and its teeing grounds enlarged and extended. Additionally, the bunkers short of the green have been reduced in size. No significant change has occurred to the hole in the last fifty years.

The opposite and opposing par 3 11th hole has also experienced relatively little change. Apart from the Championship tee being extended back for the 1927 and 1939 Opens, the only other change has been behind the green where, due to erosion, a sea wall has been constructed to keep the Eden estuary further from the green. The direct effect of this sea wall has been to reduce the chance of players who hit their ball over the green reaching the water.

HOLES 8 & 11
1900 OPEN CHAMPIONSHIP

Hole 8 = 139 yds
Hole 11 = 148 yds

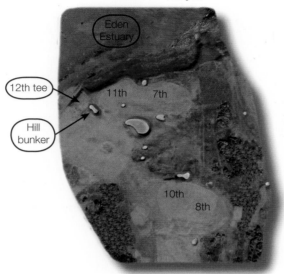

HOLES 8 & 11
2005 OPEN CHAMPIONSHIP

Hole 8 = 175 yds
Hole 11 = 174 yds

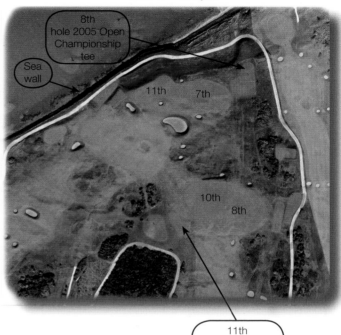

Time, Tradition and Technology: The impact on the Old Course

There are few problems more difficult to solve than the problem of what actually constitutes an ideal links or an ideal hole, but it is comparatively safe to say that the ideal hole is one that affords the greatest pleasure to the greatest number, gives the fullest advantage for accurate play, stimulates players to improve their game, and which never becomes monotonous.

– Dr Alister MacKenzie, *The Spirit of St Andrews*, 1933

The physical state of the Old Course has evolved in fits and starts. The growth spurts can be linked to such things as the various changes in the ball and implements, the improvement in Open Championship scoring, the greater distance the ball can be hit, the increasing popularity of the game, and the need to move spectators around the course during the Open Championship. The following fold-out spreadsheet has been compiled by taking snapshots of the course set-up during the 27 Open Championships it has hosted since the first in 1873. To provide further insights the length of the holes for a few other important tournaments and lengths as documented on influential maps and plans of the course have been included as well.

As for the early Open Championships, it is difficult to ascertain the exact length of the course due to the vagueness of historical records on the subject. From about 1900 however, a greater level of detail is increasingly available. And more recently, even stroke averages for individual holes are available. As a result, a picture of the distance and difficulty of each hole emerges.

To help indicate the elasticity in the course and the periods when the course has had considerable periods of change, a colour-coded system has been adopted. When any significant change to the length of a hole has occurred – significant being a change of 11 yards or more – the hole's length has been assigned a colour. If the hole was lengthened, then the change is highlighted in green, if the hole was shortened from its previous length, then the change is highlighted in blue. Looking at the chart, it is immediately obvious that in some years, such as 1905, the Old Course was only lengthened, but fifty years later some holes were lengthened, yet others shortened.

Additionally, a coloured continuum runs along the bottom of the spreadsheet showing when different types of ball came into play. It is interesting to correlate the changes in the golf ball, to the changes made to the Old Course. It can easily be concluded that the Old Course, the Open Championship and the game of golf has changed considerably in many ways.

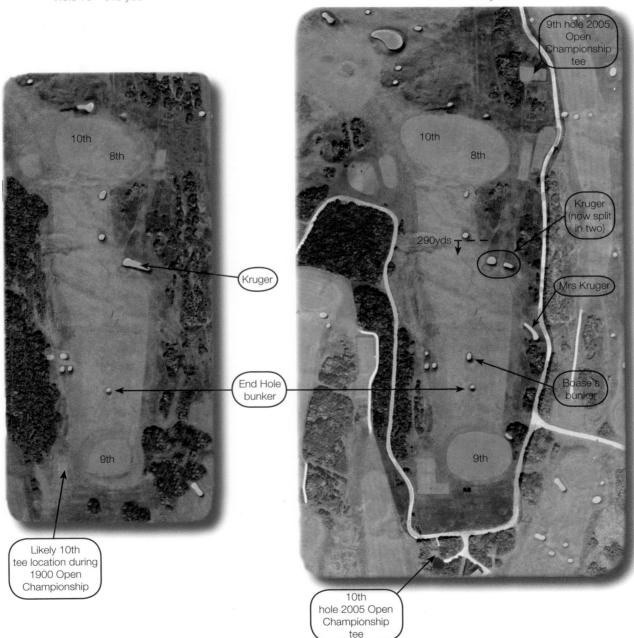

HOLES 9 & 10
1900 OPEN CHAMPIONSHIP

Hole 9 = 273 yds
Hole 10 = 312 yds

HOLES 9 & 10
2005 OPEN CHAMPIONSHIP

Hole 9 = 352 yds
Hole 10 = 380 yds

10th

8th

Kruger

End Hole
bunker

9th

Likely 10th
tee location during
1900 Open
Championship

9th hole 2005
Open
Championship
tee

Kruger
(now split
in two)

290yds

Mrs Kruger

Boase's
bunker

10th

8th

End Hole
bunker

9th

10th
hole 2005 Open
Championship
tee

189

Recent changes to the Old Course

Several bunker changes have taken place on the 9th hole. Firstly Kruger has been built and then split in two, and Mrs Kruger and Cronje added about 1901. Then – and perhaps most notably – between 1908 and 1920 Boase's bunker was cut in the centre of the fairway. The hole has also been extended in length with almost 80 yards being added in total.

The 10th hole, also know as Bobby Jones, had up to seven bunkers cut between 1900 and 2005, but only three survive today. These are located in a cluster about 100 yards forward of the tees and just to the left of the fairway. Three new back tees have caused the hole to gain 68 yards in length, with the latest tee (built in 1997) accounting for 37 of these yards.

Description of Hole Changes – 1842–2005

A good golf course is like good music or good anything else: it is not necessarily a course that appeals the first time one plays over it, but one which grows on the player the more frequently he visits it.
— Dr MacKenzie, 1920

J. Balfour Melville Report, 1887		
Hole	**Yards**	**Casting his eye back 40 years: the course in 1842**
1	360	Hole on green beside road. Its hazards were the road across the links, the burn, the bunker on one side of the putting green, as well as the turnpike road on the other. Making this a limited green, with narrow approach to it, flanked by severe hazards. (Author's note: Left hand course – Current 17th Green)
2	450	The tee of the second hole used to be, of course, near the road. There were then no separate teeing grounds, but the rule was to tee within 8 club lengths of the hole. The ground between the wall and the bunkers toward the corner of the dyke, which is now often preferred as the shortest approach to the hole, was covered with thick whins and was then quite unplayable. Consequently players were obliged to cross the course, and approach the hole by the right of the bunkers. The whins on the right made the course narrow in that direction, and the low ground to the right of the putting-green could not be played on account of the whins and rough grass, so that the hole was much more difficult both in playing and approaching than now. The putting-green, too, which was formerly on a slope, has been made quite level.
3	335	There used to be a thick bank of whins all along the left of the course by the side of the present railway, and the whins and rough grass on the right made it necessary to play straight in the centre, where was the Principal's Nose, with its little satellite of Tam's Coo. [Now filled up] The smaller bunkers, too, short of these, presented together with them dangerous traps. There was very little room indeed to pass them on either side. The hole was always in the centre of the green, so that the bunker which crosses the Links beside it had to be played over, else a considerable distance was lost by going to the right of left of it.
4	375	Formerly the whins encroached so much on either side that it was necessary that the tee stroke should be played on or over the table in front of the tee, and then a very narrow course was left up to the hole, which was on a narrower putting-green than now, and it was usually placed nearer the bunkers.
5	540	This hole is more altered than any other on the Links, and sadly destroyed. The tee stroke used always to be played to the right of the big bunker with the uncouth name (Hell), unless when now and then some huge driver 'swiped over H... at one immortal go'. The second stroke was always to the left on to the Elysian Fields, where the grass was then short and smooth like a putting-green. The third had to navigate the intricate 'Beardies', and the fourth was across a wide, staring, horrid bunker, beyond which was a beautiful putting-green. Altogether this used to be the finest golfing hole, certainly on the Links and probably in the world. There were beautiful lies when play was correct, very difficult hazards, and a perfect putting green.
6	370	
7	350	
8	150	
9	300	
10		
11		
12		
13		
14		The long hole home, like the long hole out, has been entirely changed. The big yawning bunker in front of the tee, that was ready to catch a topped ball, and to hold it, is almost entirely avoided, while the 'beardies', where so many balls used to be kidnapped, and from which escape was not always made with the loss of only one stroke, are never looked at.
15		The whins on the left, where the first stroke was played, protruded far into the links, and the ball was either caught in them or had to be played right in the centre. There was no possible play to the left of the table, and the second stroke had to fly right over that table; if that stroke were at all short, the ground, which sloped down towards dangerous bunkers, drew the ball into them.
16		
17		
18		
Total Yardage	6332*	* Measurement taken from W. Chalmers 1836 map of the Old Course.
Other Changes		

Above: Arthur James Balfour, formerly Minister in Charge of Scottish Affairs, opening the 1894 Autumn Medal meeting at St Andrews. He was later to become the British Prime Minister from 1902–1905. Note Old Tom in the background.

J. Balfour Melville Report, 1887

Hole	Yards	Description of the course in 1887
1	360	The first hole on the medal round now is quite different. It is placed just beyond the burn, on a flat smooth, broad green to the right of the course. The only hazards in the hole are the road across the Links and the burn. There are none whatever close to the hole.
2	450	At present the tee to this hole is on the right of the Links, while the whins have been driven back and the low ground to the right near the hole made quite playable, the hole can be played without any bunkers, or any hazards of any kind. Of course, if the player goes off the line, he has to encounter some hazards. The putting-green, as has been said, is now on a flat, and not a slope.
3	335	The tee is now on the right side of the green, and the ball from it is easily played to the right of the Principal's Nose, while the hole being to the right of the putting-green, it is readily approached without having to crossing the bunker.
4	375	The whins having now been driven back, the ball can be played to the right of the table. The course is clear for the second stroke, and the hole is placed to the right, far from the bunkers.
5	540	Now the play is quite different. The Elysian Fields are avoided, and the hole is played on a lower level, where high whins formerly grew, which made play there impossible. There is hardly any hazard; there are no bunkers of any consideration, and the approach to the green is a blind stroke without any bunker between. The hole is altogether much tamer, and less interesting, as well as easier. The young Laird of the Links would do the game an unspeakable benefit if he would plough up the low course, or honeycomb it with bunkers, so as to compel players to return to the old line on the Elysian Fields.
6	370	The sixth hole is also much altered. It used to be one of the most dangerous on the Links, but two or three large and important bunkers have been filled up to make a double course. The reduces the number of hazards materially, and the whins have so much disappeared that it is safe to go round the bunkers, playing well to the right, instead of being compelled to play over them. The putting-green, too, is greatly changed. Formerly it had no turf, but was merely earth, heather, and shells, from which it got its name of the heather hole, or the 'hole o' shell', but it has now been turfed and, like the other greens, is carefully kept.
7	350	The course here was a narrow one, so that the first stroke was necessarily played over – very often, unfortunately into – the bunker that crosses the green; but there was not much room to go either side of it. The putting-green of the high hole, which was always placed near the Eden, was then surrounded with thick bent grass, leaving a very limited space near the hole. Besides, the ground was sandy ad soft. The deterioration of this putting-green has been arrested by the growth of rank sea-grass on the banks of the Eden, which prevents the sand from being blown onto the Links. These bents were a serious hazard.
8	150	The short hole is not much changed, except that the putting green is wider than it used to be.
9	300	9, or last hole going out, used to be principally heather, but a large portion of that heather was some years ago taken up and relaid with turf. The putting-green is also much broader than formerly.
10		The principal difference on the first hole here is that the course was formerly narrower, and the heather has been replaced by turf. If a ball was at all drawn to the left, it used to be either lost in the whins or so embedded among them that it had to be played out at the sacrifice of at least one stroke, if not more; but now it often lies very tolerably even there, and can be played forward. Near the hole, too, the ground short of it and the left was so covered with think grass that if the ball got there it had an exceedingly bad lie. Now the ball has a fair lie where it used to be so heavy.
11		The short hole home is not much changed, except that the bents have disappeared, as already stated, while the putting-green is much harder and broader.
12		In driving this hole there is now plenty of room to pass the bunker that crosses the green on either side of it. The rough ground at both ends of the putting-green has disappeared, and the putting-green itself has been turfed as is no longer shelly.
13		The next hole used to be one of the most difficult on the Links, and more medals have been lost at it than at any other. It has a good many hazards yet, but two of the largest have been filled up to make a course to the left, as well as one to the right. In former times Allan Robertson used to play the first stroke often with the short spoon , short of all the bunkers, and the third from behind the hill with the short spoon also, on to the green. Now there is plenty of room to avoid the bunkers, both on the right and on the left: players can have a long stroke off the tee, while long drivers may be on the green in two, and some of the worst bunkers not played over at all.
14		Now the play is on the lower ground to the left of the Elysian Fields, thus crossing the bunker diagonally. This line used to be absolutely impossible. There are now no hazards there, or only trifling ones. The hole itself is always on the right or left of the putting-green instead of the centre, just between two bunkers, the approach to which used to be at the sacrifice of some distance to circumvent the bunkers.
15		Now the hole can be played to the left or right without much risk.
16		Formerly there was little room to pass the 'Principal's Nose' on either side from the tee; and it, and 'Tammy's Coo' beside it, were ugly hazards. The line of the whins alongside the present railway was an additional difficulty if the right-hand course was adopted; and if the left, the ground which is now clear was then impracticable from whins. The putting-green itself, as has been mentioned before, has been levelled, so that the hole, instead of being on a slope, as formerly, is now on a flat table, and the low ground to the left of it is no longer covered with whins. Note: "Tam's Coo" is now filled up.
17		Playing off from the hole at the dyke, the ground in front is now cleared of the dense clump of whins that used to be immediately in front of the tee. There has been no other alteration on this hole of great consequence, except that the grass, which is sometimes long and heavy after much rain, is mowed with a scythe, and a large bank of rushes has been removed.
18		The Principal difference on the last hole is in the putting-green. That has been quite changed by the formation of an artificial table-land, which forms a beautiful green. Formerly the hole was on broken ground in a hollow, with the ground sloping down on both sides. A separate teeing-ground has been provided at each hole, which preserves the putting-greens from being broken by the teeing strokes.
Total Yardage	6460	
Other Changes		

Horace Hutchinson, 1913

Hole	Yards	Comparing the 1913 medal course to Mr Balfour's 1887 course
1	365	The last paragraph may stand for a perfectly adequate description of the hole to-day.
2	402	The hole in the old days in fact was the hole as we play it now when the course is set for going out by the left, except that the whins on the left have all vanished. But we have to observe that bunkers have been put in on the right to take place of the whins which have been worn away. The hole is, I think, just as difficult now as in the latter days of Mr Balfour's memoir.
3	353	Nowdays, we play the tee shot far to the right, without (if we are lucky) getting into grave trouble, and really the approach is only made more open by doing so. Some bunkers have been cut which catch the slightly sliced tee shot; but the wildly sliced tee shot escapes them. Some catchy new bunkers have also been cut on the right of the plateau near the green; but it has always to be remembered that in 1887, the date of Mr Balfour's writing, dense whins came up to these right-hand bunkers, both those that trap the sliced tee shot and those nearer the green. All that right-hand country was unplayable.
4	417	What has happened at this hole, since the (previous) writing is again that a great pushing back of the whins has taken place; but, by the way of a little compensation, bunkers, as at the third hole, have been cut to catch the sliced tee shot, and also the approach shot, if that be sliced. I think that the cutting of these bunkers has perhaps made both this and the preceding hole a little harder than in 1887; but it always has to be noted, where bunkers have replaced whins, that the former are more "chancy": a lucky ball lies well amongst them. The whins, if closely growing, are inexplorable: they always exact the penalty.
5	533	This is a tremendous indictment, and a really heroic suggestion. It is not for a moment to be denied that it would make the hole far more dramatic, both in coming out and going home, if it were even now adopted; but we do not want the outgoing and incoming streams at St Andrews concentrated more into one channel than they now are... We now follow that lower line, so disdained by Mr Balfour, to the hole. Whins have been further worn away, even than in his time, and a sprinkling of bunkers have replaced them. But the hole, even as it is, is a very fine one... What with the new ball, and a new spirit of daring, fostered by less strict and painful necessity to keep to the narrowest line, the man who willendeavour with his second shot to steer between the bigger and the lesser of the two bunkers facing him on the hillside before the hole, or even to make a big carry of them, will find that this hole is still capable of arousing the great emotions...
6	370	The description is as of a putting-green in some dreadful nightmare... (Mr Balfour) writes to show the modern golfing man how easy life is made for him to-day... The modern alteration in this hole that we have to note is as in the proceeding – much, though not quite so much, wearing away of the whins on the right and a somewhat inadequate substitution of them by occasional bunkers. Be it noted that occasional bunkers are all that is possible in that mode, for if the heroic counsel addressed to "the Young Laird" had been followed and any extent of the course been ploughed, the winds would have scattered the sand ubiquitously and made it a Sahara.
7	345	It is at this high hole that the most considerable difference of all has been made, by the wearing away of the whins since the date of writing. It is recorder of a an eminent professor of St Andrews University that one day, in the early nineties, he was seen to come to the scene of his learned duties labouring under uncontrolable excitement. Sympathetic inquiries elicited that this was occasioned by his having discovered "a new line to the high hole". The new line is now that most familiar route to the right of the high hill: but up to date the whins on the right had come in a solid battalion to the foot of the hill and half-way up it, so the common route was to the left, on the low ground, with the tee shot; which meant a most perilous, beside a longer, second shot over that high-cliffed bunker (Hill). This hole has, therefore, become appreciably easier than at the time of Mr Balfour's writing.
8	142	In regard to that hole, there has been little change in the years that have passed since that brief comment was put on record.
9	303	As to that hole, it is to be noted that there has been a considerable further wearing away of the heather in recent years. On the other hand, several bunkers have been introduced, one to catch a topped tee shot, another to trap one that is pulled, and there is also an insidious little bunker on the left near edge of the green which often grips an approach that is slightly pulled. And now that we have arrived at the half-way house we may note that at several of these out-going holes, as well as many of the in-coming ones, new teeing grounds have been made, farther back than any ever known to Mr Balfour, so that the whole course has been stretched out to meet, more or less, the needs of the india-rubber cored balls.
10	312	The wearing away of whins and heather has now further proceeded there also, but again bunkers have been introduced. There are bunkers to catch a topped tee shot, and also one called "Kruger", signifying the date of its creation, which a sliced drive finds its way into. Where by the hole is made slightly more difficult than when Mr Balfour wrote of it.
11	148	Neither have I much change to record at this hole, but I will say, with confidence in winning general agreement for the comment, that the green is even now narrow enough to be the cause of infinite vexation of spirit and of many rent scoring cards.
12	318	To this account there is nothing to add, except that the whins are further worn back. Mr Balfour's statement of the case holds good now, as when it was first made.
13	413	...since the date of his writing there has been very extensive wearing away of the whins on the right, to the far greater ease of both tee shot and second. If a man cannot get home in two, he can lie safely on that plateau ground to the right of the little pot bunker (little but with a large "catchment area") in the centre of the valley. All that upper plateau was a dense sea of whins even in 1887, and the whins came well up to the right-hand edge of the green. The tee shot had also a far narrower space for safety to the right of the bunkers, and no one now regards this hole as inspiring any mighty terrors.
14	516	The play to this hole has undergone drastic change since Mr Balfour's writing, and in a manner which brings it back more into conformity with his earlier than his later account. The tee has been brought far back, and far out to the right, and the tee shot is very seldom played onto that lower course of which he speaks, but it is aimed to go between the "Beardies" and the wall on the right. A big drive may carry the "Beardies". From this big shot now it is possible to carry Hell bunker, and get a good lie, straight for the hole, but in 1887 if you had drawn a line from the right-hand edge of that "bunker with the uncouth name" ...straight to the hole, all to the right of that line would have been a sea of whins where now is tolerable fair lying. Still, however, the normal mode of playing the second shot is to the left of Hell, whence is an easier approach than from the right, but still a parlous difficult one, by reason of a steep cliff face to the plateau on which is the green. The steep face creates almost as great a difficulty as that which the historian records as lost by the removal of the hole from its old perilous place between the two bunkers.
15	395	No previous account bears such eloquent testimony as this to the vanishing of the whins. To get into the whin on the left, on the way to that hole now, would need a herculean pull. The menace of the right-hand whins is very much less – they have gone back by fifty yards or more – since Mr Balfour knew the hole, and this is true of their menace for the second no less than for the tee shot. A very well placed bunker has been let into the face of the brae on the left side of the line of the approach (Sutherland??). It would have been in the absolute direct line of the old second shot "straight over the table".
16	338	Except that a new tee has been made for this hole, farther back than the writer (Mr Balfour)... can ever have seen it, his comparison gives a perfectly good description of the hole as we play it to-day.
17	456	This account hardly does justice for all the terrors of this hole. Yet they have been somewhat mitigated in the years that have passed since it was written. For "scythe" we may now read "mowing machines". At that date the rule was that if the errant ball went to the right, into that grimy cabbage-patch described as "the station-master's garden", it had to be treated as "lost". Now all that extramural region falls under the far lighter penalty enacted for "ball out of bounds". Moreover, the road on the right of the green has its side banked up, and is by no means the place of utter perdition that it was in Mr Balfour's time.
18	361	...there is no more to be said in addition to his account of this last hole.
Total Yardage	6487	
Other Changes		

Guy C. Campbell, 1933

Hole	Yards	Comparing the 1933 medal course to Mr Balfour's 1887 course
1	368	Note: G.C.C. clarifies that "the bunker on one side of the putting green" Mr Balfour refers to is indeed "the famous Road-Hole pot bunker."
2	401	
3	356	
4	427	Note: The old teeing ground was at the back of the third green – immediately in line with the position of the medal hole as played nowadays – and close to the pot bunker guarding the present 15th green. The table was the table-land between Robb's bunkers and the Strath up which the direct line to the fourth hole now runs. From this table the line to the old hole lay between the long bunker from which Bobby Jones got his 2 against Roper and the "dead elephant" just short of the present green.
5	530	Note: The "Young Laird" was Cheape of Strathtyrum, and at this date the Links had not become the property of the Town. Had effect been given to Balfour's wish, the Long Hole home would, for modern conditions, have required a different fairway running to the right of the wall where the Eden Course now runs, leaving the whole massif of "Hell" to be either carried or avoided by the right with the second shot: but who shall say that in such a case the 14th hole, like the 5th, would not have been far greater?
6	367	
7	352	
8	150	
9	306	
10	312	
11	164	
12	314	Note: The bunker alluded to is the long hidden bunker that is now often found by a topped or skied tee-shot played direct at the hole. By "green" in this connection Balfour means fairway.
13	410	
14	527	Note: The two bunkers to which James Balfour refers are those which today guard the medal position of the fourth hole, one of which catches the slightly pulled second, the other the over-played straight shot.
15	409	Note: by "to be played right in the centre", He (Mr Balfour) means that the drive had to be played down an avenue flanked by whins. Note: The table is the table-land referred to in the description of the fourth hole...The dangerous bunkers are that little cluster of pots known today as Robb's bunkers.
16	348	
17	467	Note: It is interesting to see how casually Balfour dismisses what today, with all its width of fairway, is one of the most telling holes on the Links. He makes no mention of the Station-master's Garden, the Scholar's Bunker, the famous pot bunker and the road, but perhaps this is not so odd when we remember how narrow and teeming with hazards was the course as he first knew it.
18	364	Note: I wonder how many of the millions who have played this hole since the date of James Balfour's book ever considered that this wonderful green was the work of man and not of nature?
Total Yardage	6572	
Other Changes		

Hole	Yards	Comparing the modern course to the 1933 medal course
1	376	There has been no change to this hole since 1933. However in 2003–2004, a new practice putting green was constructed to the right of the teeing grounds.
2	453	There has been little change to this hole since 1933. The most significant alteration has been the addition of the new championship tee this year to the right of the Swilcan Burn in the area known as the Ladies Putting Course. It was anticipated this new tee would bring Cheape's bunker into play during the 2005 Open Championship. The whins down the right still come into play, as does the sea-shell covered path which winds its way around the outskirts of the Old Course. The hole is usually cut on top of the plateau for competitions but down to the right at other times. The tee behind the green is only occasionally used in the winter.
3	397	A new Championship tee was added to this hole about 1993, but otherwise the landing area is still very broad with only a few whins past the last bunker in the landing area and to the left of the shell-covered path which would cause any problems. However, with new equipment strong hitters can reach the green so Cartgate bunker can be in play. Most players lay-up short of the bunkers when they play this hole.
4	480	Around 1963 a back new tee was added to lengthen the hole by approximately 46 yards. A further extension was made in 2004, otherwise this hole remains similar to its state in 1933. Whins still cover the hill right of the landing area and 130 yards short of the green, and this is the most significant hazard off the tee. The line off the tee is generally at the small hut in the distance. With the ball travelling further, and players able to hit shorter irons into the green, the "dead elephant" or mound in fornt of the green caused less problems now than it did in 1933.
5	568	A new Championship has been added to this hole also, probably around 1936. Almost 50 yards were added, and the tee was pushed slightly to the right to bring the "Seven Sisters" into play on the right of the fairway. However with no changes since, this hole plays very short today. Indeed, during the 2005 Open Championship it was the second easiest hole on the course. With the average drive going 298.5 yards, almost all players reached the green in two shots. As a result it gave up 15 eagles – more than any other hole.
6	412	In the early 1940s a new back tee was added that extended the hole by 45 yards. This tee was located at what could now be described as the side of the fifth green. But what it did do is bring the bunkers cut in 1905 back into play. Time and technology eroded this relationship. For safety and to add a slight dog-leg to the tee shot, a new elevated tee was built in 1997 away from the green. This is still in play. However nowadays, particularly off the medal tees, only the last of the bunkers down the left of the fairway, if any, are in play for the longer players. It must be acknowledged that this is a relatively tame hole today and perhaps only when the flag is positioned just over the swale, is the hole problematic.
7	390	Since 1933, the Championship tee has been extended twice. The most recent change was about 1997, when it was shifted slightly to the right. Shorter hitters may still catch the thinning whins on the right and short of the plateau, but most golfers can make the carry and the professionals hit an iron to stay short of Shelly bunker.
8	175	A back tee on top of the ridge was created that lengthens the hole to 192 yards, but this is only used in casual play and occasionally in the winter.
9	352	About 1936, the Championship tee was extended back about 50 yards in an attempt to bring the End Hole bunker back into play. Kruger catches very few shots off the 9th tee (occasionally some off the 10th), but the whins down the left still swallow the pulled shot. The heather down the left is still low and relatively sparse, making it very little of a hazard. A new low profile tee has been created slightly further back and to the left of the current back tee. It's located on the New Course, but it was not used for the 2005 Open Championship.
10	380	The tenth hole has undergone little change in the past 70 years. Similar to the 9th hole, the whins still prevail down the left, though possibly a little further back than previously. The heather between the whins and the fairway is somewhat stunted by the constant wear, but otherwise the fairway, green and its bunkers remain untouched. Only the teeing ground, which was extended back almost 40 yards into the whins in 1997, is new.
11	174	While odd changes to the teeing ground have occurred there have throughout time been very few changes to this superb hole. Perhaps the greatest may be more linked to the condition of the course. With improved turf maintenance, this green often is firm and keen. Putting can be treacherous when the wind blows and the green runs fast.
12	348	The tee for this hole has frequently moved, and the teeing ground has been adapted accordingly. In 2004 the Open tee was relocated back to an area behind the eleventh green, where it was for the 1955 Open. This was in an attempt to bring the bunker in front of the green back into play and stop players hitting their drives over the green and chipping back to the hole.
13	465	The Coffins still pose an impending threat at this hole, but only in certain winds. The medal tee was moved to it current location in 1905, and has undergone very few changes since except in 1997 the tee was extended back 8 yards. However this year has witnessed perhaps the most significant change. The teeing ground has been extended back onto the Eden course gaining a further 34 yards. As the 2005 Open proved, the Coffin bunkers were in play, and as a result of that and flag positions pushed to the right of the green, this hole played second hardest overall.
14	618	Since 1933, the most recent change was about 1936 when a new Championship Tee was built. That added approximately 60 yards to the 'Long Hole In' and with the angle, brought the Beardies back into play. Hell bunker was rebuilt in preparation for the 2000 Open, and the most significant change being the inclusion of wooden railway sleepers set in concrete behind the face of the bunker. Since then, and in preparation for the 2005 Open, a new tee was constructed. Controversially, this tee was again on the Eden course, and it was hoped the extra 37 yards would again bring the Beardies and Hell bunker back into play. The extra yardage, however, made little difference. In the final statistics the hole actually played easier than it did in 2000! Many could reach the green in two shots, and only the undulations at the front of the green prevented it relinquishing more than 3 eagles.
15	456	A new back tee was added about 1936 and added fifteen yards to the Championship course and a little over 20 years later Hull bunker was filled in. Some further alterations were made to the teeing ground in 1993, but in 1997 the hole was extended over 40 yards.
16	423	This hole still proves a test for all golfers. The professionals, possibly with the exception of Daly, who in 1995 and ever since chooses to hit over the "Principal's Nose", lay up short and slightly left. The new back tee added in 1997 has been the main factor in this change of strategy.
17	455	Apart from the road behind the green being resurfaced and the constant additions to the hotel which now looms even closer to the tee – and limits the ability for the right-hander to draw the ball into the fairway – this hole remains unchanged. The difference in yardage is almost certainly a correction due to more accurate measurment devices. For the Open Championship, the rough left and right of the fairway is now grown to increase the reward for hitting the fairway. It has been suggested that the Road Hole bunker has got smaller and deeper in recent years, but that may be a factor of the regular revetting program than any malicious plot.
18	357	Again, apart from the resurfacing of Granny Clark's Wynd, this hole remains unchanged since 1933. For all medal and major competitions the tee used is that abutting the back of the seventeenth green.
Total Yardage	7279	
Other Changes		Approximately ninety bunkers were rebuilt this year and last year in preparation for the Open Championship.

Hole Changes Chronologically – 1866–2005

Hole	c1866	1869	1870	c1899	1901	1902	late 1904
				Year			
1			New 1st Green built			Several new teeing grounds.	Tee moved 15yds back.
2							Tee kept back- 'Almost at the burn'
3							Tee moved 30yds back Green partly re-turfed.
4				3 bunkers cut?			Hole extended 20yds. Green partly re-turfed
5				Right Spectacles bunker cut?			
6				New Bunker cut Right side of Fairway?			New Tee made 30yds back and right. Green partly re-turfed.
7							
8							Green re-laid
9					Kruger made*. Kruger split in two. Cronje name given to bunker by the green.		Tee back 40yds and left.
10				New Tee. 22yds added to length of hole	Probably cut c1901. Bunker (1) added short and left.		Green re-laid. New bunkers planned
11							Green re-laid
12							(Medal Tee behind Hill bunker!)
13							
14							Green re-laid
15		Sutherland bunker filled in and re-opened					New Tee made 25yds further back
16							
17							Tee heightened & enlarged
18	New 18th green						
NOTES					* Kruger bunker was named after victory in South Africa when 4000 POWs were set free. Its name is said to describe its hidden and treacherous nature.		With the medal course being set on the right-hand side, instead of forming new bunkers Hamilton proposes to narrow the course at certain points by allowing the rough to encroach upon the ground now mown, and so face the present hazards.
	1879 Swilcan Burn altered				When Kruger was split in two, the name of Mrs Kruger was given to the new bunker.		
	1880 Links Road War						
	1893 (Sept) Mr Bruce starts embankment						
	1899, Oct; proposals to cut new bunkers.						
	NB: Swilcan Burn made to curve in a NW direction.						
	Formerly it followed further to the South and debouched on a broad sandy channel near the road.						
	Course width= 30-60yds						

Hole	Year					
	1905	1906	1905–'08	1909	1910	1911
1						
2	3? Bunkers (2 fairway, 1 Green) cut at intervals along right side of fairway				Deep hollow in front of tee raised	
3	Bunkers (3?) cut at intervals along right side of fairway.		2 Greenside Bunkers cut?			
4	Bunkers (3?) cut at intervals along right side of fairway					
5			Seven Sisters Bunkers cut?			
6	(3?) bunkers cut on right side of fairway in a cluster		extra bunker cut			
7						
8						
9						
10			3 bunkers cut in fairway short left			
11	Bunker at back of green renovated					
12						
13	August – new tee to right. Whins in front of tee cut down	Landing area. Right hummock lowered.		New tee cut for Left-Hand Course		
14						Out-of-bounds on right.
15	New bunker (1) in front of green					
16						Out-of-bounds on right.
17	Green banked-up on road side					Out-of-bounds on right.
18						Out-of-bounds on right. July 17th 1911. Out-of-bounds came into play along several holes.
NOTES	13 additional bunkers added May–June 1905	Citizen May 6th, 1905: "It was agreed on recommendation of the green committee to introduce several new bunkers to the course"				
						Late 1913, last section of Swilcan Burn piped.

The Impact of Time, Tradition and Technology

St Andrews: The Evolution of the Old Course

	Year					
	1914	1920–'24	1924	1924–'32	1936	1939
1						
2				Green expanded to lower right. 4th bunker added right of green	c1936. Bridge by 2nd tee moved. Tee extended 10yds back to burn.	
3				late 1929: tee enlarged		
4		1 bunker cut next to Students' Bunker				
5			Returfing FW 180-220yds from tee completed		c1936: New tee made back 49yds. Details p.82	
6		Long bunker cut on right of fairway		1928: 'hollow at the 6th hole raised and returfed'.	Slope at north end of causeway eased (old mins). Details p.81	
7		Bunker in front of tee grassed over	Tee enlarged			
8			Tee enlarged?	Bunker short right of green reduced in size		
9	Boase's Bunker Added between 1913-1920		New tee 5yds square and 15yds NW of existing back tee made	late 1929: tee enlarged	c1936- New tee made back 53yds	
10		3 bunkers left of tee cut		late 1929: tee enlarged	Considering new back tee "in whins". Details p.81	
11			c1924: Tee extended back		Top tee raised and built. Details p.81	
12						
13			Tee enlarged	2 bunkers filled in that were located forward & left of tees		
14			c1924: Tee extended back & right		c1936: New tee made back 37yds. Details p.82	New tee made 60yds back
15			c1924: New tee		c1936: New tee made back 15yds	
16			c1924: Tee extended back		c1936: New tee made back 32yds	
17		c1923: Road tarsealed				
18		1924: Substantial returfing took place. See old minutes, P.70				
NOTES		c1923/24 Swilcan Burn cleaned out				

Hole Changes Chronologically – 1866–2005 (cont.)

	Year						
	1939–1945	1949	1947–1954	1954	c1993	1997	2003–'04
1							
2							New tee (in Ladies Putting Course) Hole extended 40yds
3				New tee 50yds behind and right of Medal tee. Details p.92	New tee made back 19yds	New tee. Hole extended 26yds	
4	New "Open" tee +45yds back. Details p.89–90						Existing tee Extended back. 16yds Added
5							
6	New tee made +45yds back					New tee to right	
7						Tee extended back +16y	
8			Tee extended back 10yds				
9						Tee rebuilt	
10				Refurbish existing tee 20yds behind Medal tee. Details p.92		New tee. Hole extended 37yds	
11							Top tee extended and levelled.
12							Revamped tee for Open on hill behind 11th Green. Hole extended 34yds
13				New tee 25–30yds behind Medal tee. Details p.92		Tee extended back +8yds	New tee. Located on Eden Course. Hole extended 35yds
14					New tee made back 14yds		New tee. Located on Eden Course. Hole extended 37yds
15		Hull's bunker filled in. Details p.84			New tee made back 43yds	New tee. Hole extended 43yds	
16						New tee. Hole extended 40yds	
17							
18							

Open Prize Money

Year	Inflation	Multiplier	Input Column Actual		Result Column Today's Money	
			1st	Total	1st	Total
2005		1	£720,000	£4,000,000	£720,000	£4,000,000
2000	3.00%	1.1	£500,000	£2,750,000	£550,000	£3,025,000
1995	3.50%	1.2	£125,000	£1,250,000	£150,000	£1,500,000
1990	9.50%	1.4	£85,000	£825,000	£119,000	£1,155,000
1984	5.00%	2	£55,000	£451,000	£110,000	£902,000
1978	8.30%	3.6	£12,500	£125,000	£45,000	£450,000
1970	6.40%	9.8	£5250	£40,000	£51,450	£392,000
1964	3.30%	13	£1500	£8500	£19,500	£110,500
1960	1.00%	15	£1250	£7000	£18,750	£105,000
1957	3.70%	15	£1000	£3750	£15,000	£56,250
1955	4.50%	17	£1000	£3750	£17,000	£63,750
1946	3.10%	26	£150	£1000	£3900	£26,000
1939	2.80%	41	£100	£500	£4100	£20,500
1933	-2.10%	45	£100	£500	£4500	£22,500
1927	-2.40%	40	£100	£275	£4000	£11,000
1921	-8.60%	31	£75	£225	£2325	£6975
1910	0.90%	75	£50	£125	£3750	£9375
1905	0.40%	77	£50	£125	£3850	£9625
1900	5.10%	78	£50	£125	£3900	£9750
1895	-1.00%	84	£30	£100	£2520	£8400
1891	0.70%	81	£10	£29	£810	£2309
1888	0.70%	83	£8	£21	£664	£1743
1885	-3.00%	82	£10	£32	£820	£2624
1882	1.00%	77	£12	£46	£924	£3542
1879	-4.40%	79	£10	£45	£790	£3555
1876	-0.30%	73	£10	£27	£730	£1971
1873	3.10%	69	£11	£25	£759	£1725

Control of the Old Course

The following information is beyond the scope of this book but is very interesting in that it briefly documents the discussion for control of the Links at St Andrews. The implications of these town minutes are thought provoking, as different decisions could have resulted in a different ownership and configuration of the courses.

Excerpts from the Town Minutes 1887–1900 sourced from St Andrews University Library.

Town Minutes 8th May 1893
Extension of Golfing Links.
A report by the committee appointed at the last meeting to consider the possibility of extending the Golfing Links was read in the following terms: '3rd May 1893. The Chairman stated that the Secretary of the Royal and Ancient Golf Club had informed him that a special Committee of the Club would meet the Town Council Committee, the same evening, at a quarter past five… Geo Murray acting Convenor.'

4th May 1893. The Special Committee Reported, as a result of their interview on the 3rd… with the Special Committee of the Royal and Ancient Golf Club; that the said Club are apparently determined to acquire the Links on their own behalf and to make a private Golf Course for the use of members of their own Club. The representatives of the Club stated that it was not their intention to abandon the use, or the upkeep of the present Golf Course, but they would come under no obligation in respect of such upkeep. They also stated that the interest of the Ladies Golf Club would be attended to, but it might be necessary to remove them from the present ground. The question of the right of the public to walk over the Links was discussed, and it was maintained on behalf of the Club that no such right existed in law, and although permitted by Mr Cheape, the present proprietor, it might be stopped at any time. The Club, however, had no intention they said if they became proprietors of the Links, of interfering with the existing state of matters, but although strongly pressed on this point they declined to give any written obligation that they would not interfere with the public walking over the Links. On behalf of the Town it was stated that the community consider that they have the right from Ancient Charters and Titles to walk over any part of the Links – that this is not a question of *acquiring* a right because there is no doubt that the right had been acquired; and it is exercised now as it has been continually from time immoral. It was represented by the Town Council Committee that the Town might acquire the Links, and in that event the Club Committee were asked whether they would continue to keep up the present course, and form a new one, paying a rent for the latter in the event of the Town agreeing that it should be private, and leasing it to them for the purpose: it was also suggested that the Town might purchase the Links and authorise the Club to form any number of new courses, to be open to the public, but the Club declined to take these proposals into consideration. The Committee recommended that this matter be referred to the Local Authority, and that

a meeting of that body be called for an early day.
(signed) Geo Murray
Acting Convenor.

A month later:

12th June 1893. Town Council
Extension of Golfing Links
A letter dated 12th from Mr Cheape of Strathtyrum was read, in reply to the communication made to him by direction of the last meeting of the Council, stating that he declined to bind himself in any way as to the disposal of the Links, and that, if the Town Council has any further communication to make on the subject, he must refer them to his agents… it was resolved to appoint a Joint Committee… to consider the advisability of purchasing the Links either under the powers of the corporation or of the local authority, with power to ascertain from Mr Cheape whether he is prepared to sell the Links to the Town or Local Authority and, if so, for what price.

25th Sept 1893
Public Meeting as to the Purchase of the Links.
[Note: After the posting of a public notice, approximately a thousand ratepayers turned up.]
Resolved: 'That this meeting cordially approves of the action taken by the Town Council with reference to the purchase of the Links, and is of opinion that it is vital to the best interests of St Andrews that the Links should become the property of the corporation.'

15th Nov 1893 – Town Council Minutes
Extension of Golfing Links
A letter dated 11th from Mr E Henderson on behalf of the Special Committee of the Royal and Ancient Golf Club was then read, a copy of which follows: 'Dear Sir, The Special Committee of the Royal and Ancient Golf Club to which that Club at their last General Meeting remitted the laying out of a new course on the ground recently purchased by them, have appointed a sub-committee (of which I am Convenor) to prepare a plan for a proposed new course.'

ST ANDREWS LINKS ACT 1894

From this point on the Links were to be under the control of various St Andrews Links Acts. The first of these, and perhaps most significant, was in 1894.

St Andrews Links Act 1894: Summary – The council to take over the ownership of the Links while the R&A would be responsible for the management of the links and construct a second course at its expense.

For more information of these Acts, and the various Acts passed afterwards, i.e., 1913, 1924, 1932, 1946, 1967 and 1974, I recommend readers read *St Andrews Golf Links – The First 600 Years* by Tom Jarrett.

Acknowledgements

I've never climbed Mount Everest, but I am wondering if there are similarities between doing that and writing about the Old Course. It seems those who did it first were great men. Failure to respect the challenge is fatal, and those who follow must stand on the shoulders of those who preceded them. If this analogy is true, I'd like to thank those who went before me, but perhaps also modestly suggest that this research takes a previously unchartered route.

However before I turn the oxygen off, loosen the crampons and put away the ice axe, I'd like to acknowledge my support team.

Firstly this book is as much Susannah's as it is mine. Susannah is the beautiful woman who somehow overlooked my considerable failings and agreed to marry me during this research.

Secondly, the inception of this study was born through discussions with an architect, Denis Griffiths, whose talents are widely under-recognised. Thanks Denis for your time and friendship.

If my research got me to the Himalayan Base Station, I hold two men wholly responsible for encouraging me up the icy slopes – Greg Turner and John Huggan. They thought the research I had produced for greater personal enlightenment would be appreciated by a wider audience, and insisted that with a few words and the odd photo, a book wouldn't be too hard to produce. While the jury is out on the matter of appreciation, gentlemen, you are none-the-less guilty of gross understatements... and I thank you. Had I known the truth, I may not have made an attempt on the peak. You were the oxygen when the going got tough.

Scottish book collector Rhod McEwan was most generous with his time and collection, as was Dr David Greenhough.

Thanks to Kel Devlin at Nike Golf for his help and for putting me in touch with people who could answer technical questions. Remaining Sherpas include those at the British Golf Museum, St Andrews University Library and the USGA, including Patty Moran and Emma Jane McAdam. Also Mr Peter Dawson, Secretary of the Royal and Ancient Golf Club, and Gordon Moir at the St Andrew Links Trust.

I also need to thank my friends in St Andrews: David Joy, Iain Lowe and Rhodri Price for their time, support, and passion… and for silently putting up with a myriad maddening questions.

A special mention must go to Peter Thomson. Thanks for your time and support in Melbourne and in St Andrews. My respect for you can be no deeper.

Last but not least to my publisher and his team at Hazard Press, my friends and family: you have all been important cogs of various sizes in the realisation of this research. Thank you. To the many people whose path has crossed mine and contributed to the research, sorry most of you must go unnamed, but to you I offer my deepest thanks.

Finally, I have two last thoughts. I have attempted to contact all those whose works were included in this research. For those who have kindly granted permission, you have my most sincere appreciation. But regarding the few images for which the owner cannot be traced, should you not be identified, I would like to thank you also. And last of all a note to providence – may I receive mercy from those whose knowledge of this almost inexhaustible subject exceeds my own. I welcome any new information that may help us traverse the cracks in the glacier and only hope this study will let us all get a little higher and see a little further.

Periodicals

Blackwoods Magazine, Edinburgh, 1913, Blackwood, Edinburgh
Chambers Journal, 1906, W&R Chambers Ltd, Edinburgh
Country Life Magazine
Field and Stream, 1910, 1921
Golf Illustrated Weekly, 1990
Golf Illustrated, London, 1890–
Golf Monthly, 1938–40, 1978
Golf Weekly, 1984
Golf Word, 1984–1995
Golfers Handbook, 1947, 1956, 1958, 1961–2001
Harper's New Monthly Magazine, European Edition, Harper Brothers, London, 1894
Nisbet's Golf Year Book, Edited by John L. Low, James Nisbet & Co., London, 1908
Sportsmans Yearbook, 1905
The Field, 1875, 1895, 1927
The Gofer's Year, 1955, 1957, 1960
The Golfing Annual
The Golfing Year, 1955, 1957, 1960, 1964

Newspapers

Manchester Courier
New Zealand Herald
St Andrews Citizen, St Andrews
St Andrews Times
The Scotsman, Edinburgh
The Times
Westminster Gazette, London

Library

British Golf Museum
National Library of Scotland
Rhod McEwan Library
Royal and Ancient Golf Club Library
St Andrews Golf Club Library
St Andrews University Library
USGA Library

Maps

The Old Course St Andrews Surveyed, designed and drawn by D. Hogg, 1987
The Old Course surveyed by Alister MacKenzie, 1924

Books

Balfour, James. *Reminiscences of Golf on St. Andrews Links*, David Douglas, 1887
Browning, Robert. *History of Golf: The Royal and Ancient Game.* Dent, London: 1955
Clark, Robert. *Golf: A Royal and Ancient Game*, Edinburgh: 1875
Cotton, Henry. *This Game of Golf*, Country Life Ltd, London: 1948
Darwin, Bernard. *A history of Golf in Britain*, Cassell, London: 1910
Darwin, Bernard. *British Golf, Jarrold and Sons*, Norwich: 1946
Dye, Pete. *Bury Me in a Pot Bunker*, Contemporary Books, Illinois: 1999
Hackney, Stewart. *Bygone Days on the Old Course*, Ravensbay Publications, Dundee: 1990
Hamilton, David. *Golf: Scotland's Game*, The Patrick Press, 1998
Hotchkiss, John F. *500 Years of Golf Balls.* Antique Trader Books, Iowa: 1997
Hutchinson, Horace et al. *British Golf Links*, J.S. Virtue & Co, London: 1897
Hutchinson, Horace et al. *Golf.* The Badminton Library, Longmans, Green, London: 1890
Jarret, Tom. *St Andrews Golf Links: The First 600 Years.* Mainstream Publishing, Edinburgh: 1995
Joy, D. et al. *St Andrews & The Open Championship.* Sleeping Bear Press, Michigan: 1999
Kirkaldy, Andrew. *My Fifty Years of Golf: Memories*, T. Fisher Unwin Ltd, London: 1921
Low, J. *Concerning Gold*, Hodder and Stoughton, London: 1903
MacKenzie, Alister. *Dr MacKenzie's Golf Architecture*, Simpkin, Hamilton and Kent, London: 1920
MacKenzie, Alister. *The Spirit of St Andrews*, Sleeping Bear Press, Michigan: 1995
Mackie, K. *Golf at St Andrews*, Arum Press, London: 1995
Martin, John S. *The Curious History of the Golf Ball: Man's Most Fascinating Sphere*, Horizon Press, New York: 1968
McPherson, J. Gordon. *Golf and Golfers, Past and Present*, W. Blackwood, Edinburgh: 1891
Nicklaus, Jack. *My Story*, Ebury Press, London: 1997
Olman, Morton & John. *St. Andrews & Golf*, Market Street Press, Cincinnati: 1995
Salmond, J.B. *The Story of the R&A*, Macmillan, London: 1956
Smith, Garden G. *The World of Golf*, Isthmian Library, Innes: 1898
Tillinghast, A.W. *Reminiscences of the Links*, Treewolf Productions, USA, 1998
Ward Thomas, Pat. *The Royal & Ancient*, Scottish Academic Press, 1980
Warren Wind, Herbert. *The Story of American Golf*, Farrar Straus, New York: 1948
Young, D. St Andrews, *Town and Gown, Royal and Ancient*, Cassell, London: 1969

Index

R. and A. Golf Club House and Links, St. Andrews

RIVER EDEN

THE EDEN COURSE

OLD COURSE

NEW COURSE

JUBILEE COURSE

WEST SANDS

THE SHEDS 17TH

1ST GREEN OLD COURSE

SWILCAN BURN

18TH FAIRWAY

GRANNIE CLARK'S WYND

RUSACK'S HOTEL

1ST TEE OLD COURSE

ST. ANDREWS GOLF COURSES FROM THE AIR.

18TH GREEN

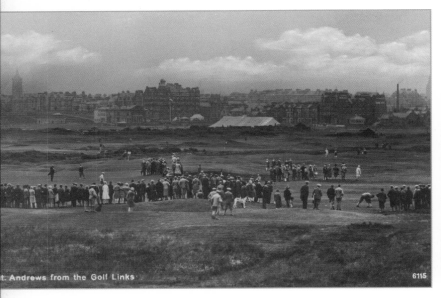

St. Andrews from the Golf Links

6115

17th Hole (Road Hole), Old Golf Course, St. Andrews
Length of Hole, 456 yards; Bogey, 6